"*The Shaping of Things to Come* is a theological splinter in the Western church's collective mind. But it is a holy splinter, because it calls us forward to a grander view of the church-in-mission than the one to which we have become all too accustomed. I am personally grateful for this new edition."

—Mark Batterson, lead pastor, National Community Church;
author, *The Circle Maker*

"Not often does a title of a book prophesy itself. But *The Shaping of Things to Come* has shaped things to come in the global Christian world like perhaps no one book published in the past decade. It truly is a 'classic,' and this new edition promises to continue its tradition of shaking and shaping."

—Leonard Sweet, author; professor, Drew University
and George Fox University

"*The Shaping of Things to Come* has been a window of hope and motivational boost for bringing change to the church for so many of us. Just when we were about to lose hope in today's organized church, Mike and Alan show us that perhaps we unintentionally developed a limited understanding of what the church is even supposed to be. But they don't stop at simply pointing out the problems of the church; they give us vision and ideas for joining in together and creating the future church. Not a future church based on trends or human strategies either, but one based on going back to the beginning to see what was the New Testament vision for the church on mission in the world. *The Shaping of Things to Come* is one of those rare books that you don't just read and place nicely back on your shelf. It gets deep into your psyche and alters your perspective on what it means to be the church today, what it means to follow Jesus on his adventurous mission."

—Dan Kimball, author, *They Like Jesus but Not the Church*

"*The Shaping of Things to Come* by Michael Frost and Alan Hirsch was a pivotal book in 2003 for me and many others who take the mission of God seriously. This new and revised edition will play a monumental role in bringing even more leaders and readers into the missional conversation. I would encourage you to take a first or second look at this landmark text and discover your part in the Jesus mission."

—Dave Ferguson, lead pastor, Community Christian Church;
movement leader, NewThing

"The first edition of *The Shaping of Things to Come* helped reshape the missional thinking for many church planters and congregations around the globe. It challenged us to recognize the extent to which change was necessary in our approach to church and faith and helped us think about how this might be possible. This new edition of Frost and Hirsch's groundbreaking book does not disappoint. It reinforces the messages of the first edition with new insights and updated examples that speak well into our current context with messages of hope for revitalization within the church. I think that this new edition is particularly helpful for those within the established church who seek to reinvent their approach to the mission of the church."

—Christine Sine, cofounder, Mustard Seed Associates

"As we look at the depth and breadth of the missional movement, I continually direct people back to *The Shaping of Things to Come*. Things have definitely shaped around the concepts of this book, and it continues to be a plumbline for missional thought leadership and practice.

—Hugh Halter, author, *The Tangible Kingdom* and *Sacrilege*

"*The Shaping of Things to Come* has achieved landmark status in the missional church conversation. Ten years after its first printing, it remains the starting point for many of the concepts we are fleshing out to this day. So welcome to this revised edition. And I eagerly look forward to new insights!"

—David Fitch, author, *Prodigal Christianity*; BR Lindner Chair of Evangelical Theology, Northern Seminary

"*The Shaping of Things to Come* was one of the early warning cries to the Western church that the world we are responsible to engage with the love of Christ is radically changing. Though it caused discomfort, we had to face the truths expressed, and open our minds and hearts to what 'the Spirit is saying to the Church.' Though we still have much that needs shaping to become as effective as we need to be, the missional conversation has significantly transformed many of us."

—Tammy Dunahoo, general supervisor, The Foursquare Church

"*The Shaping of Things to Come* is a seminal book that has profoundly influenced the missional conversation. To truly understand where the conversation is now, it is essential to retrace its roots and embrace anew the concepts that were introduced by Hirsch and Frost a decade ago."

—Linda Bergquist, church planting catalyst and coach; coauthor, *Church Turned Inside Out*

"Passion, imagination, and clear analysis; organization theory and historical perspective; biblical depth and cultural sensitivity—the first time I read *The Shaping of Things to Come*, I was stunned. Where had these guys come from? They quoted my favorite authors and wove it together with a perspective on the captivity of the church that was both prophetic and pastoral. And they saw where it needed to go because they were on the ground working for change while participating in a global conversation. The astonishing thing is how current the book remains. This update celebrates the ongoing story of missional recovery as the world moves deeper into post-Christendom. If this is your first read, fasten your seatbelt and open your heart. Listen for the Spirit; you won't be disappointed."

—Len Hjalmarson, adjunct professor of ministry, Northern Baptist Theological Seminary; author, *Missional Spirituality*

REVISED AND UPDATED

THE
SHAPING
OF THINGS
TO COME

Innovation and Mission
for the 21st-Century Church

*Michael Frost
and Alan Hirsch*

BakerBooks

a division of Baker Publishing Group
Grand Rapids, Michigan

© 2003, 2013 by Michael Frost and Alan Hirsch

Published by Baker Books
a division of Baker Publishing Group
P.O. Box 6287, Grand Rapids, MI 49516-6287
www.bakerbooks.com

ISBN 978-0-8010-1491-8

Printed in the United States of America

Original edition published in 2003 by Hendrickson Publishers and Strand Publishing

Library of Congress Cataloging-in-Publication Data is on file at the Library of Congress, Washington, DC.

Unless otherwise indicated, Scripture quotations are from the Holy Bible, New International Version®. NIV®. Copyright © 1973, 1978, 1984 by Biblica, Inc.™ Used by permission of Zondervan. All rights reserved worldwide. www.zondervan.com

Scripture quotations labeled NASB are from the New American Standard Bible®, copyright © 1960, 1962, 1963, 1968, 1971, 1972, 1973, 1975, 1977, 1995 by The Lockman Foundation. Used by permission.

Scripture quotations labeled RSV are from the Revised Standard Version of the Bible, copyright 1952 [2nd edition, 1971] by the Division of Christian Education of the National Council of the Churches of Christ in the United States of America. Used by permission. All rights reserved.

Italics in Scripture quotations signifies authors' emphasis.

The internet addresses, email addresses, and phone numbers in this book are accurate at the time of publication. They are provided as a resource. Baker Publishing Group does not endorse them or vouch for their content or permanence.

18   19   7   6   5   4

To my students at Morling Seminary,
who help me trial all these ideas before they ever get to print.

—MF

To my various comrades at missional.com (a newly formed collaborative
network comprising of ForgeAmerica, Exponential, Future Travelers,
Missio, New Thing Network, GCM, Entermission).
You are the shaping of things now.

And especially to Debs,
who has always inspired me for the journey.

—AH

A church which pitches its tents without constantly looking out for new horizons, which does not continually strike camp, is being untrue to its calling. . . . [We must] play down our longing for certainty, accept what is risky, live by improvisation and experiment.

—Hans Küng

Contents

You Must Read This Bit First

The first edition of *The Shaping of Things to Come* was published in 2003, although we had begun what turned out to be the lengthy and laborious process of writing it several years before that. It has also subsequently been translated into German and Korean, and has been read across the globe. Given this exposure, and that it was penned over a decade ago, we are regularly asked whether we still agree with what we wrote then, and if there's anything we'd change if we could write it over. Our answer is invariably the same: we still totally stand by the central tenets of this book, but there are three changes we'd make if we were rewriting it:

1. update the anecdotes and snapshots of missional projects outlined in the original edition;
2. soften the polemical edge of the early section that appears to dismiss all traditional approaches as inherently non-missional; and
3. be less pessimistic about inviting the leaders of established churches to incorporate missional principles into their churches.

On the first point, the need to update our illustrations should be evident. More than ten years after our search for missional experiments took us across the US and the UK back in the early 2000s, we can now report that the missional paradigm is being widely discussed and indeed accepted by church planters around the world. There are many more fresh stories to tell, and with the help of our colleague and friend, Lance Ford, we have now included them throughout this edition.

The second and third points are related. We acknowledge that we were rather too quick in dismissing existing traditional churches and their leaders from being able to re-missionalize what they were doing. Part of the reason for this is that we wrote the book primarily for church planters and missionaries in the West—a group of people who needed material that took us beyond contemporary church growth approaches to being genuine cross-cultural missionaries in our context. It was built on the curriculum we had developed for Forge Mission Training Network. There was no such text available at the time. All we had was the Church Planter's Toolkit, a resource that was great for people in non-missional environments, but no longer worked for those of us who found ourselves isolated from mainstream Western culture. We never thought that the book would be read by established church leaders. None were more surprised than us when it became something of a defining text for the missional church movement as a whole.

As a result, the tone of the first edition can be read as being somewhat dismissive (some might say, obnoxiously so) of prevailing forms of church. Consequently we do think it is appropriate to soften the stridency without underplaying the intended revolutionary invitation originally sounded by *The Shaping of Things to Come*.

Indeed, we suspect the book garnered the readership it did partly because we were so raucous in our call to the church to embrace wholesale change. We laid all our cards on the table and called it as we saw it. Many people didn't like that, but it did keep them reading. Maybe our original tone was shockingly appropriate back in 2003, but a decade later we think a less strident, but no less radical, call is more in keeping with our times.

We are also seeing encouraging shifts within existing churches toward a greater embracing of the missional paradigm. In 2003 we confessed our belief that the planting of new, culturally diverse missional communities was the best way forward for the church, acknowledging that the challenging missional context in the West required us to adopt a fully incarnational stance, a stance we openly doubted most established churches could embrace. We had seen some churches become revitalized, but felt that such success was so rare that the greater hope lay in a missional church planting movement. Today, we certainly don't back off from our hope for such church planting movements to emerge, but we are rather more optimistic about missional revitalization within the established church.

In fact, Alan in particular has been working with large churches across the US in the Future Travelers project, exploring principles for the adoption of a missional stance in large established churches. These principles were detailed in his book with Dave Ferguson, *On the Verge* (Zondervan, 2011). The signs are much more promising than we would ever have anticipated in 2003.

Nonetheless, we are hopeful that this second edition of *The Shaping of Things to Come* can remain the incendiary shot across the bow of the church that it was ten years ago. In our introduction to the first edition we wrote,

> In this book expect to encounter revolutionary ideas that will sometimes unnerve you. We hope to reawaken the latent apostolic imagination at the heart of the biblical faith and to exhort God's people to courageous missional engagement for our time—living out the gospel *within* its cultural context rather than perpetuating an institutional commitment *apart from* its cultural context. In writing this book we are advocating a wholesale change in the way Christians are *doing* and *being* the church, and because of this ours is not necessarily a popular message.

We don't wish to soft-sell that unpopular message today and have been careful not to tamper with the rousing tone and clarion call it contains. We trust this second edition will be as combustible as was its original incarnation.

P A R T   O N E

THE SHAPE WE'RE IN

1

Evolution or Revolution?

There is nothing more difficult to carry out, nor more doubtful of
success, nor more difficult to handle, than to initiate a new order
of things. For the reformer has enemies in all those who would
profit by the old order, and only lukewarm defenders in all those
who would profit by the new.

—Machiavelli

A Bad Day in Black Rock?

Something's up in the Nevada desert outside Reno. A movement is gathering
force and it is not leaving its participants untouched. Its influence is now stretch-
ing across the US. On the playa, the four-hundred-square-mile, flat-floored
basin known by artists and musicians around the world as Black Rock Desert,
the annual pilgrimage to Burning Man builds to a crescendo. Burning Man
is perhaps the ultimate postmodern festival. Each year thousands of artists,
musicians, bohemians, punks, taggers, rappers, and other artistes or simply
interested bystanders journey into the 107-degree heat of the desert for a festival
like no other. It is a temporary community of people committed to generosity,
environmentalism, celebration, spirituality, and above all, art. Burning Man
has been so successful over the past twenty or so years that it has come to represent those trends that pose the greatest challenges to the Christian church. It
dares to offer acceptance, community, an experience of god, redemption, and

atonement. In short, it resembles everything the church is supposed to offer. But many people are finding the transformative power of Burning Man to be far and away more effective than anything they experience in church.

Although Christians might be tempted to focus on and condemn Burning Man's patently pagan elements—the near-deification of art, nature, and the individual, not to mention the quasi-sacred rite in which both a human effigy and "confessional cards" are burned—we should rather examine what takes place at Burning Man in order to learn why thousands of people flock to the event every year. It is actually quite easy to denigrate Burning Man as a counterfeit religious experience, but Christians who content themselves with this will never understand what exactly draws participants to live under the Man's watchful gaze in Black Rock Desert. They will never discover what people today are searching for and thus will never offer the authentic spiritual experience that people crave.

Eager to understand this experience and the cravings behind it, Alan and his wife Debra recently journeyed to the desert themselves. Along with members of their church, The Tribe of LA, they entered fully into the Burning Man experience for its own sake, but also as a kind of exercise in anthropological research. What drew people to Burning Man? What longings were met on the floor of the Black Rock Desert? What they found confirmed what participants have previously told us. According to participants at this postmodern festival, six key elements make up the Burning Man experience.

Belonging: Says the official Burning Man website,

> You belong here and you participate. You're not the weirdest kid in the class-room—there's always somebody there who's thought up something you never even considered. You're there to breathe art. Imagine an ice sculpture emitting glacial music—in the desert. Imagine the Man, greeting you, neon and benevolence, watching over the community. You're here to build a community that needs you and relies on you.[1]

In a society that has been fractured by economic rationalism, globalization, racial disunity, ideological differences, fear, and violence, the Burning Man community claims to offer solace, welcome, and acceptance.

Survival: Burning Man is not for the fainthearted. It involves venturing into the desert and surviving without restaurants, air conditioning, or shopping

---

1. This and all subsequent quotations about Burning Man are from Molly Steenson, "What Is Burning Man?", http://burningman.com/whatisburningman/about_burningman/experience.html.

malls. Why is this important? With all the comforts of home stripped away, participants have no choice but to look deep within themselves, to discover who they truly are, and to summon up from within themselves the will and the power to survive—both in the desert and after they return to the world outside.

Empowerment: Again, to the website:

> You're here to create. Since nobody at Burning Man is a spectator, you're here to build your own new world. You've built an egg for shelter, a suit made of light sticks, a car that looks like a shark's fin. You've covered yourself in silver, you're wearing a straw hat and a string of pearls, or maybe a skirt for the first time.

Some artists create massive, highly sophisticated art installations. Others develop smaller works. Some people simply paint their naked bodies or their cars. Others, who have come expecting merely to spectate, are cajoled into expressing themselves creatively throughout the week. No one is deemed to be without talent.

Sensuality: Burning Man is a highly sensual, experiential community.

> You're here to experience. Ride your bike in the expanse of nothingness with your eyes closed. Meet the theme camp—enjoy Irrational Geographic, relax at Bianca's Smut Shack and eat a grilled cheese sandwich. Find your love and understand each other as you walk slowly under a parasol. Wander under the veils of dust at night on the playa.

Celebration: The crescendo of the festival is the burning of the large human effigy in the middle of the camp. Participants have told us that as the Burning Man goes up in flames, they experience a deeply spiritual sensation. As the founder of Burning Man, Larry Harvey says,

> As the procession starts, the circle forms, and the man ignites, you experience something personal, something new to yourself, something you've never felt before. It's an epiphany, it's primal, it's newborn. And it's completely individual.

Artists cast their art works into the flames. There is apparently a purging, a form of atonement, and a sense of liberation and joy.

Liminality: The word *liminal* from the Latin *limen* (threshold) signifies an in-between time. Often used by anthropologists to describe the period between childhood and adulthood, it refers to the transitional, temporary period of human transformation. The Burning Man community appears in August and takes over the seemingly untouched playa, then leaves in September, removing any trace that it was ever there. First-timers are instructed,

> You'll leave as you came. When you depart from Burning Man, you leave no trace. Everything you built, you dismantle. The waste you make and the objects you consume leave with you. Volunteers will stay for weeks to return the Black Rock Desert to its pristine condition. But you'll take the world you built with you. When you drive back down the dusty roads toward home, you slowly reintegrate to the world you came from. You feel in tune with the other dust-covered vehicles that shared the same community. Over time, vivid images still dance in your brain, floating back to you when the weather changes. The Burning Man community, whether your friends, your new acquaintances, or the Burning Man project, embraces you. At the end, though your journeys to and from Burning Man are finished, you embark on a different journey—forever.

We open this book with our impressions of the Burning Man phenomenon because it and festivals like it around the world seem to be saying something important to the world in general and to the church specifically. Burning Man is not just a bad day in Black Rock (to quote a great movie title). It's a cry from an emerging postmodern generation for a community of belonging, spirituality, sensuality, empowerment, and liberation. And yet, once you've been to the Nevada desert and tasted something as overwhelming as Burning Man, what does the contemporary traditional church have to offer you? We, the authors, take the view that the transformative power of the gospel of Jesus Christ is greater than anything offered at Black Rock. But we are realistic enough to admit that unless the church recovers its role as a subversive, missionary movement, no one who has been to Burning Man will be the least bit interested in it. We are both missionaries to the core. And like all missionaries we cannot stand by and watch the contemporary church become a pale, anemic version of its former self. What is required to reach the Burning Man generation is nothing less than a complete paradigm shift for the Western church.

The same people who first told us about Burning Man also spoke with gusto about their favorite film, *Fight Club,* starring Brad Pitt and Edward Norton. In that film a subversive community of young men begins to gather around the charismatic figure Tyler Durden (played by both Pitt and Norton—if you haven't seen the film, don't ask). Under his manic leadership the club members meet to fight each other and to inflict random acts of seditious violence on society. Theirs is a community of male empowerment with a strongly anticonsumerist sentiment. Like the Burning Man festival, it is also about belonging, liberation, rebellion, and the rejection of middle-class American values. There is an untamed energy about Durden's fight club. It has a dissident wildness about it, and we know many young men who have been deeply affected by the film. It might seem unsavory to many Christian people to be asked to learn something about the need for an emerging missional church by exploring Burning Man or *Fight Club*. But we are convinced that both are prime examples of the desperate yearning that has been unleashed in the Western world over the past few decades. During that time, the advent of postmodernism has raised within the West many expectations for an experiential, activist form of religious, mystical experience. The Christian church has not met these expectations, though it could be argued that for a brief time some forms of Pentecostalism came closer than the rest of the church. The contemporary traditional church is increasingly seen as the least likely option for those seeking an artistic, politically subversive, activist community of mystical faith. The church can no longer write the emerging Burning Man generation off as a small subculture. While the activities at Burning Man might not be everybody's cup of tea, the yearnings it seeks to meet are much more common than the church gives credence to. D. H. Lawrence said as long ago as 1924, "The adventure has gone out of the Christian venture." He then proposed that humankind create a new venture toward hope. His aspirations are still being played out to this day.

Evolution or Revolution?

We've become increasingly convinced that what the church needs to find its way out of the situation it's in at the beginning of the twenty-first century is not more faddish theories about how to grow the church without fundamentally reforming its structures. What the church needs is a revolutionary new approach. Therefore, it is our intention to tell stories about the local heroes we've encountered on our travels around the world. Because we do not advocate a one-size-fits-all approach to church planting and church growth, the various models we'll discuss are presented not as a panacea, not as *the* recommended way forward for the church, but as examples of what certain missionaries have done in their quests to reach Melbourne, San Francisco, Los Angeles, or Glasgow, and many other cities in the Western context with the gospel. We will present a number of principles and suggestions for church leaders wanting to morph into what is now openly being called the missional church. The Gospel and Our Culture Network (GOCN) says, "The missional church represents God in the encounter between God and human culture. It exists not because of human goals or desires, but as a result of

God's creating and saving work in the world. It is a visible manifestation of how the Good News of Jesus Christ is present in human life and transforms human culture to reflect more faithfully God's intentions for creation. It is a community that visibly and effectively participates in God's activity, just as Jesus indicated when he referred to it in metaphorical language as salt, yeast, and light in the world."[2]

In case this sounds like the mandate for just about every church (whether consciously "missional" or not), GOCN furthers its definition by stating that a missional church "seeks to discern God's specific missional vocation for the entire community and for all of its members." In other words, such a church makes its mission its priority and perpetually asks itself, *"What has God called us to be and do in our current cultural context?"* The issue of cultural context is essential because the missional church shapes itself to fit that context in order to transform it for the sake of the kingdom of God. By definition, the missional church is always outward looking, always changing (as culture continues to change), and always faithful to the Word of God. In many places it is so radical it barely resembles church as we know it. In other cases it might appear conventional but is in fact incarnating itself into its community in surprising and exciting ways. Above all, we're convinced that what will ultimately be required is Christian leadership that values imagination, creativity, innovation, and daring.

Albert Einstein, one of history's greatest thinkers, once noted that "the kind of thinking that will solve the world's problems will be of a different order to the kind of thinking that created those problems in the first place." This was no mere wordplay for Einstein. It was the defining motif in his life as a paradigm shifter. His ability to think with radical originality precipitated no less than two, and some argue three, major paradigm shifts in our understanding of physics and of the cosmos, and in so doing changed the course of history and shaped the thinking of generations. We are proposing that a similar paradigm-busting imagination is needed for the emergence of the missional church of the twenty-first century in the West.

If Einstein was right, then the problems of the church, like all real problems in any context, cannot be solved at the same level of awareness that created those problems in the first instance. In other words, boxlike thinking simply cannot resolve the problems created by the box itself. We are in dire need of some Einsteinian originality if we are going to engage the issues of the twenty-first century with any real missional effectiveness. It's time to step out of the box of Christendom in order to take on the problems raised by Christendom.

2. See http://www.gocn.org/.

Christendom—Get Over It!

Christendom is the name given to the sacral culture that has dominated European society from around the eleventh century until the end of the twentieth. Its sources go back to the time when Constantine came to the throne of the Roman Empire and granted Christians complete freedom of worship and even favored Christianity, thereby undermining all other religions in the empire.[3] In virtually an instant, Christianity moved from being a marginalized, subversive, and persecuted movement secretly gathering in houses and catacombs to being the favored religion in the empire. Everything changed! The emperor had changed from being the principal persecutor of Christianity to being the chief sponsor of the church. With the Edict of Milan, the age of the missional-apostolic church had come to an end. Things were to be very different from then on.

In the fifth to tenth centuries Christianity grew from infancy to adulthood throughout Western Europe, emerging in the eleventh century as fully grown and in control of the culture. By the Middle Ages, the church-state symbiosis was formalized into an institutional interdependence between the pope and the ruler of what was then called the Holy Roman Empire, effectively Western Europe today. This institutional partnership between church and state changed forever the social behaviors and religious patterning of Europe. In the *corpus Christianum* (viz. Christendom), church and state became the pillars of the sacral culture, each supporting the other. Even where there existed conflicts between church and state, it was always a conflict *within* the overarching configuration of Christendom itself. Christendom had by this stage developed its own distinct identity, one that provided the matrix for the understanding of both church and state. It had effectively become *the* metanarrative for an entire epoch. A metanarrative is an overarching story that claims to contain truth applicable to all people at all times in all cultures. And while the Christendom story no longer defines Western culture, it still remains the primary definer of the church's self-understanding in almost every Western nation, including and perhaps especially the United States.

That metanarrative not only defined church and state, it defined all the individuals and social structures in its orbit of influence. Members of that society were assumed to be Christian by birth rather than by choice. Christianity was

3. When we proclaim Christendom dead, we use that term—Christendom—advisedly. We don't proclaim Christianity dead, nor the church. Jesus promised that he would build his church and the gates of hell would not prevail against it. But Christendom, that period of Western history during which the church held sway as the moral and spiritual centerpiece of civilization, has effectively vanished.

an official part of the established culture of Europe. In some countries, the king or queen actually became the head of the church. Overall, Christianity moved from being a dynamic, revolutionary, social, and spiritual movement to being a religious institution with its attendant structures, priesthood, and sacraments.

Taken as a sociopolitical reality, Christendom has been in decline for the last 250 years, so much so that contemporary Western culture has been called by many historians (secular and Christian) as the *post-Christendom* culture. Society, at least in its overtly non-Christian manifestation, is "over" Christendom. But this is not the case within the Western church itself. Christendom, as a paradigm of understanding, as a metanarrative, still exercises an overweening influence on our existing theological, missiological, and ecclesiological understandings in church circles. In other words, we still think of the church and its mission in terms of Christendom. While in reality we are in a post-Christendom context, the Western church still operates for the most part in a Christendom mode. Constantine, it seems, is still the emperor of our imaginations.

Apostolic and Post-Apostolic Mode (AD 32 to 313)	Advance and Triumph of Christendom Mode (313 to current)	The Missional Mode (past 20+ years)
Didn't have dedicated sacral buildings. Often underground and persecuted.	Buildings become central to the notion, and experience, of church.	Rejects the concern and need for dedicated "church" buildings.
Leadership operating with a fivefold ministry-leadership ethos.	Leadership by an institutionally ordained clergy operating primarily in a pastor-teacher mode.	Leadership embraces a pioneering-innovative mode including a fivefold ministry-leadership ethos. Noninstitutional by preference.
Grassroots, decentralized movement.	Institutional-hierarchical notion of leadership and structure.	Grassroots, decentralized movements.
Communion celebrated as a sacralized community meal.	Increasing institutionalization of grace through the sacraments.	Redeems, re-sacralizes, and ritualizes new symbols and events, including the meal.
Church is on the margins of society and underground.	Church is perceived as central to society and surrounding culture.	Church is once again on the fringes of society and culture. The church reembraces a missional stance in relation to culture.
Missionary, incarnational-sending church.	Attractional / "extractional."	Missional, incarnational-sending church.

A Tale of Two Pubs

To understand the difference between Christendom-like thinking and the missional model, the following examples might help. Recently it was reported that a congregation in a small rural town in Australia had taken an innovative step toward reaching its community. A Melbourne newspaper announced, "Patrons of the Hamilton Hotel will soon be offered spirit of a different kind. In an unusual conversion, the town's Baptist congregation—who are teetotalers—have taken over one of the six pubs."[4] The Hamilton community watched in amazement as the pub, located on the main street opposite the local post office, was bought by the Baptists and renovated into a church and conference center. Its front bar was turned into a recreation area for young people and its dance area was rebuilt into a chapel and meeting room. The bar was transformed into a coffee bar, the old pub now becoming an alcohol-free building.

In the article, various church leaders from Melbourne and the pastor of the Hamilton Baptist Church spoke of the relocation as innovative, creative, and daring. However, one sour note was sounded. Midway through the newspaper article a local from Hamilton is quoted. "One of the hotel's former regulars, farmer Bruce McKellar, 71, said he would miss his corner of the bar. 'I would walk in and straight to it; we all had our own space,' he said." The implied sadness of this comment wasn't lost on us. Farmer McKellar had been displaced from his personal seat at the bar, and though he had probably moved on to one of the other pubs, he would never again be welcomed at his favorite watering hole. In Australia, like England, the local pub is a place of acceptance and friendship. Patrons develop allegiances to their pubs and though they might visit another one occasionally, they feel a deep connection to *their local* (as it's called). Though American bars can be less friendly, more foreboding places, the myth perpetuated in the successful television show *Cheers*, about a place "where everybody knows your name," is true of most English and Australian pubs. In Hamilton, farmers, tradesmen, and business people had been shooed out of the Hamilton Hotel to make way for the Baptists.

This project, though appearing innovative, in fact reflects Christendom thinking. It assumes that the church belongs prominently on the main street, and it claims that the church has the right to take over a public space and clean out the local people while creating a so-called sanctified religious zone. Whether it's in a pub, a school auditorium, or a two-hundred-year-old cathedral, it

4. *Sunday Herald Sun*, Melbourne, Australia, 15 October 2000, 3.

represents the same thinking. As we will seek to demonstrate, what is needed is the abandonment of the strict lines of demarcation between the sacred and profane spaces in our world and the recognition that people today are searching for relational communities that offer belonging, empowerment, and redemption.

On the other side of the planet, in the English town of Bradford, another pub has been transformed by Christians. The Cock & Bottle is a yellow, two-story English pub at the bottom of the street on the corner of Bradford's inner ring road. Two years ago it was rented by the Bradford Christian Pub Consortium. Bradford is a hardscrabble, working-class town. It has been noted in recent times for its racial conflict and street violence. But the Cock & Bottle represents a place of sanctuary and solace. Malcolm Willis has been employed by the consortium to manage the pub, and he and his wife live upstairs above the bar. He proves himself to be a genuinely missional leader when he says, "Jesus said go into all the world. And this includes pubs. He didn't say sit in your church and wait for people to come to you."[5] The Willises and their staff (all Christians) have set about creating a loving, welcoming environment, where locals are cared for, listened to, and ministered to. Says Willis, "Initially, many won't accept you talking about Jesus. Maybe after you've listened to them ten or twenty times—which can be exhausting—they might say 'Can you pray for me?' And then you see things happen."[6] The missional church always thinks of the long haul rather than the quick fix.

Of course, the dilemma about whether Christians should be serving alcohol or not is bound to arise. Willis is himself a teetotaler, but he has an earthy and realistic outlook on the issue of drinking: "Yes, we're selling booze to people who could do without it, but if we don't, they'll just go somewhere else—at least if they're here, we can get alongside them. I knew that when I came here I personally had to be seen not to drink, but I'm not everybody. Someone once showed me Proverbs 31, which says, 'Beer and wine are only for the dying or for those who have lost all hope. Let them drink and forget how poor and miserable they feel. But you must defend those who are helpless and have no hope.' So I have to ask, What would Jesus have done? I think the Lord would have been here in the pubs."[7]

There is a world of difference (and not just geographically) between the Cock & Bottle and the Hamilton Hotel. The former is missional, incarnational, and very risky. The latter is safe. It demonstrates sound financial management

5. Sarah Chapman, "Last Orders," *Interact*, SMG (July–September 2001): 14.
6. Ibid., 16.
7. Ibid., 17.

(it was cheaper for the Baptist Church to renovate the pub than to build a brand-new building). But it is classic Christendom thinking.

GOCN, to whom we referred earlier, has fostered much research into cultural trends and the revisioning of a new (missional) approach to church. They have come up with twelve hallmarks of a missional church:

1. The missional church proclaims the gospel.
2. The missional church is a community where all members are involved in learning to become disciples of Jesus.
3. The Bible is normative in this church's life.
4. The church understands itself as different from the world because of its participation in the life, death, and resurrection of its Lord.
5. The church seeks to discern God's specific missional vocation for the entire community and for all of its members.
6. A missional community is indicated by how Christians behave toward one another.
7. It is a community that practices reconciliation.
8. People within the community hold themselves accountable to one another in love.
9. The church practices hospitality.
10. Worship is the central act by which the community celebrates with joy and thanksgiving both God's presence and God's promised future.
11. This community has a vital public witness.
12. There is a recognition that the church itself is an incomplete expression of the reign of God.

We can't fault any of these features, but we would like to propose three more, overarching principles that give energy and direction to the above-mentioned marks. In fact, we will use these three features as the headings for three of the broad sections of this book. These three principles are:

1. The missional church is *incarnational*, not attractional, in its ecclesiology. By incarnational we mean it does not create sanctified spaces into which unbelievers must come to encounter the gospel. Rather, the missional church disassembles itself and seeps into the cracks and crevices of a society in order to be Christ to those who don't yet know him.
2. The missional church is *messianic*, not dualistic, in its spirituality. That is, it adopts the worldview and practices of Jesus the Messiah, rather than that of the Greco-Roman empire. Instead of seeing the world

as divided between the sacred (religious) and profane (nonreligious), like Christ it sees the world and God's place in it as more holistic and integrated.

3. The missional church adopts an *apostolic*, rather than a one-dimensional top-down, mode of leadership. By apostolic we mean a mode of leadership that recognizes the fivefold model detailed by Paul in Ephesians. It abandons the triangular hierarchies of the traditional church and embraces a biblical, flatter leadership community that unleashes the gifts of evangelism, apostleship, and prophecy, as well as the currently popular pastoral and teaching gifts.

We believe the missional genius of the church can only be unleashed when there are foundational changes made to the church's very DNA, and this means addressing core issues like ecclesiology, spirituality, and leadership. It means a complete shift away from Christendom thinking, which is attractional, dualistic, and hierarchical.

Many Christians seem to have great difficulty giving up on the old Christendom-based assumptions. They fear that to finally abandon Christendom means we cast the church into oblivion or chaos. They would ask, How could a bunch of Christians running a pub in Bradford be a church? Well, we think they can be. Many of the ways the missional church is emerging around the world look messy, chaotic, and dynamic. They don't always meet in the same room on a Sunday for church services, but they are worshiping God, building Christian community, and serving their world. They meet the biblical criteria for a church, but they don't often look like church as we are used to thinking of it. A helpful way of looking at the post-Christendom church is to see not disorder but a diaspora. This is the view of theologian Douglas John Hall who prefers to think of the contemporary church as a diaspora rather than as an institution. He sees this as a more positive reformulation than the resignation or defeatism of seeing Christendom's end as chaotic. He says:

> If we once have the courage to give up our defense of the old facades which have nothing or very little behind them; if we cease to maintain, in public, the pretense of a universal Christendom; if we stop straining every nerve to get *everybody* baptized, to get *everybody* married in church and onto our registers (even when success means only, at bottom, a victory for tradition, custom and ancestry, not for true faith and interior conviction); if, by letting go, we visibly relieve Christianity of the burdensome impression that it accepts responsibility for everything that goes on under this Christian topdressing, the impression that Christianity is a sort of Everyman's Religious Varnish, a folk-religion (at the

same level as that of folk-costumes)—*then* we can be free for real missionary adventure and apostolic self-confidence.[8]

Touché! We couldn't have said it better! So then, what are the effects that Christendom has had on our understanding of the church and its mission, and why is it so important to "get over it"?[9]

Christendom in its essence is a certain stance in relation to its context, a mode of engagement, and a way of thinking about the church. Given its privileged status at the center of culture, its view of mission is fundamentally distorted. What's more, it has a very fixed, very *concrete*, notion of the church—one normally associated with (distinctly designed) buildings, liturgies, denominational templates, and clergy. Its missional mode is primarily attractional/extractional rather than sending or incarnational. It assumes a certain centrality as the official religion of the culture, and its placement of buildings (usually the tallest building in the medieval setting) symbolizes that centrality. Its type of leadership can generally be described as priestly, sometimes prophetic to insiders but almost never to outsiders (no one "out there" is listening), and rarely apostolic. Christendom has moved Christianity into a maintenance mode.

Christendom, when viewed from a missiological perspective, is more than the symbiotic relationship between church and state that resulted in a move away from the normative apostolic-missionary mode of the New Testament. When Christianity was recognized and accepted in 313 and then gained favored status with the imperial courts, it altered the fundamental *mode* of the church's self-understanding and its conception of its unique task in the world. Because a type of "contract" now existed between the church and the political powers, the church's understanding of itself in relation to that state, culture, and society was profoundly changed. We don't mean to discount the incredible mission movements that occurred sporadically in the fifth to the tenth centuries. But it is fair to say that by the triumph of Christendom in the eleventh century, mission was no longer seen as necessary within Europe. It was delimited to identifiable non-Christian religions both inside and outside of the realm, but no longer to those baptized by the official church. Theology was now used as a powerful political tool. So too were missions. Mission was used as a means of colonization and advancement of various state interests. Christendom set up a certain correlation, a complex of assumptions, about the association

---

8. Douglas John Hall, "Metamorphosis: From Christendom to Diaspora," in Craig Van Gelder, ed., *Confident Witness* (Grand Rapids: Eerdmans, 1999), 67.
9. The effects of Christendom on our theological perspective in general are outside of the focus of this book. In this discussion, we will focus primarily (and briefly) on the effects on our notion of the church and of our understanding of its mission.

between the realms of politics, geography, church, spirituality, and mission. As a result the gospel was politicized, regionalized, as well as *racial*-ized. There was no longer any real place for the subversive activity associated with the New Testament gospel. The "revolution" was quelled from the inside. The historical institution of the church from then on would brook little prophetic criticism of the political realm that threatened the church's elite status in the empire and vice versa.

The Bankruptcy of Christendom

The fact that the Christendom paradigm has presided over the last seventeen centuries in the West provides us with a substantial basis with which to test its success or failure. As we stand here at the roots of the 21st century, we believe that we must, at long last, give up trying to rejig the paradigm to suit the massively changed missional contexts of the Western church. *It simply has not worked.* In fact, in the increasingly complex situations we now find ourselves, it has likely created more problems than it has solved. The church is in decline in almost every context in the First World. In this situation, naïve applications of traditionalist paradigms create problems . . . they don't resolve them.[10] For those holding on to the Christendom mode, it is as if they were trying to interpret the cosmos with a pre-Copernican view of the world. The paradigm doesn't fit. The emperor has been shown to have no clothes.

It's now a matter of record that one of the reasons for the loss of influence exercised by the church in the West has been its flirtation with modernity and the ideas of the Enlightenment. Says John Drane, "No persecutor or foe in two thousand years has wreaked such havoc on the church as has modernity."[11] By the end of the era of modernity in the mid-twentieth century, the Christian faith was no longer the center of Western culture. It had been swept away by the very movement it had sought to befriend. Where once the church in Europe occupied a place of significant influence, by the end of the twentieth century it was almost completely irrelevant. In Europe, the United Kingdom, and its colonial outposts, Australia, New Zealand, and Canada, the church had been displaced from its central position.

10. For an excellent exploration of how simply applying solutions formulated in a different era creates more problems than it solves, see Joshua Cooper Ramo, *The Age of the Unthinkable: Why the New World Disorder Constantly Surprises Us And What We Can Do About It* (New York: Little, Brown & Co., 2010). See also the introduction of Alan Hirsch and Dave Ferguson, *On the Verge: The Future of the Church as Apostolic Movement* (Grand Rapids: Zondervan, 2011).

11. John Drane, *Evangelism for a New Age: Creating Churches for the Next Century* (London: Marshall Pickering, 1994), 13.

Martin Robinson cites the Swedish church as an example.[12] He notes that even though a law that prohibited Swedish citizens leaving the Church of Sweden was lifted in 1860, very few actually do. In fact, a huge 95 percent of the population are members of the national church. However, a recent study found that only 8 percent of all Swedes adhere to a Christian worldview. When you consider that that figure would undoubtedly comprise a good number of the 5 percent who have opted to join another church, there are very few official members of the Church of Sweden who hold to its tenets. The national church exists in name only. It is an artifice. The same can be said of other Western European nations.

We must admit that Christendom, particularly its ecclesiological and its missiological manifestations, amounts to something of a failed experiment. To reiterate, by the term Christendom, we are referring to a period in history when the church assumed influence by its connection to temporal, secular power. Its high watermark occurred in the Middle Ages and continued beyond the Reformation well into the 1700s. Since the emergence of the Enlightenment it has been in decline, disappearing in the latter part of the twentieth century. It is time to move on and find a new mode of understanding and engagement with surrounding contexts. We can no longer afford our historical sentimentality, even addiction, to the past. Christendom is *not* the biblical mode of the church. It was/is merely one way in which the church has conceived of itself. In enshrining it as the sole form of the church, we have made it into an idol that has captivated our imaginations and enslaved us to a historical-cultural expression of the church. We have not answered the challenges of our time precisely because we refuse to let go of the idol. This must change! The answer to the problem of mission in the West requires something far more radical than reworking a dated and untenable model. It will require that we adopt something that looks far more like the early church in terms of its conception of the church (ecclesiology) and its core task in the world (missiology).

The Rise of the Missional Church

When there are megashifts in a culture, there tends to be a reconceptualization of the church. The more profound the cultural shift, the more thorough is the shift in the church's notion of itself. The most noteworthy example of this was the innate connection between the Renaissance of the fifteenth century and the Reformation of the early sixteenth century. The Renaissance, particularly

12. Martin Robinson, *The Faith of the Unbeliever* (London: Monarch, 1997), 13.

with its new hermeneutics, set in motion cultural forces that led inexorably to Luther's revolution, which in turn unleashed a massive recalibration in both church theology and praxis. The church is inseparably related to its cultural milieu. This provides a vital lesson for our day. We are living in an epoch-shifting period in the West (and globally) as we shift from the modern to the postmodern. There is every indication that this cultural shift will be even more profound and radical than was the shift precipitated by the Renaissance, which took place within the auspices of Christendom. What is happening now is entirely outside of any discernible Christian influence.

We propose that what will emerge from the chaos of the current social-historical shift to the postmodern is likely to be a second reformation as the church rediscovers itself as an apostolic movement. In fact, we suggest that if the church in the West does not embrace such a radical recalibration, it will find itself increasingly imperiled. The standard Christendom model will simply not engage the new generations.[13] To reach them and all other innumerable subcultures, the church should abandon its role as a static institution and embrace its initial calling to be a missionary movement. What is the nature of this apostolic movement? Whereas Christendom has unraveled because of its captivity to Western culture, the missional church must see itself as being able to interact meaningfully with culture without ever being beguiled by it. This is the classic task of the cross-cultural missionary: to engage culture without compromising the gospel. We cannot emphasize this enough. In fact, the whole tenor of this book will be to call post-Christendom to see itself again as a *missionary movement* rather than as an institution.

Essentially the early church was a missional movement to its core. It understood that personal conversion implied the embracing of the *missio Dei*—the redemptive mission of God to the whole world through the work of his Messiah. It is in this sense that we use the word *apostolic*, and it is this redemptive mission that we seek to recover for our own day. Forging apostolic movements will require massive paradigm shifts in the Christendom-based church. It requires a different kind of thinking that innovates new modes of doing and being church and recasts its notions of leadership, structure, and mission.

The church by its very nature has an indissoluble relationship to the surrounding cultural context. This relationship defines the practical nature of its mission. But the reason for mission comes from somewhere else. To say it more theologically, Christology determines missiology, and missiology determines ecclesiology, which in turn returns back to Christology in a continuous cycle of

13. See the latest research by Dave Kinnaman of the Barna Research Group, *You Lost Me: Why Young Christians Are Leaving Church . . . and Rethinking Faith* (Grand Rapids: Baker, 2011).

renewal. It is absolutely vital that the church gets the order right. We will deal with the christological issue in a later chapter and then present the practical implications in another chapter. It is Christ who determines our purpose and mission in the world (discipleship), and then it is our mission that must drive our search for modes of being-in-the-world.

We began with the question "Evolution or Revolution?" Actually, while some forms of evolutionary development are necessary, the real answer is *revolution*. The church that Jesus intended was clearly meant to be a permanent revolution and not a codified civil religion, mere chaplains to the prevailing empire. As we will point out in the next chapter, we feel that we are living in an incredibly urgent time that can be described as the greatest spiritual awakening in the history of Western culture, and the message of the church is not even getting any airplay. We cannot expect to impact Western culture by simply renovating disused pubs. A completely alternate model is required. If we fail at this point, history will judge us very harshly. It is likely, in our home of Australia at least, that it will spell the church's demise as a significant spiritual force in our land, and the church will be consigned to being a footnote to history. The statistics bear this out right across the West. This is not a time for evolutionary approaches alone, as if another desperate reworking of the old model is going to fix our problems and start a revival. It is time for a revolution in the way we do and are church.

2

The Missional Church

It is necessary for the Church to rethink its stance entirely and to become a missionary church within the West.

—Martin Robinson

Hope of Post-Christendom

A missional church is the hope of the post-Christendom era. Many of the new Protestant church movements of recent years are simply variations on the old Christendom mode. Whether they place their emphasis on new worship styles, expressions of the Holy Spirit's power, evangelism to seekers, or Bible teaching, these so-called new movements still operate out of the fallacious assumption that the church belongs firmly in the town square—that is, at the heart of Western culture. And if they begin with this mistaken belief about their position in Western society, all their church planting, all their reproduction will simply mirror this misapprehension. When we reflect on the 1990s, the declared Decade of Evangelism, we are given cause for deep concern. For all the flurry of activity across the West, in particular in the US and the UK, church numbers have continued to decline. When once it was assumed that church planting was the strategy for reaching a postmodern West, church-growth experts are now having second thoughts. Church membership has been flagging, and as the Decade of Evangelism proceeded, fewer and fewer churches were being planted. Stuart Murray and Anne Wilkinson-Hayes, in their booklet *Hope from the Margins*, identify a number of reasons why the church-planting boom has gone bust.

- Most churches which were able to plant another church early in the 1990s have not yet recovered sufficiently to do so again;
- Few newly-planted churches have yet grown quickly enough to plant another church;
- The dominance of personnel-intensive models of church planting has discouraged smaller churches from becoming involved;
- A disturbing number of church plants have failed, have remained small and weak, or have attracted only those who were already Christians;
- Church planting has generally been restricted to areas where churches are already flourishing, leaving many urban and rural areas untouched.[1]

The heart of the problem is that we have been planting churches that are (smaller) carbon copies of the already beleaguered, failing Christendom-style church. The Christendom virus is passed on. It's like Dr. Evil, in Mike Myers's ridiculous *Austin Powers* movies, creating a clone called Mini-Me. By duplicating a failing system, we are digging the same hole deeper in our attempt to dig somewhere else. In fact, it's more often than not been the case that Sunday services are planted rather than missional Jesus communities. A missional church on the other hand has abandoned the old Christendom assumptions and understands its role as an underground movement, subversive, celebratory, passionate, and communal. Mission is not merely an activity of the church. It is the very heartbeat and work of God. It is in the very being of God that the basis for the missionary enterprise is found. God is a sending God, with a desire to see humankind and creation reconciled, redeemed, and healed. The missional church, then, is a sent church. It is a *going* church, a movement of God through his people, sent to bring healing to a broken world. North America is as much a mission field as any other nation or people group on the face of the earth. The existing church, which is invariably static, rooted in one place, institutionalized, needs to recover its *sent-ness* in order to become the missional church.

The overly reproduced Christendom-mode church has at its core a number of fundamental flaws. These flaws occur in the model's very DNA. The way forward is not to tinker with its external features, but to rebirth a new

1. Stuart Murray and Anne Wilkinson-Hayes, *Hope from the Margins* (Cambridge, England: Grove, 2000), 4–5.

movement on different ground. Those flaws can be generally categorized into three broad areas. Although we will introduce them here, we will deal with them fully throughout various sections of this book.

Attractional, Dualistic, Hierarchical

As mentioned, the Christendom-mode church has these three flaws in its DNA—it is attractional, dualistic, and hierarchical. First, by attractional, we mean that the traditional church plants itself within a particular community, neighborhood, or locale and expects that people will come to it to meet God and find fellowship with others. We don't claim that there's anything unbiblical about being attractive to unbelievers. The early church was attractive to the wider community (Acts 2:47), though there is much more evidence that the church was reviled and avoided in its early days. Nonetheless, when we say it is a flaw for the church to be attractional, we refer more to the missionary stance the church takes toward the broader host communities and cultures it inhabits. By anticipating that if they get their internal features right, people will flock to the services, the church betrays its belief in attractionalism. It's like the Kevin Costner character in the film *Field of Dreams* being told by a disembodied voice, "If you build it, they will come." Viewed in this light, we can best call this approach "extractional" or perhaps even "excarnational."

How much of the traditional church's energy goes into adjusting their programs and their public meetings to cater to an unseen constituency? If we get our seating, our parking, our children's program, our preaching, and our music right, they will come. This assumes that we have a place in our society and that people don't join our churches because, though they want to be Christians, they're unhappy with the product. The missional church recognizes that it does not hold a place of honor in its host community and that its missional imperative compels it to move out from itself into that host community as salt and light.

When we have consulted with churches that recognize the need to embrace a missionary stance in their communities, we are amazed at the number of times, when asked to discuss specific ways they can recalibrate themselves to become missional churches, they begin talking about how to change their Sunday service. It betrays their fundamental allegiance to being attractional. We believe the development of indigenous, contextualized worship occurs in partnership with new believers from one's host community. The tailoring of worship services is a lot further down the priority list for missional church leaders. The Come-To-Us stance developed over the Christendom period is unbiblical. It's not found in the Gospels or the Epistles. Jesus, Paul, the disciples, the early church leaders all had a Go-To-Them mentality.

Second, the Christendom-mode church is dualistic. It separates the sacred from the profane, the holy from the unholy, the in from the out. What we have said so far about the sickness of attractionalism finds its roots in the church's dualistic spirituality. We will apply this more fully to the missional church model in the third section of this book. But in brief, we are convinced that the church has so fully embraced its attractional stance because of its dualistic spirituality. We talk routinely about the "world out there." What else can that mean other than that we, the church people, are "in here"! This dualism has over 1,700 years created Christians that cannot relate their interior faith to their exterior practice, and this affects their ethics, their lifestyles, and their capacity to share their faith meaningfully with others. In Robert Banks's groundbreaking book, *Redeeming the Routines*, he identifies the enormous gap between belief and everyday life. He points out that this gap shows up in ten worrying ways:

1. Few of us apply or know how to apply our belief to our work, or lack of work.
2. We only make minimal connections between our faith and our spare time activities.
3. We have little sense of a Christian approach to regular activities like domestic chores.
4. Our everyday attitudes are partly shaped by the dominant values of our society.
5. Many of our spiritual difficulties stem from the daily pressure we experience (lack of time, exhaustion, family pressures, etc.).
6. Our everyday concerns receive little attention in the church.
7. Only occasionally do professional theologians address routine activities.
8. When addressed, everyday issues tend to be approached too theoretically.
9. Only a minority of Christians read religious books or attend theological courses.
10. Most churchgoers reject the idea of a gap between their beliefs and their ways of life.[2]

Banks quotes occasionally from an old book called *Christianity and Real Life*, written by William Diehl, the sales manager of a major overseas steel

2. Robert Banks, *Redeeming the Routines: Bringing Theology to Life* (Wheaton: Bridgepoint, 1997), 50–65.

corporation. Diehl, as a layman (terrible word, but you understand its meaning), writes about the gap between the secular and the sacred in church circles:

> In the almost thirty years of my professional career, my church has never once
> suggested that there be any type of accounting of my on-the-job ministry to oth-
> ers. My church has never once offered to improve those skills which could make
> me a better minister, nor has it ever asked if I needed any kind of support in what
> I was doing. There has never been an inquiry into the types of ethical decisions
> I must face, or whether I seek to communicate the faith to my coworkers. I have
> never been in a congregation where there was any type of public affirmation of
> a ministry in my career. In short, I must conclude that my church really doesn't
> have the least interest whether or how I minister in my daily work.[3]

This credibility gap between the church world and the real world is, as theologian Helmut Thielicke calls it, a modern form of Docetism.[4] We believe that
it is so endemic in the contemporary church that it has worked its way into
the very fabric of all aspects of church life. Remove this Docetism, or dualism,
from church and a great deal of what the church has built and developed over
1,700 years will fall away. Because the missional church, by its very nature,
exists organically within its host community, it has had to abandon Western
Christianity's dualistic worldview in favor of a whole-of-life spirituality.

Third, the traditional church (Christendom) is hierarchical, deeply indebted
to what we see as an overly religious, bureaucratic, top-down model of leadership, as opposed to one that is more structured around grassroots agendas.
While some denominations are ideologically committed to a very top-down
hierarchical model that includes archbishops, bishops, priests, and parish
councils, others (who call themselves low church) are equally indebted to
top-down approaches via regional superintendents, senior pastors, associate pastors, youth pastors, and deacons. From Pentecostals to the Orthodox
Church, from Baptists to Episcopalians and Presbyterians, the hierarchical

3. William Diehl, *Christianity and Real Life* (Minneapolis: Fortress, 1976), v–vi, quoted in
Banks, *Redeeming the Routines*, 59.
4. "Docetism is in essence a Christology heavily influenced by basic Greek assumptions of
both the Platonic and Aristotelian varieties. Plato taught the idea of gradations of reality. Spirit
or mind or thought is the highest. Matter or the material is less real. With this distinction of
ontological gradations of reality, there came to be ethical gradations as well. Thus, matter came
to be thought of as morally bad. Aristotle emphasized the idea of divine impassability, according
to which God cannot change, suffer, or even be affected by anything that happens in the world.
These two streams of thought have significant differences, but both maintain that the visible,
physical, material world is somehow inherently evil. Both emphasize God's transcendence and
absolute difference from and independence of the material world." Millard J. Erickson, *Christian Theology* (Grand Rapids: Baker, 1985), 713.

model seems to be universal. For how much longer can the church ignore Paul's radical dissolution of the traditional distinctions between priests and laity, between officials and ordinary members, between holy men and common people? Says English pastor Rob Warner:

> The first Christians radically reshaped the language of "priesthood" and "sacrifice." In one sense all are priests; believers are their own priests for all have immediacy of access to God's grace in Christ. What priests have performed for others before, believers can now do for themselves. In another sense, none can be appointed priests in the Christian church, for Christ has fulfilled the priestly role once for all.[5]

Some younger leaders are discovering that in the emerging global cultural context the hierarchical model has little to say to a generation that values egalitarianism and community. Dan Mayhew, who works with Summit Fellowships in Portland, Oregon, has come to understand that to minister to an emerging generation of young people with authenticity, he has had to completely flatten his organization's leadership style. He says, "I make a distinction between hierarchy and 'heir-archy.' We are to be fellow heirs with one another. It's a bit of a play on words, but I think it conveys something very real. We are used to the systematic approach to things, so we create hierarchies. But the organic approach is more to create heir-archies where you are all fellow heirs to the grace of God."[6]

What Should We Do Instead?

Gerard Kelly, in his timely book *RetroFuture*, takes issue with the current conception of church when he says, "I believe the church must change. The church is not trend-driven; it is God's family and lives by other rules. But it is also a cultural and social institution, rooted in a given place and time. If we have any concern for the rising generations—and for those who will follow them—we must look with urgency to the future shape of our church."[7] He goes on to quote Tom Sine's oft-rehearsed warning, "Every denomination and religious organization I have worked with does long-range planning. Ironically, they do long-range planning as though the future will simply be an extension of the present. . . . As a result, we are chronically surprised by change. In the future, we can no longer afford this luxury."[8]

5. Rob Warner, *21st Century Church* (London: Hodder & Stoughton, 1993), 131.
6. Dan Mayhew and Brad Sargent, *Summit Fellowships Update* (October 1997): 67.
7. Gerard Kelly, *RetroFuture* (Downers Grove: InterVarsity, 2000), 17.
8. Tom Sine, *Wild Hope* (Crowborough, England: Monarch, 1992), quoted in Kelly, *Retro Future*, 17.

So, what will the future shape of the church look like? If it takes the form we propose for the missional church, it will look vastly varied in its many different contexts. But we can be sure that there will be some common values across the board. It will place a high value on communal life, more open leadership structures, and the contribution of all the people of God. It will be radical in its attempts to embrace biblical mandates for the life of locally based faith communities without feeling as though it has to reconstruct the first-century church in every detail. We believe the missional church will be adventurous, playful, and surprising. Leonard Sweet has borrowed the term "chaordic" to describe the missional church's inclination toward chaos and improvisation within the constraints of broadly held biblical values. It will gather for sensual-experiential-participatory worship and be deeply concerned for matters of justice-seeking and mercy-bringing. It will strive for a type of unity-in-diversity as it celebrates individual differences and values uniqueness, while also placing a high premium on community. Bishop Gladwin, expressed in his book on the postmodern church, believes that the emerging missional church will have these four features in common:

1. focus on the journey of faith and the experience of God;
2. desire for less structure and more direct involvement by participants;
3. sense of flexibility in order and a distinctly nonhierarchical culture;
4. recognition that the experience of church is about the sustaining of discipleship.

He concludes, "So the church will focus on core faith, on minimum essential order, on people and their gifts, on flexible patterns of life held together in communion and on a shared sense of community."[9] And this from a bishop!

We appreciate that working models are often more informative than theoretical ones. What follows are a few case studies of the missional church around the world.

Church in the Missional Mode

When Tim and Kristy Cobillas set out to begin a church in the northern landscape of Saint Louis, Missouri, in 2001, they had no idea that it would evolve into an outlaw biker haven. Joshua House began as an informal worship gathering around a backyard bonfire on a two-acre plot of suburban

9. John Gladwin, *Love and Liberty: Faith and Unity in a Postmodern Age* (London: Darton, Longman & Todd, 1998), 209.

wilderness that included Tim and Kristy's house and a converted two-story garage that served as a sort of clubhouse and worship sanctuary all in one.

Tim's "real job" as a motorcycle builder kept him connected to the biker culture throughout the years, and as Joshua House began to develop into a community of faith, more and more of Tim's clients began showing up around the campfire. The presence of so many bikers caused Tim to eventually found and lead the Faithful Few, an outlaw Christian motorcycle club.

The Faithful Few is not a collection of middle-age suburban dads living out their Wild Hogs fantasies on the weekends. Far from it. These guys are the real deal. Tim shared with us that just a couple of days before we visited with him, he had baptized an outlaw biker he had been cultivating a relationship with for five years. This particular biker was known as an *enforcer*. We will leave the definition of that title to your imagination. Tim points out, "When these dudes come to Christ, they do so radically. They are radical cats, and just as radical as they were in the outlaw biker lifestyle, they go just as hard for Christ." One of his hardest jobs in discipling outlaw biker converts is for them not to "enforce" Christ upon their unconverted buddies. The objective is to create a circle of relationships among guys who have lived the outlaw biker life and want to become faithful and committed followers of Christ while still living in the biker culture.

Tim stresses that Joshua House is not a biker church per se. "We don't look at bikers as tokens for us to claim or highlight. But they have found a refuge and a community here." Joshua House is made up of an eclectic mix of straight-laced college students, middle-aged couples, single moms, and the biker crowd. It would be a gross understatement to say a Sunday morning at Joshua House is not your normal church service. Depending on the season, folks gather either outside nearby the organic garden and campfire or inside the downstairs clubhouse for pancakes, bagels, or other breakfast fare. Eventually the whole troop makes its way to the *upper room* for singing, prayer, and a typical sermon type of teaching.

Joshua House has no website or advertising other than the lives of its people who live to incarnate the message of the gospel in the midst of a culture that is somewhat hostile to the Christian idea. Speaking of the combination of Joshua House and the Faithful Few, Tim says, "We are an armpit in the body of Christ. We are not just an *everybody* church. We are an *anybody* church. Jesus went out and invited the tax collectors and outcasts to join him. We do the same thing."

This is missional church thinking. Instead of planting a traditional, at-tractional church, Tim and Kristy engage in the very rhythms and life of a host culture to genuinely listen to their hopes and fears. A similar experiment is the Hope Community in Wolverhampton, England. Three Roman Catholic sisters were asked by their parish church to conduct a community survey in Heath Town, an impoverished public housing project comprising nine high-rise buildings. They began simply by listening to the voices of the community. What they heard was a litany of despair, pain, and great social need. Unable to continue the "survey" and then return to their comfortable chapter house in a nearby middle-class suburb, they rented an apartment on the third floor of one of the bleak towers. There, they continued their regular life of community and prayer, making themselves much more available to the local people. The missional church assumes that proximity to a host community is essential.

Interestingly, as Sister Margaret Walsh reports it, none of the sisters set out to initiate anything.[10] They simply lived with and listened to their neighbors. But their gracious presence catalyzed many social changes. Housing project church services have begun, planned and led by local people. The sisters offer computer courses and literacy training, and have hosted holiday events—all contributing greatly to an improved quality of life for the residents. The integrity of their community and the power of their sense of mission have been salt and light in the public housing community. While the sisters resist calling what they're doing "church," the rest of the community clearly identify the nuns' apartment as their chapel. Like Tim and Kristy, the sisters have not come to impose anything on their host community. But by being Christ in the midst of their respective people groups, they make the assumption that God is already present and already touching people's lives. They don't presume to "bring" God to St. Louis or to Heath Town, but they do desire to be used by the Spirit to transform individuals and cultures for Christ's sake by the God who was already there.

Proximity Spaces

With these two working models as background, we are able to identify some of the shared traits that we observe in various missional churches. Four characteristics deserve special consideration: proximity spaces, shared projects, commercial enterprise, and emerging indigenous faith communities. By proximity spaces, we mean places or events where Christians and not-yet-Christians can interact meaningfully with each other.

Located in the small midwestern town of Newton, Kansas (population 15,000), is Norm's Coffee Bar. Robert Palmer began it as a place for people of a multiplicity of backgrounds to gather and experience community. He also

10. Margaret Walsh, *Here's Hoping!* Urban Theology Unit, New City Special No. 8, 1991.

pastors Stone Creek Community Church, which meets in the same building that houses Norm's Coffee Bar—but unless you knew the church also meets there, you would never know it. There are no church advertisements in the space. This is to say, the space has not been *Christianized*. It is neutral territory.

Dreaming of a space that would promote the type of community evoked in the mythical *Cheers*, a Boston pub from the 1980s television show by the same name, Palmer's team named the place Norm's, after *Cheers* patron Norm Peterson, whose entry to the pub is routinely met with a group greeting of "Hi, Norm!" Robert said, "A bar is really a counterfeit for the church. Everybody is welcome. Everyone does know your name. They're accepting. It doesn't matter what your background is or where you've come from. And there is always someone to talk to who doesn't judge you but just listens to your story. And the idea for us was to create Norm's Coffee 'bar' and to see if that could happen. And it has. Here, people come to us. And they just share their stories. I stand behind this counter and people open their hearts up." Norm's has become a public space being used by groups and organizations throughout the city, including the Chamber of Commerce.

Around the world, Christians are developing cafés, nightclubs, art galleries, design studios, football teams, etc., to facilitate such proximity and interaction. If the church service is the only space where we can meaningfully interact with unbelievers, we're in trouble. In Birmingham, England, Pip Piper, the founder of a design studio called One Small Barking Dog (great name!), runs a monthly gathering in a local café, the Medicine Bar. He has negotiated permission from the landlord to deck the premises out as a "spiritual space." Using incense, projected images, and ambient religious music, he designed a spiritual zone he calls Maji, where artists who would normally patronize the Medicine Bar as well as invited friends can hang out, experience the ambience, and talk about faith, religion, and spirituality—it's a classic proximity space.

Shared Projects

Second, missional church thinking values the development of shared or joint projects between the Christian community and its host community. Proximity spaces are excellent for casual interaction. Shared projects allow the Christians to partner with unbelievers in useful, intrinsically valuable activities within the community. In the context of that partnership, significant connections can be established. The church can initiate these shared projects though presented as a community-wide activity. Or the Christian community can simply get behind existing projects. The important thing is to find joint projects that put Christians and not-yet-Christians shoulder-to-shoulder in a lengthy partnership.

Time is an issue here. We need to find or develop projects that allow the time for important friendships to form.

Allan Tibbels was a 26-year-old quadriplegic in the mid-1980s when he moved into Sandtown, one of the toughest neighborhoods in Baltimore. He and his wife Susan were inspired by the writings of evangelist and civil rights worker John M. Perkins to live incarnationally by moving into the ghetto. What they found in Sandtown was nothing but overpriced rental units, every one of them a firetrap leased by an absentee landlord. Transience, homelessness, and the constant threat of eviction were everyday experiences there. And yet the neighborhood was pockmarked by vacant lots. Even though he couldn't move his arms or legs, Tibbels believed he could build affordable housing for his neighbors on this land. He turned to Habitat for Humanity for help.

Although he knew nothing about housing and couldn't swing a hammer himself, Tibbels scrounged enough donations and local volunteers to get a Habitat house built in 1990. Such was the response to this minor miracle across Baltimore that the funds for more houses began to flow and soon Tibbels announced he would build another hundred houses, with mortgages of about $300 a month, less than half the typical rent. Committed to partnering with the residents of Sandtown, Tibbels only hired from the neighborhood, which meant his staff grew to include ex-cons, addicts, and dealers. It also meant that he lost something in building efficiency and excellence, but in its place grew love. Maybe it was Tibbel's own brokenness that inspired the broken men and women of Sandtown to trust him in this foolhardy venture.

As a result, over two decades, a man who couldn't lift his arms built 286 houses. He also helped plant the New Song Community Church that grew out of the relationships Allan and Susan had built with their neighbors. One thousand people attended his funeral there in 2010, a service that saw politicians sitting next to drug dealers. The *New York Times* reported, "Someone once described Tibbels as 'saving Sandtown,' which made him wince. God saves; neighbors share."[11]

While in San Francisco, we had the opportunity to take a walk through the Hispanic mission district with Mark Scandrette, a bohemian artist who moved to the Bay Area to plant a church. He has discovered that by joining the neighborhood mural co-op (one of the oldest in the country), he literally stands shoulder-to-shoulder with non-Christians as they apply paint to murals across the city. He can also have input into what shape public art takes in San Francisco. In cities without a strong culture of public art, a Christian

11. Obituary, *New York Times*, cited 24 December 2010, http://www.nytimes.com/interactive /2010/12/26/magazine/2010lives.html#view=allan_tibbels.

community might want to initiate such a cooperative. The missional church doesn't immediately think in terms of strategies, but in terms of people and places. As Bono from U2 says, "If Jesus were on earth you'd find him in a gay bar in San Francisco. He'd be working with people suffering from AIDS. These people are the new lepers. If you want to find out where Jesus would be hanging out it'll always be with the lepers."

Commercial Enterprise

Third, commercial enterprise is important. Bringing positive and tangible change speaks volumes to the host community. If we come to plant a church in a particular area, we're not perceived as doing anyone any favors. But if we're starting a café, an internet launderette, or a day-care center, we're seen as bringing some intrinsic value to a community. We're serving those to whom we're sent.

In Sheffield, England, a woman named Jane Grinnoneau has established a community-based business called the Furnival in a derelict English pub of the same name. Her story is one of sheer hard work as well as the miraculous provision of God (a great combination). The Furnival pub had been stripped, vandalized, and abandoned by the time Jane came across it while wandering lost in the notorious Burngreave public housing project one day. How she acquired the building and fully fitted it out to meet the needs of the local community is a story of God's miraculous grace. Now the Furnival is a skills center for local young people, with a training kitchen and café. There are plans for a launderette and a multiagency health and advice center. Burngreave was so nefarious that formal Christian witness had ended there when the Methodist Church finally pulled out years before Jane got there. If anyone had announced that they were planting another traditional church in the project, the local community would have wondered why and the denominational churches would have questioned the waste of resources. But the Furnival is a Christian community serving the host community and seeing the kingdom being extended in ways a conventional church could never have seen.

Even at a denominational level, people are beginning to see the incarnational value of planting service industries within a host community. As Robert Palmer has discovered, the right local business can create significant and intimate relationships with people not normally interested in church-based programs.

Emerging Indigenous Faith Communities

Fourth, indigenous faith communities ought to emerge from all this interaction with a host subculture. While it is a noble and, indeed, a godly activity for a Christian businessman to run a shoe shop and to try to be Christ to his customers, something is missing if a Christian faith community isn't part of the equation. The Christian businessperson can engage colleagues, clients, and customers in a discussion of faith questions, but the best hermeneutic of the gospel is a community of Christians living it out. Robert Palmer, Margaret Walsh, Allan Tibbels, Jane Grinnoneau, and Pip Piper have developed their proximity spaces and their commercial ventures as missionaries. Their desire is to see the kingdom come and to see lives transformed by the power of Christ. Some have already developed faith communities from their incarnational activities, while for others it is still in the early days.

Some critics of the missional church ask, "When is the Bible taught? How do people learn doctrine?" We recognize these as valid questions. But we believe such learning takes place much more effectively when the Christian faith community is involved in active mission. Too much existing Bible teaching happens to passive groups of Christians, many of whom are not involved in any kind of risky missional activity. A missional church mobilizes all its members to be sent into the community. Like Jesus' first followers discovered, learning occurs when we need to draw on information because a situation demands it. This isn't to say that there shouldn't be formal teaching times, but these formal occasions will allow the teaching to be related to the missional experience gained by the church itself. It is important to note that the missional church combines the concern for community development normally characterized by the liberal churches and the desire for personal and community transformation normally characterized by the evangelical movement. This blurring of the old lines of demarcation between theologies, doctrine, and ideology within the church makes the way open for much more integrated mission to occur. It's like saying that we want to prepare like an evangelical; preach like a Pentecostal; pray like a mystic; do the spiritual disciplines like a Desert Father, art like a Catholic, and social justice like a liberal.

In fact, we have found that among many missional church leaders and thinkers there is a concern to balance ideas that are normally considered opposites. It is called both/and thinking and has been a feature of the emergent postmodern culture. Missional church thinking allows the dialogue between liberation theology, which says *context* is everything, and the post-liberals like Hauerwas and Brueggeman who say we need to get our *story* right. The missional church will take context seriously, but will also work on recovering the biblical narrative with its richness and potency for today's world. When story and context are equally embraced, we are beginning to think and act missionally. In San Francisco, a group calling itself ReImagine has been meeting to explore how this dialogue works itself out practically. To do so, ReImagine refs to different colored spaces. Yellow space refers to a Christian spirituality that is only concerned with the personal, interior world of faith. It characterizes the classic individualized form of faith that focuses on personal quiet times, Bible study, church attendance, and personal moral/ethical behavior. Blue space refers to an exclusively other-focused form of Christian spirituality, one that takes context seriously and features such activities as social concern, justice-seeking, activism, and public moral/ethical behavior. It is only in the dialogue between them, says ReImagine, that we come close to biblical missional activity and spirituality, as illustrated in figure 1.

FIGURE 1

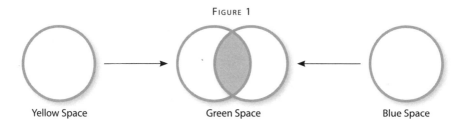

Yellow Space   Green Space   Blue Space

Since the combination of yellow and blue on the color chart does make green, it's a clever way to think about missional spaces. They are *green spaces*. And missional Christians might rightly be referred to as *green people*. In a green space, story and context, the individual and the communal, the interior world and the exterior world, the religious and the non-religious, find genuine meeting. At ReImagine references to green people and green spaces are common.

Getting It Right

In sleepy suburban Pomona in Los Angeles, the front lawns are freshly cut and their edges trimmed. The streetlights glow a warm amber hue throughout the quiet evenings. Street signs announce that Pomona is a neighborhood-watch zone and tell would-be intruders that "we report any suspicious persons or activities to our police department." But on downtown Second Street, something's up! Some years ago Second Street was transformed into an Arts Colony (an imposing sign over the street announces it as such), and now there are a number of dance venues, nightclubs, art studios, and hip clothing stores. There is a college of the arts in town, and Second Street is crawling with bohemians, punks, hip-hoppers, taggers, and performance artists. Posters in windows advertise everything from acting classes to stained glass making, poetry readings, and mosaic table workshops. When we were visiting Pomona, there was a "Beginning Wicca" workshop and a panel discussion on "Woman in the Arts" happening that night. Music styles available in the various venues include blues, hip-hop, rock, house, punk, rockabilly, and Latino.

Right in the middle of this carnivalesque atmosphere of art and music, new age religion, and commercialism we discovered the Millennia Co-op at 181 Second Street. Although it no longer exists, we found that its cohesion in the community offered several wonderful elements of a faith collective existing as servant to the host community. It was the brainchild of the radical missionaries John Jensen and the late Brian Ollman, and was a mission experiment that combined proximity spaces, shared projects, business enterprises, and indigenous faith communities. Their mission statement read, "The Millennia Co-op advances cultural renewal and personal transformation through the integration of the arts, community, spirituality, business and public service. The Millennia Co-op consists of several inter-connected projects, all centered in the Pomona Arts Colony. Each Millennia Co-op project provides opportunities for creative expression, employment and connecting in a healing community centered around Jesus."

Each Millennia Co-op project was designed to incorporate one or more of the four features we mention above.

Millennia art lounge: The Lounge was the Millennia Co-op's storefront project (literally)—a street-level store right on Second Street, converted into a performance space/dance venue hosting a weekly poetry night, live bands, hip-hop music, and house music events. All these regular events offered free or low cost and provided an alcohol- and drug-free space for a diverse group of young people to hang out and create community. The Millennia Lounge also hosted occasional art exhibitions as local artists, including the homeless, could gain exposure to their work and expression (note: proximity space, with an element of shared project).

Millennia art studio: This space offered beginning and experienced artists a place to create together in a community environment. Free studio space was available, as were art workshops and vocational training courses. The artists who used the studio (Christians and not-yet-Christians) occasionally took their work to the streets by producing murals and art installations to beautify the city. It's from the studio that much of the work for the exhibitions in the Lounge came (note: shared project and proximity space).

Millennia design group: Established in an open-plan office in a loft above the Lounge, the lab specialized in creative graphic designs that attracted customers

from an assortment of businesses in Pomona and beyond. It produced business cards, websites, letterheads, and other business collateral (note: business
enterprise).

Innerworld: Millennia's electronic dance culture collective, hosting a weekly
house music event in the Lounge and also making a positive impact on the host
community through projects like picking up trash and serving the homeless
(note: shared project).

Millennia JiuJitsu: In the front of the basement under the Lounge, there were
weekly jiujitsu wrestling classes promoting community relationships and personal fitness (note: business enterprise and proximity space).

Ichthus: At the core of the Millennia Co-op, an indigenous faith community
called Ichthus. Originally one small group meeting in Brian Ollman's home,
grew to three cell churches and continued to burgeon. Members of the church
shared responsibility for several of the Millennia projects, and the leadership
network (not elected, merely recognized) met regularly to consider the future
direction of the mission. Those members of Ichthus that we met saw their
involvement as that of missionaries. The people who came to Ichthus and
then made a commitment to Christ were first accessed through the Lounge
or jiujitsu or the Studio. In fact, some of those who came to Christ had been
about as far from the church as Western kids could be.

We don't present the Pomona experiment as *the* way forward nor as the
only expression of the missional church. It is *one* of the forms the missional
church takes, and there will be as many forms as there are subcultures or people
groups or neighborhoods to reach. And we applaud the courage, tenacity, and
creativity shown by Brian and his team in getting something as effective as the
Millennia Co-op launched. It was genuinely green space.

Incarnational, Messianic, Apostolic

What we propose is a reversing of the three mistakes made by the Christendom-
mode church. The missional church, by its very nature, will be an anticlone
of the existing traditional model. Rather than being primarily attractional, it
will be incarnational. It will be willing to leave its own comfortable religious
zones and live in direct contact with non-churchgoers, seeping into the host
culture like salt and light. It will be an infiltrating, transformational community.
Second, rather than being dualistic, it will embrace a messianic spirituality.

That is, a spirituality of engagement with culture and the world in the same mode as the Messiah himself. And third, the missional church will develop an apostolic form of leadership rather than the traditional hierarchical model.

We will explore each of these modes of being missional in the following three sections of this book. In fact, we prefer the term mode to that of model. We are not commending a new model at all. The church is surely tiring of the latest model being offered by church-growth theorists. As we just pointed out, the missional church will value diversity and should look significantly different depending on which subculture it has felt called to serve.

PART TWO

INCARNATIONAL ECCLESIOLOGY

3

The Incarnational Approach

Ivan Illich was once asked what is the most revolutionary way to change society. Is it violent revolution or is it gradual reform? He gave a careful answer. Neither. If you want to change society, then you must tell an alternative story, he concluded.

—Tim Costello

Reinventing the Church

We recently saw the cover of a book about reinventing the church that's an icon of just what we think is wrong with the post-Christendom church. It depicts a classic church building, replete with a tall steeple, long stained glass windows, and a white picket fence. Leaning over the building from behind is a giant man in a white, long-sleeved shirt and a tie (we think he's meant to be a minister—very clean cut) and a gigantic wrench in his hand. He is tightening a huge bolt on the front of the steeple. When we talk about reinventing the church, too many people assume it's as simple as tightening a bolt here, oiling a hinge there, slapping on a new coat of paint. But we are proposing a monumental change to the way we think about being and doing church.

All the tinkering with the existing model of church that's going on will not save the day. Simply making minor adjustments like replacing pews with more comfortable seating, or singing contemporary pop songs instead of hymns will not reverse the fundamental decline in the fortunes of the Western church.

If you think of the church as a car, we cannot simply take it in for service. We need a whole new model. Or think of the church as a DVD player. If you have a newer Blu-ray disc, you can't play it on your old DVD player—you need an entirely different device. As we pointed out in the previous chapter, we believe this new mode should be incarnational, messianic, and apostolic. We will turn our attention now to the first of these primary aspects of the missional church.

Coming to Grips with Being Incarnational

For us the Incarnation is an absolutely fundamental doctrine, not just as an irreducible part of the Christian confession, but also as a theological prism through which we view our entire missional task in the world. So when we talk of incarnational mission, we hope to, in some real way, directly draw inspiration and motivation from that unique act whereby God entered into our world and into the human condition in the person of Jesus Christ.

Some reflection on this unique event is therefore necessary before we can draw out some of the profound implications that this should have on our engagement with the world in which we live. When we talk of the Incarnation with a capital *I* we refer to that act of sublime love and humility whereby God took it upon himself to enter into the depths of our world, our life, and our reality in order that the reconciliation and consequent union between God and humanity may be brought about. This "enfleshing" of God is so radical and total that it is the bedrock upon which rests all subsequent acts of God in his world. A halfway house on the way to God would not do for a lost humanity, and so God had to come down to man, not halfway but the whole way.

To say that this event is fundamental to a true conception of the Christian faith is surely an understatement. Without it, the work of Jesus lacks its redemptive merit. Orthodox Christian belief rightly stresses that the atonement is directly linked to Christ's divinity and to his humanity. Jesus had to be God to be able to lift us out of our sin, but had to be fully human to create the right conditions for such redemption to take place. It is *from inside* the human condition and experience that God fulfills his own requirements for the salvation of the human race. Therefore we rightly confess that God is love, and that this is a love that has resolutely pursued us to the point at which it overtakes us—in the depths of our sin and lostness. Thus the course of human sin determines the history of God's love.

While recognizing that in the Incarnation we are dealing with something of a holy mystery and a paradox that in some ways is inexplicable, we wish to highlight here some of the theological implications for us to consider in the context of this book.

Identification: The Incarnation embodies an act of profound identification with the entire human race. The medium is entirely the message. The human form which God takes in Jesus is no mere outer garment, like a beggar-cloak of a king who dresses up in order to seek out the love of a beggar-girl in the local village, a garment that flutters loosely about him and so betrays his real status as a king. No, rather it is his true form and figure. In an act of unspeakable humility, God actually takes upon himself all the conditions, even the limitations, the struggles, and the doubts of humanity (Phil. 2:6–8; Heb. 5:7–8). And it is God's distinct greatness that in Jesus his love encompasses not just the great and the strong, but even the smallest—all of the little and inconsequential people who suffer in their quiet corners. Nothing is so small that he overlooks it. That is the extent to which God becomes human—the extent to which he loves us and wills to experience unconditionally what it means to be human. Therefore we can believe in his love and be sure that he is completely *for* us.

Locality: It has been said, "If we want to make a thing real we must make it local." That is precisely what God did in Jesus Christ—the divine love took on a local habitation and a name. The coming of God among us was not just a momentary theophany, but constituted an actual "dwelling" among us (John 1:14). In the light of such a dwelling, place—geography itself—took on a sacred meaning: He became known as Jesus *of Nazareth*. It is interesting to ponder whether Nazareth itself, a poor town in ancient Israel, actually had a role in the formation of Jesus and, through him, the world. To be theologically true to the meaning of the humanity of Jesus, we have to recognize that Jesus was who he was, not only because he was God, but because he was formed through his real engagement with his social milieu. As an authentic human being, Jesus was Jesus precisely because of Mary and Joseph, his twelve disciples, the poor to whom he ministered, and all the others who interacted with him in the myriad ways common to human life. He was changed in some way by all those he came in contact with in precisely the same way that we are changed by our relationships—for good or ill. To be a genuine human being, Jesus must have had such relational encounters, and to continue as a person (as he indeed still is), he must somehow retain them. If this is not true, then his humanity was a sham, a make-believe. And so the life of God incarnate in Jesus could not be locked secretly within his heart; rather it became a spreading complex of *personal being* centered in Jesus and annexing his companions. This, as we will see, has massive implications for the way in which we engage our world and the people around us.

The Beyond-in-the-midst (2 Cor. 5:19): Here resides the paradox at the heart of the Incarnation. The eternal transcendent God was and is right here, in our midst. In Jesus, God came into direct personal contact with the human race which he so loves. He was/is not "above" us any longer. He is one of us. The presence of God in Jesus will henceforth define God's mission to the world. Those who seek God will now find him in Jesus the man. The Incarnation is an event in heaven as well as on earth. In Jesus, God meets each of us personally. Henceforth all people, whoever they are and whenever or wherever they live, have the possibility of a personal relationship with God.

The Human image of God (Col. 1:15): It has been noted that in the light of the New Testament, the remarkable truth is not so much that Jesus is Godlike, but rather that God is actually Christlike. (God is Christlike and in him is no un-Christlikeness at all.) In the light of the New Testament revelation, all who would wish to know who God is and what he is like need look no further than the person of Jesus (John 1:18; 14:9). From now on, all true perspectives of God must pass through the very particular lens of the man called Jesus of Nazareth. To say this more technically, all theology must now be understood through Christology. The genius of this aspect of New Testament revelation is that in Jesus God provides for us the basis of all imitation of him. From our perspective as human beings Jesus becomes the reference point for all genuine knowing, all true loving, and all authentic following of God. This, too, will have massive implications on the church's life and mission.

The above points are only a poor attempt to outline some of the theological implications of the *enfleshing* of God as we perceive them. And we have outlined them here to somehow trace ways that we believe the Incarnation should inform our mission in God's world—how we, as the fruit of God's Incarnation, should ourselves be and become *incarnational*. When we use the word *incarnational* (and we do all the way through this book), we use it in such a way as to gather up all or any of these motifs into the concept. We believe it must define and change the way we do mission in any context.

First, the Incarnation provides us with the missional means by which the gospel can become a genuine part of a people group without damaging the innate cultural frameworks that provide that people group with a sense of meaning and history. David Bosch is right when he notes that "it should not bother us that during different epochs the Christian faith was perceived and experienced in new and different ways. The Christian faith is intrinsically incarnational."[1] Therefore unless the church actively resists the demands of incarnational mission, it must always enter fully into the context in which it happens to find itself. To birth, for instance, a full-fledged denominational church with all its associated Western-style liturgies, symbolic system, and worldview in the middle of Africa is a distortion of the incarnational principle of mission. The same is true for every missional context, including that of our now profoundly tribalized Western cultures. Thus the incarnational criteria must guide the church's cultural expression in all its diverse contexts.

Second, incarnational mission will mean that in reaching a people group we will need to identify with them in all ways possible without compromising the truth of the gospel itself. The power implicit in this act of identification is forcefully portrayed in movies with religious themes like *Of Gods and Men*, *The Mission*, *The City of Hope*, and *Romero*. It is also a grand theme in mythology and in general literature precisely because there is a great "magic" in it. There is a mysterious power that is unleashed in the act of becoming part of a people group for the sake of the gospel. Why? Because it involves a personal "buy-in," a partaking, a stakeholding, and a real sympathy. And it is a powerful tool for mission in any context. For instance, for the members of Urban Neighbours of Hope (UNOH) in Melbourne and the InnerCHANGE workers in San Francisco, identification with the poor is an absolutely fundamental principle to their mission among the poor. All the missionaries and workers in these two missionary orders voluntarily live under the poverty line and refuse to be paid by their organizations for their work among the poor lest the people say, "You are paid to be kind to us." They choose to live like the people with all the struggles and problems that poverty creates for people without power and resources. This incarnational act not only creates credibility for the missionaries, but it thus creates the relational-social context within which they can meaningfully and humanly share their faith. Because it means that for all intents and purposes, they have actually become part of the people group that they are trying to reach and have thereby overcome a very significant cultural barrier to the communication of the gospel. To identify incarnationally with a people will mean that we must try to enter into something of the cultural life of a "people"; to seek to understand their perspectives, their grievances and causes, in other words their real existence, in such a way as to genuinely reflect the act of identification that God made with us in Jesus.

But the practice of incarnational identification with a group of people should not be limited to work among the poor. We insist that in some ways

---

1. David Bosch, *Transforming Mission* (Maryknoll, NY: Orbis, 1991), 190–91.

it should apply to all forms of genuine mission whatever the context. Not only because it "works" but because it somehow reflects that primal act of identification that was an intrinsic part of Christ's Incarnation. It is because of this that incarnational identification retains its inherent gospel power to transform the myriad subcultural tribes that now face us in our task of mission in the West.

The great danger in failing to practice mission *incarnationally* is cultural imperialism. This form of imperialism, itself a sin, is easily observed in so many countries where Western missionaries import without critical reflection their cultural forms of the gospel and impose them on a people group. Even though conversions often result, the long-term outcome is the loss of a genuinely local, indigenous culture. The Christians of that group appear to be more like *wannabe* westerners than genuine incarnational expressions of the Christian faith among their own people group. The "church" thereby becomes an isolated, somewhat alien body in the midst of a people. And with this demise of a shared culture, there sadly comes an overall loss of meaning and connectedness. Perhaps the worst result is, however, that the gospel, which itself cannot be understood apart from a shared meaning system (culture), cannot thereby sustain itself organically and meaningfully among the original people group over the long term because the relational connection is severed.

Thus, short-term success gives way to long-term ineffectiveness, leading us to believe that all non-incarnational (excarnational?) missions are in the end self-defeating. Perhaps this is one of the reasons that so many missionary efforts have failed—in that so many missionaries, indeed the church itself, remained aliens to the target group rather than being an incarnated presence with all that this implies. What is now clear to us about non-Western contexts is also becoming appallingly clear regarding our own context. We so easily impose a cultural form on the people and the groups we hope to reach with the love of Jesus. We so often make the gospel synonymous with a bland middle-class conformity and thereby alienate countless people from encountering Christ. How often have we seen public opinion polls that reflect the attitude of "Jesus, Yes! Church, No!"

Third, incarnational mission implies a *real and abiding* incarnational presence among a group of people. Quite simply, it means that if you want to reach the local *gangstas*, you are going to have to live where they live and hang out where they hang out. Or it might mean that if you want to plant a church in a given suburb, you should really think about living there. Why? Because you cannot become part of the organic life of a given community if you are not present to it and do not experience its cultural rhythms, its life, and its geography. The idea of incarnational presence corresponds to the idea of locality that was outlined above in our reflections on the Incarnation. Jesus moved into the neighborhood; he experienced its life, its rhythms, and its people *from the inside* and not as an outsider. It is sobering to think that for thirty years Jesus practiced this presence before he actually started his ministry. Nazareth had indeed become a living part of him and defined him in so many unaccountable ways. If this was so for Jesus, then, we believe, we, too, need to practice the missional discipline of presence and identification with any of the groups and people we hope to engage with. This is true whether they are the local ravers or members of bohemian art cooperatives, sports clubs, common interest groups, or parent groups—we need to identify a whole lot more before we can expect to really share Jesus in a meaningful way with them.

Fourth, in terms of its missional stance in relation to context, incarnational mission implies a *sending* impulse rather than an extractional one. The New Testament impulse of mission is therefore centrifugal rather than centripetal.[2] God is a missionary—he sent his Son into our world, into our lives, into human history. Incarnation therefore implies some form of sending in order to be able to radically incarnate into the various contexts in which disciples live. And while not all of us are called to cross-cultural forms of mission, we do believe that all of us are called to some form of incarnational expression of faith. We are not all meant to look and sound alike in every context! We are not meant to be part of a stifling monoculture. And why is this so? Because mission is always conditioned by that act whereby God reached out to us in a meaningful way when he moved into our neighborhood. We will have more to say about the missional mode of the Christendom church as being "attractional-extractional" in the pages to come, and so we leave the argument until then. But, suffice to say at this point that, in our opinion, the vast majority of churches in the West engage their contexts in an attractional, and therefore *extractional,* way. We believe that this insight provides a clue into why so much of our outreach and evangelism in the US, UK, and Australia actually ends up being ineffective and self-defeating. We believe that this situation *must* change if we are to be faithful witnesses in the new millennium.

And finally, incarnational mission means that people will get to experience Jesus on the *inside* of their culture (meaning systems) and their lives because of our embodying the gospel in an incarnationally appropriate way. For us, this is perhaps the most important aspect to consider in our attempts to genuinely

2. These terms derive from physics: *centripetal* means moving or tending to move toward a center whereas *centrifugal* means moving or tending to move away from a center.

re-evangelize the Western world. If Jesus has become so unfamiliar to most people, perhaps it is because he is perceived by many as a tame "churchgoer" and a teacher of moralistic platitudes. Most attitudinal research on the subject indicates that in terms of the public perception of outsiders (the "unchurched"), to become a Christian is synonymous with becoming a somewhat happy but bland, usually white, almost always middle-class, middle-of-the-road kind of person. This kind of person is exemplified by Ned Flanders in Matt Groenig's immensely popular and insightful cultural critique, *The Simpsons*. One might well say that Ned is a caricature, but if he is, it only serves to exaggerate the reality that underlies all caricaturing. Ned Flanders is all too real to allow us to be at all comfortable. The problem we face is that this is precisely the way in which evangelicals are perceived by the non-churched culture 'round about us. It is sobering to consider that on these grounds, Jesus himself would likely have been deeply alienated from the church as it generally expresses itself in the US, the UK, and Australia. This puts a new spin on that text "Behold, I stand at the door and knock."

Missional churches all around the world are now trying to find ways in which to embody the gospel in an incarnational way. Whether it be Third Place Communities in Tasmania, where the community commits to always gather in public social spaces and never in private sacred buildings, or the church of which Michael is part (marvelously named Small Boat, Big Sea) where people experience a culturally seamless expression of Jesus, or the Breakfast Club in Pomona where the experience of church is built around the natural conversation of a breakfast table. For us at least, it is in these struggling little communities that the hope of the gospel in the West resides. For in such ways the biblical prophecy of the Incarnation of God in Jesus will once again be true in our day, that people living in darkness might once again see a great light (Matt. 4:16).

It is absolutely vital for the gospel to be incarnated into the thousands of subcultures that now exist in our complex, postmodern, tribalized, Western contexts. It is vital that these multiform people and subcultures encounter Jesus from *within* their own cultures and from *within* their own communities, for only there can they truly comprehend him. It is now critical for the sake of the gospel itself that these people experience salvation in a way that does not dislocate them from their organic groups but rather allows them to encounter Jesus in a way that is seamlessly connected with life as they have come to understand it through their own histories and experiences.

But the greatest argument for the case of incarnational mission in the end is the undeniable fact that it was the missional mode in which God himself engaged the world; it should be no less ours!

Attractional Versus Incarnational

As we've already pointed out, the relationship between the traditional Christendom mode of church and the world around it can best be described as being fundamentally *attractional*. That is, the church expects people to be willing to come to some centrally located religious institution at the heart of the culture to hear, respond, and be nurtured in the gospel. The church bids people to *come and hear* the gospel within the holy confines of the church and its community. This seems so natural to us after seventeen centuries of Christendom, but at what price and to what avail have we allowed it to continue? If our actions imply that God is really only present in official church activities—worship, Bible studies, Christian youth meetings, ladies fellowships—then it follows that mission and evangelism simply involve inviting people to church-related meetings.

In fact, this is one of the core assumptions that the attractional church is based upon—the assumption that God cannot really be accessed outside sanctioned church meetings or, at least, that these meetings are the best place for not-yet-Christians to learn about God. Evangelism therefore is primarily about mobilizing church members to attract unbelievers into church where they can experience God. Rather than being genuine "out-reach," it effectively becomes something more like an "in-drag."

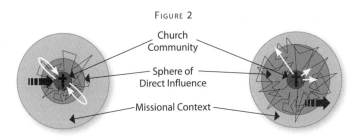

FIGURE 2

Church Community

Sphere of Direct Influence

Missional Context

Christendom & Church Growth	Incarnational & Missional
• Mission mode & impulse is inward (attractional)	• Mission mode & impulse is outward (sending)
• Cells and evangelism exist to get people into church	• Cells and mission exist to create organic communities
• Christians cluster at center	of faith in the context of mission
• Appropriate for outreach to sphere of direct influence	• Christians spread out in context
	• Appropriate for all forms of mission

Now, we are not suggesting that people can't experience God in a church service. Of course they can, for in the preaching of God's Word and the worship of God's people his true voice can be heard. But if the church limits God's agency in this world to particular times and places that the vast majority of not-yet-Christians have no access to, or no desire to attend, then the gospel is effectively hobbled. God becomes mute to the vast majority of people in the Western world, people who cannot interpret the church culture that has effectively imprisoned the good news within its cultural system. The only means to evangelize people becomes organizing little "patrols" to go into the world in order to rescue them and bring them back to the safety of "church." Many Westerners in our post-Christendom era report that they've tried church and found it wanting. If they don't want to go back, what then?

If they won't come to us, we have to go to them. This approach, being incarnational, is the opposite of being attractional. It implies something of a Go-To-Them approach to mission and evangelism. Instead of asking non-Christians to Come-To-Us, to our services, our gatherings, and our programs on our terms, the incarnational church seeks to infiltrate society to represent Christ in the world.

That is why we propose that a radical shift needs to take place in this time— a shift from the attractional mode to an incarnational one. This is no mean request, because the vast majority of churches in the West (95 percent?) operate in a nonincarnational mode of mission. An incarnational mode creates a church that is a dynamic set of relationships, friendships, and acquaintances. It enhances and "flavors" the host community's living social fabric rather than disaffirming it. It thus creates a medium of living relationships through which the gospel can travel. It emphasizes the importance of a group of Christians infiltrating a community, like salt and light, to make those creative connections with people where God-talk and shared experience allow for real cross-cultural Christian mission to take place.

The missional-incarnational church starts with the basic theological understandings: God constantly comes to those who are the most unlikely. For example, the Hebrews were the world's outcasts. God chose them. The Old Testament story of Ruth is profoundly missional. It is part of the continuing story of God's future plans emerging through the strangest and most unlikely people and places. In that story God revealed that his future for Israel was to be fulfilled in and through a Gentile (Ruth). If we are to take incarnational mission seriously, then we must see that God's future—his new creation—is not just among "his people" (churchgoing Christians) but it is among the "ordinary" people—the lost, strugglers, and listless ones of our world.

Going to Ignored People

Some time ago I (Michael) was watching my daughter play soccer in a local park. Next to the field was an asphalted area where a group of model-car enthusiasts had set up a track and were using remote controls to race their cars against one another's. The constant buzz of the miniature motors caught our attention and we wandered over to watch what they were doing. We soon realized we had encountered a lost suburban tribe. Everyone looked the same. They all wore tight black jeans and checkered flannel shirts. They wore baseball caps with car manufacturers' logos on them. They had parked their cars—virtually all drove pickups—beside the track, and their wives or girlfriends sat in one of the truck beds talking and laughing loudly. It was a tribe in every sense of the word—dress code, language, culture, and customs. We learned that once a month on a Sunday morning they met to race each other, to discuss the latest designs in model cars, and to drink and laugh and build community.

If the nearby church decided that this suburban tribe needed to hear about the saving work of Christ, how would they reach them? The attractional church would hold special services for model-car racers. It would design an excellent flyer explaining that Jesus loves model-car enthusiasts, and they would place one under the windshield wipers of each pickup. It would try to find a recently converted model-car enthusiast and have him share his testimony one Sunday morning. The attractional church would seek to do anything it could to draw the car racing fraternity into its church building. This might even work if you're dealing with a localized community with some geographic proximity to the church building. But a car club community usually draws people from a very large geographic area. The model-car club is probably a citywide community, and its members probably drive great distances to come to its monthly meetings. They are not drawn together by some geographic proximity, but by a commonly held interest. And to complicate matters further, they meet on Sunday mornings!

The attractional church is stuck! Even though it has a close-knit community of people (likely non-churchgoers) right outside its door, it has no mechanism for sharing Christ with them. Since they (the car club members) are not likely to turn up at the church service one Sunday (doesn't the attractional church *love* stories of people miraculously turning up at the church service searching for meaning and purpose!), the only way to share Christ's love with them must be to go to them. It would be a decidedly incarnational choice if a few members of a local church, so moved by compassion for the car enthusiasts right across the road, chose to buy a model car and join the club! This would be the kind of thinking and acting we're talking about. If the spirit of our missionary God were to sweep through such a church, we don't doubt that the church itself might buy a few model cars and commission some of its members to miss the morning service so they can fully enter into the community of the car club. By racing cars and repairing cars, they could earn the right of relationship to share their thoughts on life and their love for Jesus. This is the incarnational church in action. If a few car racers came into relationship with Christ, they should not be encouraged to leave the club and join the church. Rather, a home church could be established, and the brand-new Christian car enthusiasts could worship God in the context of their tribal identity.

The Missional Church Is Incarnational

The missional-incarnational church adopts a stance totally different from the attractional one. Rather than investing time in the creation and development of sacred religious spaces for people to meet God, this mode recognizes that church is a much more organic, dynamic, and non-institutionalized set of relationships than the old Christendom mode allows for. If the attractional mode sees the world as divided into two zones, the "in" and the "out," the incarnational model sees it more as a web, a series of intersecting lines symbolizing the networks of relationships, friendships, and acquaintances of which church members are a part.

It was Jesus who, in calling the first members of his faith community, the disciples, invited them to become fishers of people (Mark 1:16–18). By calling fishermen and inviting them to fish for humans, he used language that made sense to his hearers. But he did more than that. He used an image or a metaphor that conveyed a great deal more than some simple idea that he was concerned with "catching" people. He made reference to an activity that fishermen engaged in regularly, and by doing so created a sense of the missional community that was to come.

When we refer to fishing in our Western context, we think about a single person with a single rod and a single hook on the end of a single line. The fisherman is attempting to catch one fish with each cast of the line. It is a one-on-one engagement, and good fishermen know how to read the weather, the tides, the presence of weeds, and the use of lures to catch that one fish. So when we read about Jesus inviting the first disciples (and by inference us) to fish for people, we might assume it's a similar one-on-one affair. We have thought of evangelism like this in recent years. We have been sent out to fish for someone we can bring into our church. Getting someone to attend a service with us or come to an evangelistic breakfast or youth rally has formed the foundation of much Western evangelism. But unfortunately, a good many people in the West believe they have tried church and were left unsatisfied or they aren't interested at all in church attendance.

But if we think about fishing during Jesus' time, it wasn't done with rods and reels. It wasn't one-on-one. Jesus' disciples would have thought of fishing with a net. They would have cast their nets out into the water, and dredged or dragged the sea as they hauled the net back onto the boat. Whatever happened to be swimming in the way of the net as it was lugged back on board w ʔ¹ have been caught. The key to successful fishing wasn't in the technical details of tides and weather patterns, but in the strength of the nets. For this reason, Jesus' fishing disciples spent most of their working day, not out on the lake's surface, but on shore, mending their nets. If their nets were strong and tight, anything caught in them couldn't escape.

If we relate this image to the missional-incarnational church today, it has important implications. Instead of adopting a stance that requires a Christian to leave a sacred zone to go and fish for an individual to return with him to that zone, it releases the church to see its "fishing" as a more relational exercise. If the disciples spent so much time on their nets to ensure a catch, what might those nets be for us today? We propose that the web of relationships, friendships, and acquaintances that Christians normally have makes up the net into which not-yet-Christians will swim. We believe the missional-incarnational church will spend more time on building friendships than it will on developing religious programs.

Charles Ringma, from the Philippines Theological Seminary, makes this point about the emphasis on programs over relationships:

> A telling example is where a church committee develops a special plan for service and action by the church in the community and then tries to sell it to church members for their involvement and support. . . . It is this plan that receives all the publicity, the prayers and the church's money. This is the official project.[3]

Most church members can relate to this aspect of the attractional church. The church board or the deacons have decided that Alpha from Holy Trinity Church, Brompton, is the answer, or that they need to develop seeker services like Willow Creek Church. All the church's energies go into making the program work. Usually it is a strategy or a program that has been transplanted from somewhere else. And even though the program might be sound and biblical and is obviously very effective in its original context, it nevertheless smacks of something artificial. This is because it is not an indigenous, locally-based, "homegrown" initiative. But Ringma continues:

> But no thought is given to establish what church members are already doing in their neighborhood and places of work. No attempt is made, for example, to

3. Charles Ringma, *Catch the Wind: The Shape of the Church to Come* (Sydney: Albatross, 1994), 61.

identify the medical practitioner who has changed the approach to patients by providing counseling and practical support rather than just curative care. No attempt is made to identify the local [public official] in the congregation who is tackling certain important quality of life and social issues in the community. No attempt is made to support the lady who is conducting an informal neighborhood Bible study group. No attempt is made to support prayerfully the teacher who has just started work in an inner-city school with many pupils from broken families. And no attempt is made to see one family's care for their disabled child as a ministry worthy of the church's support and prayers.[4]

More than that, we don't see businessmen, students, youth workers, lecturers, plumbers, electricians, and homemakers as having missional roles in their worlds. If a businessman starts a prayer breakfast in a local restaurant, the church will notify its members and support the program. But if a businessman attempts to use his influence to develop ethical schemes through his business to serve the needy or create jobs for the unemployed we traditionally don't see this as mission. We don't see the strong creation of friendships that parents make through the local school as being anything to do with mission (unless they're inviting them to church). We can't see the regular gathering of surfers at their local beach as part of the net that catches people into the kingdom of God.

In a conversation with theological stirrer and author Leonard Sweet, we were stimulated to think about how the church's stance is always so inward. Len told us about how he will often get Christians who come to his conferences to stand in a large circle around the room. He said that they always stand shoulder-to-shoulder facing inward. When he points this out, they immediately adopt the opposite stance and face outward. But, Leonard Sweet reminds them, a totally outward-facing church isn't being everything a church should be. He then asks them to stand facing each other with one shoulder facing the center of the circle and the other facing out. It might seem like a small shift, but by standing in this less natural position they gain a powerful reminder of the missionary stance. It's both inward and outward looking.

Birds of a Feather . . .

In his magnificent book on the church, Jurgen Moltmann identifies the principle that undergirds much of how we do church today as "birds of a feather flocking together."[5] We believe this principle is inherent in the attractional mode of

4. Ibid., 61–62.
5. Jurgen Moltmann, *The Open Church: Invitation to a Messianic Lifestyle* (London: SCM, 1978), 27–36.

church. When the church is seen as a distinct category, completely separate from the world, it naturally develops an us-versus-them mentality. The missional church, with its incarnational approach, on the other hand, has built into its thinking a Go-To-Them stance. It sees itself, not as a closed system, but as an infiltrating community. Therefore it cannot tolerate the birds-of-a-feather principle. In explaining, Moltmann says, "'Birds of a feather flock together.' But why? People who are like us, who think the same thoughts, who have the same things, and who want the same things confirm us. However, people who are different from us, that is, people whose thoughts, feelings and desires are different from ours, make us feel insecure."[6] This might sound like basic group psychology. But it has serious implications for the church. If the church is simply a community of like-minded people, inviting other like-minded people to join them, then it will always be severely impeded in its attempt to win the world for Christ. This sort of church, then, according to Moltmann, has no ego-strength, no self-confidence. It is a form of self-justification. Moltmann proposes that the biblical mode is very different. Instead of being birds of a feather, the church should embrace Paul's injunction for the church, "Accept one another, then, just as Christ accepted you, in order to bring praise to God" (Rom. 15:7). Accepting others isn't just some wise and useful injunction for the good of the church. The acceptance of others emerges directly out of our having been accepted by Christ. When we know he has accepted us, we are freed from the need for self-justification. This liberates us to accept others. Says Moltmann:

> Accept one another "*as Christ has accepted you.*" Only this attitude can give us a new orientation and break through our limitations so that we can spring over our narrow shadows. It opens us up for others as they really are so that we gain a longing for and an interest in them. As a result of this we become able actually to forget ourselves and to focus on the way Christ has accepted us.[7]

The missional-incarnational church is well aware of the importance of the web of relationships, friendships, and acquaintances for mission. Christian mission is a relational activity that happens through the conduit of human relations. The incarnational church is opposed to the idea of simply developing churches full of people looking for the affirmation of other, like-minded people. Accepting others, whether Christian or not, is imperative. The stronger a church can build the nets of friendship with other Christians and not-yet-Christians, the greater the likelihood of effective mission occurring.

6. Ibid., 30.
7. Ibid., 30–31.

Wells and Fences

It is important here to distinguish between centered sets and bounded sets, for this goes to the heart of the difference between the two modes of church we've been discussing. The attractional church is a bounded set. That is, it is a set of people clearly marked off from those who do not belong to it. Churches thus mark themselves in a variety of ways. Having a church membership roll is an obvious one. This mechanism determines who's in and who's out. The missional-incarnational church, though, is a centered set. This means that rather than drawing a border to determine who belongs and who doesn't, a centered set is defined by its core values, and people are not seen as in or out, but as closer or further away from the center. In that sense, everyone is in and no one is out. Though some people are close to the center and others far from it, everyone is potentially part of the community in its broadest sense.

A useful illustration is to think of the difference between wells and fences. In some farming communities, the farmers might build fences around their properties to keep their livestock in and the livestock of neighboring farms out. This is a bounded set. But in rural communities where farms or ranches cover an enormous geographic area, fencing the property is out of the question. In our home of Australia, ranches (called stations) are so vast that fences are superfluous. Under these conditions a farmer has to sink a bore and create a well, a precious water supply in the Outback. It is assumed that livestock, though they will stray, will never roam too far from the well, lest they die. This is a centered set. As long as there is a supply of clean water, the livestock will remain close by.

Churches that see themselves as a centered set recognize that the gospel is so precious, so refreshing that, like a well in the Australian Outback, lovers of Christ will not stray too far from it. It is then a truly Christ-centered model. Rather than seeing people as Christian or non-Christian, as in or out, we would see people by their degree of distance from the center, Christ. In this way, the missional-incarnational church sees people as Christian and not-yet-Christian. It acknowledges the contribution of not-yet-Christians to Christian community and values the contribution of all people. Jesus' faith community was clearly a centered set, with him at the center. There's evidence that some disciples drew closer to the center than others (Peter, James, and John) and that at least one disciple drew away from the center. The gospels speak of the women who traveled with them. Acts makes reference to numerous faith communities. It seems that the community of Christ was not as simple as thirteen guys roaming the countryside. There was a rich intersection of relationships with some nearer the center and others further away, but all invited to join in the kingdom-building enterprise. If the modern church followed this biblical model, the church would be more concerned with relationships than with numbers.

If we return to the metaphor of the net, we might see a group of very committed Christian people befriending a number of not-yet-Christians in a variety of settings. Some will know each other, others will not, but the network of friendships will intersect at a variety of levels and degrees. Some of these not-yet-Christians will be close to identifying themselves as Christian, and others will not want to at all. But it's in the commitment to strengthening these bonds that the missional-incarnational mode functions best. As we've seen, some incarnational churches are operating as dance venues, bookshops, or cafés, places where the intersecting of relationships can happen naturally. Alan's ministry through the fully functioning café is a great example. In the café the regular clientele can include those closer to the center and others far from it, but with an incarnational community eating and drinking regularly at the café there is a greater chance of that net of relationships sweeping more into the search for God.[8]

For us the center should be Jesus himself. The gospel is the central imperative for Christian mission. Since at the core of a centered set is Christ, a church should be concerned with fostering increasing closeness to Jesus in the lives of all those involved. We believe that a centered-set church must have a very clear set of beliefs, rooted in Christ and his teaching. This belief system must be nonnegotiable and strongly held to by the community closest to its center. A centered-set church is not concerned with artificial boundaries that bounded-set churches have traditionally added. In bounded-set churches all sorts of criteria are determined for the acceptance or rejection of prospective

8. It's helpful to think of the well-known Engel Scale in this regard. See James F. Engel, *Contemporary Christian Communications: Its Theory and Practice* (Nashville: Thomas Nelson, 1979), 77–83. This scale identifies the usual process a person goes through in becoming a Christian, with zero being close to the center and -10 being far from it. Although it's a very cognitive model, and we think people move closer to the center through relationship, not necessarily just through knowledge, it's a useful guide for thinking of people moving through a process:

-10 Awareness of the supernatural;
-9 No effective knowledge of Christianity;
-8 Initial awareness of Christianity;
-7 Interest in Christianity;
-6 Awareness of the basic facts of the Gospel;
-5 Grasp of the implications of the Gospel;
-4 Positive attitude to the Gospel;
-3 Awareness of the personal implications;
-2 Challenge and decision to act;
-1 Repentance and faith;
 0 Regeneration.

members (smoking, drinking alcohol, living together outside marriage, differing views on Christ's return). In a centered-set church it is recognized that we are all sinners, all struggling to be the best people we can be. But we also believe that the closer one gets to the center (Christ), the more Christlike one's behavior should become. Therefore core members of the church will exhibit the features of Christ's radical lifestyle (love, generosity, healing, hospitality, forgiveness, mercy, peace, and more), and those who have just begun the journey toward Christ (and whose lives may not exhibit such traits) are still seen as "belonging." No one is considered unworthy of belonging because they happen to be addicted to tobacco, or because they're not married to their live-in partner. Belonging is a key value. The growth toward the center of the set is the same as the process of discipleship.

Let's face it, there are many paid-up members of respectable churches who might not "live in sin," but whose lives are marked by greed or gluttony. The bounded-set church has determined a socially acceptable standard by which to exclude certain peoples. The centered-set church will see everyone as equally fallen. It will accept all people but will make Christlikeness a key community goal. Becoming more Christlike is more likely to happen in community than in isolation. As our relationships with not-yet-Christians strengthen, and they meet others in our community, they soon discover our values. They may not embrace our calling to Christlikeness, but they will see it as central. Will the missional church at times have members whose lives don't reflect the lifestyle of Jesus? Of course. So does the traditional church. But in the traditional church it's easier to hide our foibles and fallenness. In the missional church, where relationship is the conduit for mission, things will be different. We, in fact, believe that discipleship could well be more rigorous in the missional church than in the traditional church, because transparency and proximity are key values.

A bounded-set church and a centered-set church also think in fundamentally different ways about evangelism. Evangelism in the bounded set is focused heavily on getting people into the religious zone. As we've already pointed out, this is represented by the unyielding allegiance to the work of getting people to come to church. We stress again that we don't object to inviting people to worship meetings. Even in the missional (centered-set) church, there should be the opportunity to invite not-yet-Christians to experience Christian community and worship. But in the incarnational mode the emphasis is well and truly on a cross-cultural Go-To-Them mentality. It assumes that in every human being there is a longing to know the reason for their existence, the purpose of their lives. Leo Tolstoy once despaired, "The question was: Why should I live? Or: Is there anything real or imperishable that will come from my illusory and perishable life? Or: What kind of meaning can my finite existence have in this infinite universe?" Some people, like Tolstoy, embark upon a search with energy derived from honest despair. Some refuse to search and lose themselves in any number of diversions—from material possessions to personal achievement to collecting new experiences. But still some others have simply not woken up to the realization that there is a search to be made. As a centered set, the missional-incarnational church sees that its role is not just to "present" Christ in one fell swoop, but to tantalize not-yet-Christians into beginning the search. As long ago as the 1970s Vincent Donovan was advocating such an approach: "In working with young people in America, do not try to call them back to where they were, and do not try to call them to where you are, as beautiful as that place might seem to you. You must have the courage to go with them to a place that neither you nor they have ever been before."[9] The idea that Christians can learn about God, life, faith, truth, honesty, and so forth from unbelievers is never given credence in a bounded set. It takes the openness of the centered set to do this effectively. The following table is a useful summary of the differences between the two approaches:[10]

Bounded-Set Approach	Centered-Set Approach
The evangelizer is the expert who has special knowledge regarding God that the lost person must take in to be saved.	Each person is the expert on his or her own life and has the God-given ability to seek for the truth. The evangelizer respects this.
The "lost" person is viewed as flawed in character and sinful.	Each person is viewed as created in the image of God—precious, valuable, and loved by God.
Seeing people as simply lost or saved, it tries to paternally "fix up" sinners and make them like us.	Seeing people as seekers, it tries to stimulate others to ask, seek, and knock, while understanding we don't know it all ourselves.
The goal is to get them to sign on, to profess belief, to become part of our team.	The goal is for the process of discovery of Christ and the search for truth to be furthered in the person.
A cataclysmic change occurs in people called "conversion."	Conversion is also seen as a process that does not begin and end with the profession of faith in Christ but begins with the Holy Spirit's prevenient grace on the person's life and continues through repentance for a lifetime—the Kingdom comes.
We Christians know and have the whole truth.	We don't know everything about life or God—humility and wonder remain.

9. Vincent J. Donovan, *Christianity Rediscovered* (Maryknoll, NY: Orbis, 1978), vii.
10. For this framework we are indebted to Chris Harding from Youth for Christ, Sydney. It appears in an unpublished policy document for YFC staffworkers.

For the centered-set approach to work in the church, it must be grounded in an incarnational mode. If we persist with the attractional approach and then try to think of our church as a centered set, we won't reach anybody. If you must stick with the traditional-attractional mode, then you are obligated to see your church as a bounded set. In that case, evangelism and outreach will consist of telling others that it's better inside the set than out and trying to get them over the line, into the church. Only when a community of faith is prepared to leave its space and enter into another subculture will it be able to effectively see itself as, and be, a centered set.

Perhaps an example will help here. Adam and Amy (real people, true story) are a young Christian couple. For Adam's birthday, Amy gave him a voucher for a parachute jump from a light plane (why, we don't know!). In order for Adam to take the jump, they had to drive into the country a couple of hours away from their home. As they were making the early Saturday morning trip, they noticed dark storm clouds building on the horizon, and by the time they pulled into the airstrip, a fierce thunderstorm had hit. They were ushered into the hangar by the skydiving instructor, who told them they could not go up in that weather. However, the instructor reported that the forecast was for the downpour to blow over by lunchtime. If they liked they could have breakfast in the hangar with various members of the skydiving club and wait out the storm. Adam and Amy took him up on his offer.

As they tell it, Adam and Amy ate a hearty meal with a collection of pilots, skydivers, base-jumpers, wives, girlfriends, babies, and toddlers. As the morning wore on, more and more people came to the isolated hangar in the middle of a field in the country. Adam said he and Amy were welcomed into this community with open arms. Some people worked on airplane engines, while others repaired and maintained various types of equipment. There was much laughter and a real sense of family as the rain thundered down on the hangar's tin roof. On more than one occasion Adam was told that he and Amy would be welcome to join them every Saturday. In fact, Adam says they were thoroughly "evangelized" by this group of extreme sports enthusiasts.

How would Amy and Adam best reach this subculture, this legitimate community, with the gospel? In the attractional mode, they would set up a church service or similar gathering in a nearby church and hold a "Skydivers Welcome" meeting. They might use skydiving jargon in their advertising. They might invite a Christian skydiver to speak at the meeting. They might even set up their own church-based skydiving club. Can you see any of this being effective? An incarnational mode would take seriously the fact that the local skydiving association is an unreached people group, requiring cross-cultural skills to minister to it. In an incarnational church Adam and Amy and maybe some other Christians would be commissioned to join the skydiving club, to eat breakfast with them every Saturday, to develop a web of friendships, to share their faith, and hopefully activate a search for truth in the existing club members. A church, a community of faith, centered in Christ, would then effectively be planted in that hangar. The goal would not be to bring a few newly converted skydivers into the church (whereupon they gradually replace all their skydiving friends with churchgoing ones and thus lose their places in their original "tribe"), but to develop an incarnational Christian community within the skydiving fraternity.

Such an incarnational outreach would require all the elements New Testament writers experienced and taught as normative: the leaving of one's comfort zone, sacrifice, hard work, the possibility of persecution, endurance, and putting others first. On the other hand, it's possible for Christians in traditional churches to attend services at no real cost to themselves at all.

Not the HUP!

Whenever we raise the need for the missional church to be incarnational and to focus on subcultures, we hear church leaders reminding us of the evils of the homogeneous unit principle (HUP). This principle was devised by missiologists, in particular those from the Fuller Seminary School of World Mission, in the 1970s. The HUP posits that people are best reached with the gospel in people groups of the same language, customs, culture, and beliefs. Critics of this principle, most notably the highly regarded South African missiologist, David Bosch, believe that a slavish devotion to the HUP leads to churches of like-minded people who are unable to embrace the biblical principles of unity in diversity, acceptance of others, and brotherly love. Bosch's attack on the HUP was so convincing that today many church leaders regard heterogeneity as the ultimate test of a church's biblical worthiness.

We have been attacked by church leaders who've heard us present our ideas about the missional-incarnational church and claimed that we would end up with completely homogenous churches, like cultural ghettoes of people unable to relate to Christians from different subcultures. While we acknowledge this as a possible danger, and we defer to David Bosch's scholarship, we have not heard the critics of the HUP propose any effective missional alternative to it. Invariably, those church leaders who are most critical are leading churches that might be generationally heterogenous, but are made up of entirely white, middle-class families. While we admit that having the elderly and little children all worshiping together is a good thing, we feel that the leaders of suburban, middle-class churches are being hypocritical when they dismiss the proposal for the missional church because of its missional imperative to reach people groups.

We believe the only way forward is to embrace the HUP as a mission strategy, while working toward heterogeneity with mature Christians in community. In other words, heterogeneity is a discipleship issue, not a missional one. A church that has worked on developing this balance is St. Thomas Crookes Church, in Sheffield, England. One cold, wintry day, we trudged up the hill to the old stone chapel to meet Mal Calladine, one of the leaders, and put this very issue before him. Over coffee and hot chocolate, he showed us the following diagram. The figure on the left is a non-Christian. Mal says she or he needs to cross two divides before she or he can embrace the demands of Christian discipleship.

FIGURE 3

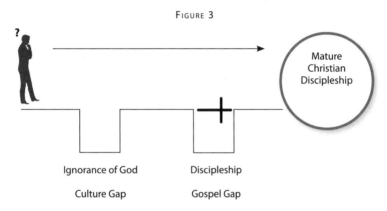

Ignorance of God   Discipleship

Culture Gap   Gospel Gap

In order for the person above to reach the point where he or she is mature enough to accept others from different cultural contexts and embrace unity in diversity, he or she must leap these two gaps. The first of these is the culture gap. Since the person we are asking to traverse this gap is not a Christian, the onus is on *us,* not him or her, to make this leap easier. By initiating culturally specific, homogeneous mission within a host community, we help not-yet-Christians to move over the culture gap and closer to the essential issue of the gospel. It is the work of the cross of Christ (see diagram) and the ministry of the Holy Spirit that navigates someone over the second gulf. Only when transformed by the work of God in their lives are they in a position to embrace heterogeneity as an important value of Christian fellowship.

St. Thomas has organized itself into a combination of homogenous and heterogeneous gatherings. It emphasizes three levels of fellowship, worship, and mission. All those people who claim St. Thomas's as their church must belong to a cell. These cells are entirely homogeneous and very missional. They are committed to ministering and serving particular people groups in Sheffield. There are cells focused on reaching the indoor rock-climbing community; others, the football community; and others still, the nightclubbing crowd. The cell is the basic unit of fellowship and mission, and it meets weekly. At the next level, the cells gather together in clusters called congregations. A congregation will comprise five or more cells and number no more than one hundred members. It meets weekly. In congregations the cells worship, receive teaching, share resources, and enjoy fellowship. Congregations are less homogeneous than cells, though they are not completely heterogeneous either. The forum for heterogeneity and diversity is the celebration gathering where all the congregations meet in a weekly service in a local nightclub. At this meeting there could be up to two thousand people in attendance. The celebration is a time for large-scale worship, motivation, and vision casting. Mal told us that while attendance at cell meetings was considered to be a weekly commitment, he didn't expect members of his church to attend the celebration any more than once or twice a month. The essential work of discipleship and mission happened at the cell level. In this way, a balance between homogeneity and heterogeneity can be struck.

A Biblical Approach to Incarnational Evangelism

If the Christian church is to be incarnational and missional, as we believe the New Testament anticipates, and if it's to abandon an us-and-them mentality, it will need to rediscover the biblical mode of impacting the world around it. The traditional-attractional church thinks about evangelism as sending out church members to share their faith with others and to bring them into the church. But the New Testament writers saw it much more organically. While recognizing the gift of the evangelist, the New Testament seems to see the engagement of the church with its world as two-tiered. That is, there is a place for gospel proclamation and the role of the gifted evangelist (though he/she need not necessarily be a pulpit-based preacher), but there is a second tier, the incarnational infiltration of society by all Christians. This infiltration, in order for it to be missional (and not just social), must be marked by the following commitments.[11]

Holiness

Jesus said, "Let your light shine before [everyone] that they may see your good deeds and praise your Father in heaven" (Matt. 5:16). Built into the very

11. We acknowledge the scholarship of John Dickson (PhD, Macquarie University), whose unpublished paper, "Our Differing Roles in God's Mission," forms the basis for these points.

fabric of New Testament teaching on the extension of the kingdom is the assumption that when the Christian community embraces a godly, holy life-style, it will so tantalize the wider community that they will seek after God. And yet so much of what typifies the so-called holiness movement in the fundamentalist-evangelical churches has had the opposite effect. When the wonders of life in Christ are boiled down to teetotalling, it's hardly likely to arouse great interest in the community about us. If by holiness we simply mean no drinking, no smoking, and no dancing, we have a very limited view of the concept. In his letter to Titus, Paul encouraged him to teach his congregation to be respectful, self-controlled, kind, loving, and faithful. He told him to discourage drunkenness, slander, gossip, and disrespect. To Titus himself, he commended integrity, seriousness, and soundness. Why? "So that in every way they will make the teaching about God our Savior attractive" (Titus 2:1–10).

The missional-incarnational church will make Christian teaching attractive by living it under the very noses of those who have not yet embraced it. What impact can a church that has withdrawn from society have on that society? The traditional-attractional church often quotes, "Come ye out and be ye separate," a reversal of Jesus' command to be salt and light in the world. Rather, our lives, which must be marked by commitments to acting justly, loving mercy, and walking humbly with God (Mic. 6:8), must be lived in close proximity to those we are seeking to reach. It might be all very good to choose to abstain from the consumption of alcohol as an act of devotion to God, but if our lives are marked by greed, self-centeredness, arrogance, and fear, in what way is our light shining forth? To impact a post-Christendom culture, the church must jettison its wealth, side with the poor, speak up for the wronged, and live as a kind, loving community. Moltmann calls this a "new kind of living together" that affirms:

- That no one is alone with his or her problems,
- That no one has to conceal his or her disabilities,
- That there are not some who have the say and others who have nothing to say,
- That neither the old nor the little ones are isolated,
- That one bears the other even when it is unpleasant and there is no agreement, and
- That, finally, the one can also at times leave the other in peace when the other needs it.[12]

12. Moltmann, *The Open Church*, 33.

Prayer

While living holy lives, the church is also commanded to pray. When it comes to praying for those not-yet-Christians in their nets, the New Testament is pretty clear on what we are to pray for.

First, we are to pray that God would gift the church with more evangelists. We believe there is the spiritual gifting of the office of the evangelist. Interestingly the Bible doesn't speak about the gift of evangelism (as it does with faith, healing, teaching, and so forth), only that there is a gift (to the church) of the evangelist. The evangelist, he or she, is the gift. We will speak more fully about the role of the evangelist in an incarnational church in our section on leadership later in the book. Suffice to say here that we cannot ignore the biblical role of the evangelist. God has gifted our churches with them, and it is incumbent upon us to pray that God will raise up more. (Fuller Theological Seminary church growth studies indicate about 10 percent of any congregation believe they are evangelists.)[13] In Matthew 9:36–38, Jesus invites his disciples to pray that God will unleash more harvesters (evangelists, proclaimers). This text is typically only quoted in church by returned overseas missionaries who are trying to recruit more missionaries. And it's quite appropriate for them to do so, but it can also be equally applied to a local congregation. Each church should ask God to give them more gifts of evangelists.[14]

Next, we are to pray for God's blessing on the evangelists' ministries. You might be quite surprised who God gives your congregation when you pray for more proclaimers, but the injunction on a local congregation is to pray for the success of their ministries. Paul, writing to the church at Ephesus, asked, "Pray also for me, that whenever I open my mouth, words may be given me so that I will fearlessly make known the mystery of the gospel" (Eph. 6:19). Perhaps you may find it easier to pray for an extraordinarily gifted apostle like Paul, than for the less extraordinary evangelists in your church. But bear in mind that Paul himself was an unusual character in his time too, occasionally

13. Quoted by Pete Gilbert, *Breaking the Mould*, Gerald Coates, ed. (Eastbourne, Australia: Kingsway, 1993), 125.
14. Though we will discuss the function of the evangelist much more fully later, we should preempt our later discussion by noting here that we don't limit the term evangelist to the pulpit-based preaching evangelist like Billy Graham. Of course we recognize that Dr. Graham is a gift to the worldwide church, but we acknowledge that evangelists in local congregations might be quite poor pulpit preachers. We see the term encompassing the public proclaimer and any Christian who naturally and normally as an outworking of their giftedness is able to present the gospel and elicit a response of repentance and faith from not-yet-Christians. This might be done in one sitting, but more normally will be part of a longer process. Our personal experience is that many evangelists are inept preachers and sometimes are quite eccentric characters, but the hand of God is on them and people come to faith through their ministries.

in conflict with other Christians, regularly criticized for his lack of preaching ability and his unimpressive presence. Incarnational churches are committed to praying for more evangelists and for their success.

Last, the church is expected to pray for the salvation of their not-yet-Christian friends and neighbors. Paul, writing this time to Timothy, urged him to pray for *everyone,* including kings and those in authority, that they might come to know that Jesus is the only mediator between God and humankind (1 Tim. 2:1–6).

Socializing

This is the third primary commitment of a missional-incarnational church's infiltration of society. If the church is living an intriguing new lifestyle that is so marked by goodness that it makes the gospel attractive, then to truly be effective it follows that this lifestyle must be lived in close proximity to not-yet-Christians. Paul took this seriously in his mediation of the Corinthian factions that had split over the issue of eating food offered to idols (1 Cor. 10:27–11:1). On the one hand the debate about "clean" and "unclean" food was a philosophical-theological issue. It concerned the inherent godliness (or lack thereof) of the material world. But on the other hand, it was a social-missional issue. It concerned the question, "At whose table can I eat?" Paul attempted to address the issue at the theological level (1 Cor. 10:25–26), but his chief concern seemed to be the missional perspective. He was primarily concerned that the Corinthian church not cut itself off from not-yet-Christians by refusing their hospitality if their food had been offered to idols. He wrote, "If some unbeliever invites you to a meal and you want to go, eat whatever is put before you without raising questions of conscience" (1 Cor. 10:27). Paul was defending his theological position regarding the liberty of the Christian, but he was also writing like a missionary.

Paul was obviously eager to encourage Christians to engage fully in close interactions with those not yet part of the faith community. In 1 Corinthians 5:9–10, speaking this time of sexual immorality, he drew the distinction between disciplining a destructively immoral Christian and the church's attitude toward not-yet-believers. "I have written you in my letter not to associate with sexually immoral people—not at all meaning the people of this world who are immoral, or the greedy and swindlers, or idolaters. In that case you would have to leave this world." Alan's ministry at South Melbourne Restoration Community featured significant contact with the gay community of Melbourne. Following the advice of Paul, the church maintained as good and open a relationship with that community as they could. But there were times when someone claiming to be a Christian began meeting with the church and was openly sexually provocative with those new believers who had left a gay life-style to follow Christ. Under those circumstances, the leadership of the church felt it was right and proper to deal with the "immoral brother" (as Paul calls him) while remaining in relationship with many other gay not-yet-Christians.

Robert Banks, in his two volumes on the early church, *Going to Church in the First Century* and *Paul's Idea of Community*,[15] helped to relocate the early church back in the home and around the table, recovering the central place of the love feast. The shared table is a powerful symbol of intimacy, generosity, and acceptance. And yet many churches do not welcome unbelievers to their table and thus perpetuate the us-and-them mentality.

Michael knows of a church in a new housing area of Sydney that was trying to hold two Sunday services each week and getting very little interest in the evening service. The morning worship meeting drew a good number, but at night they usually had 6 to 10 people turning up. Sensing that it was silly to spend their limited reserves this way, they decided to close the evening service. This isn't an unusual story. Many small or new congregations have only a Sunday morning service. But the manner in which they closed the ser-vice was unique. They invited the dozen or so people who were attending the service to covenant to use the time they would normally be in church to do something missional instead. Some people committed themselves to serving in the local soup kitchen, others volunteered to take calls at a child sponsorship program. One couple decided to spend the hour they normally sat in church on Sunday evening pushing their newborn child in a baby carriage around the streets of their neighborhood. Of course everyone stops young parents in the street to coo at a new baby. As they watered their lawns or washed their cars, people started up conversations with the Christian couple. The couple told Michael they have made more friendships, shared Jesus more often, and generally been more effective as salt and light in their community since they stopped going to church and started pushing a baby carriage. Many churches close services and their members are free to take a Sunday evening stroll, but by inviting people to see their substitute activity as *mission,* this church saw a whole raft of new possibilities emerging. Our point is that socializing must be intentional, missional, grace-filled, and generous. It must be seen as part of a broader pattern of infiltrating a community.

From the three broad commitments we've discussed so far, we can see a pattern emerging: The missional-incarnational church should be living, eating,

15. Robert Banks, *Going to Church in the First Century: An Eyewitness Account* (Sydney: Hexagon, 1980), and *Paul's Idea of Community*, rev. ed. (Peabody, MA: Hendrickson, 1994).

and working closely with its surrounding community, developing strong links between Christians and not-yet-Christians. It would be best to do this in the homes of not-yet-Christians and in their preferred public spaces (the skydiving hangar, the favorite coffee shop, etc.) but also in the homes of Christians. By creating a net of deep, loving friendship, more and more people will be swept into the community, though some will be more closely connected than others (this is the socializing commitment). While these relationships are being built, Christian believers should be demonstrating a holy lifestyle through acts of generosity and kindness, by a preference for the poor and suffering, and by a love for the scorned (this is the holiness commitment). As this complex, even messy set of relationships is being sustained, the incarnated Christian community must be constantly in prayer, praying for the salvation of their friends and that God would raise up and bless more evangelists (this is the prayer commitment).

It would follow that as these nets of friendship and service are strengthening, the ministry of the gifted evangelist comes into play. He or she shouldn't have to be a visiting preacher at a church service, but one of the links in the net. As I am building ever closer bonds between my Christian and not-yet-Christian friends, I should assume that God has gifted our church with an evangelist, one who can naturally and effectively proclaim Jesus in a contextualized and attractive manner. As the net is being repaired and tightened, my not-yet-Christians are bound to come into contact with my evangelist friend. We believe that if our not-yet-Christian friends were swept into a series of friendships with a number of incarnational Christians, at least one of whom is an evangelist, God will do his work of bringing people into a relationship with him. This leads us to the fourth element of this biblical pattern.

Supporting Evangelists

"Don't you know that those who work in the temple get their food from the temple, and those who serve at the altar share in what is offered on the altar? In the same way, the Lord has commanded that those who preach the gospel should receive their living from the gospel" (1 Cor. 9:13–14). So wrote Paul, though he was quick to point out that he was not feathering his own nest. He told the Corinthians that he personally was not after any remuneration, only that the church should financially support the work of evangelists generally. It can be debated that this passage refers specifically to the early office of apostle and is therefore no longer applicable. If it is applied these days, it seems to take a stand for ministerial stipends for professional clergy. But the missional-incarnational church will recognize that the gifted evangelist will be in hot demand for dinner parties, lunches, late-night discussions, and gatherings of parents at the school gate after school. If the evangelist can surf, she should be at the beach regularly. If he skydives (to use an earlier illustration), he should be at the airstrip every Saturday. If the evangelist is an artist, a classic-car enthusiast, a great cook, or an expert gardener, he or she must be free to interact with other members of the like-minded community. If this means working part-time to be free to work the nets created by the church's friendships, then that church should consider supporting the evangelist financially.

Supporting those who proclaim the gospel, when applied to Western culture today, could be a healthy corrective for many people for whom the cycle of work, family, and church is so consuming that they never have time for building friendships with not-yet-Christians. Ironically, full-time clergy in the traditional-attractional churches often find themselves so run off their feet with the busyness of serving on various committees, attending myriad meetings, and running worship services, that they have very few social contacts with unbelievers. We think this is one of the great blights of the institutional church; it covertly withdraws its clergy from casual, social contact with the neighborhood community. The propensity for clergy to move regularly to different parishes means many don't have long-term friendships in any one area. And when a minister joins the local jogging club or the book-reading society at a local bookshop, he or she is often accused, by the congregation, of not doing the Lord's work.

Jesus-Talk

While it is the gifted evangelist's primary role to proclaim the gospel, the New Testament exhorts all believers to talk about Jesus. We don't think this should take the form of running someone through a prescribed four-step road to salvation. Rather, it seems that the New Testament writers imagined such Jesus-talk would occur in the everyday conversation between friends. Wrote Peter, "Always be prepared to give an answer to everyone who asks you to give the reason for the hope that you have. But do this with gentleness and respect" (1 Pet. 3:15). As the net of friendships expands, so in casual, ordinary ways should the subject of our hope come up. This might be a conversation that emerges from a film you've seen together, a reflection on a common experience, or at a time of grief, suffering, or even great joy. Peter saw this happening in such an everyday way. Paul was no less casual about it when he wrote, "Be wise in the way you act toward outsiders; make the most of every opportunity. Let your conversation be always full of grace, seasoned with salt, so that you may know how to answer everyone" (Col. 4:5–6). It seems apparent that the two-tiered approach we mentioned earlier is behind Paul's statement here. Paul, in verses 3 and 4, announced that he was an evangelist (proclaimer), and that the Colossians were to *pray* for his evangelism (v. 4), live *godly lives* before unbelievers (v. 5), and give gracious *answers* to unbelievers' inquiries (v. 6).

If we're living holy lives, praying for not-yet-Christian friends, socializing regularly and building friendships with them, and introducing them to our evangelist friends, we will be creating the fertile soil for God to do his exclusive work, giving people the gift of faith. This is the incarnational approach to outreach.

4

The Shape of the Missional Church

> The only statistic I can ever remember is that if all the people who go to sleep in church were laid end to end they would be a lot more comfortable.
>
> —attributed to Queen Victoria

The Chocolate Shop Church

For a clearer understanding of what we mean by the missional-incarnational church, rent a copy of Lasse Halstrom's delicious comedy/romance, *Chocolat*. The film is set in a small French village completely dominated by an austere, overbearing form of Catholicism as championed by the intimidating mayor, the Comte de Reynaud (Alfred Molina). The Comte is a controlling and frightening character, and the whole town lives under a blanket of fear and uncertainty. Halstrom's art director has created a town center without a single tree or flower. The stone walls and cobblestones are almost completely shrouded in dust or snow or wind. Everything is gray, mirroring the dryness associated with the strict form of religion that the Comte uses to silence everyone. As a result of this blanket of austerity, the relationships of the townspeople are fractured and strained.

We meet a couple whose marriage has drifted into a passionless arrangement of cleaning house and preparing meals. Another couple, who own the lease on the town's café, are torn apart by violence and alcoholism. The Comte's secretary won't allow her frail son to see his grandmother because of a simple disagreement years before. An aged man who longs for a local widow cannot express his love because she is still in mourning for her dead husband, even though he died over forty years before. And the Comte himself has been abandoned by his wife. Unable to be honest with the town, he tells everyone that she is holidaying in Italy. Deceit and fear are the products of the rigorous and stern religious beliefs of the Comte.

Into this austere, gray community comes a woman called Vianne Rocher (Juliette Binoche), blown in by a "sly wind from the north." She arrives unannounced with her young daughter, both enveloped in bright red capes, the redness of their appearance making a striking contrast to the gray bleakness of the stone village. It is her foolhardy intention to open a chocolaterie in this sad town. What's more, she has arrived just as the Catholic season of Lent is beginning. The townsfolk are to deny themselves certain pleasures as an act of contrition and devotion to Christ. The Comte is so rigorous about Lent that he virtually refuses all food. Vianne's chocolate shop is the antithesis of everything the town stands for. Her store is soon stocked with the most decadent and exotic chocolate creations ever seen. She and the Comte are headed for a showdown over the souls of the village people.

Some reviewers noted that the Comte represents traditional Christianity while Vianne represents classic paganism. The showdown, as they saw it, was a contest between Christ and paganism. But we saw it differently. We see the Comte and the stone Catholic church that stands in the middle of the town square as symbolizing the Christendom-attractional mode. It has positioned itself in the center of things and demands allegiance and attendance. Vianne and the chocolaterie, on the other hand, represent the missional-incarnational church. She is positioned at the edge of the community in an old disused patisserie. Instead of worrying about selling her chocolates, she sets about building friendships with the community. She creates what resembles the web or net of friendships we spoke about in the previous chapter. She has an astonishing knack for guessing each potential customer's favorite chocolate. And she prescribes certain chocolate remedies to mend the townfolk's ills. To the sad middle-aged couple whose marriage has grown cold, she prescribes a chili-laced chocolate treat to "awaken the passions." Soon their love has been reawakened. She uses her creations to bring the old man and his love, the widow Madame Audel (Leslie Caron) together. And she eventually secretly reunites her landlady, Armande Voizin (Judi Dench), with her frail grandson, despite the wishes of his mother.

In her efforts to mend relationships and create an atmosphere of honesty and openness, Vianne faces her greatest challenge with the lot of the oppressed Josephine Muscat (Lena Olin). Josephine's husband, Serge (Peter Stormare), is viciously violent toward her. So horrid is his oppression of her that at first she seems incapable of normal human relations. She is frightened and completely broken by Serge's abuse. When she presents herself at the chocolaterie to escape from Serge (note her choice of sanctuary), Vianne takes her in and rehabilitates her, teaching her the trade of chocolate making and rebuilding her confidence. When the Comte hears of this situation, he is galvanized into action. As a committed Christian man he cannot abide the severing of the sacrament of marriage, but neither can he accept domestic violence. As Vianne is rebuilding the broken Josephine, the Comte accepts the challenge to reorient the violent Serge and make him a good Christian man. He forces Serge into the confessional, buys him a new suit and gives him elocution lessons. A contest has been joined. Vianne is redeeming Josephine with love, acceptance, and mercy. The Comte is redeeming Serge with education, penances, and discipline. It might not surprise those who haven't seen the film that Vianne is successful with loving Josephine back to life, while the Comte's efforts with the despicable Serge fail hopelessly.

Vianne Rocher's chocolaterie is our vision of an incarnational church. She is warm, nonjudgmental, and compassionate, offering grace and peace to the troubled community. Her shop is a haven, but she doesn't simply wait for people to enter. She engages the lives and troubles of her community and offers practical help as well as space for honesty and truthtelling to happen. She celebrates life, good food (Armande's seventieth birthday party includes a devilishly exotic menu), loud laughter, love, romance, storytelling, fantasy, and imagination. In fact, Armande's birthday party reminded us of Matthew's party for Jesus (Mark 2:15) where the outcasts, sinners, and tax collectors celebrated with the Messiah. Like Jesus, Vianne has collected the outcasts, the misfits, and created a veritable feast in their honor. In a telling moment of truth the parish priest, Father Henri, admits that the town has "measured goodness by who we exclude."

A secondary storyline in the film brings a group of gypsies who arrive by boat and camp by the riverbank. They share Vianne's vision of a life of passion and celebration, acceptance and love. But they are itinerants. Their leader, Roux (Johnny Depp), tries to coax Vianne to leave the stifling village, but Vianne is a true missionary. Though finally enticed to leave when the next north wind blows through, at Josephine's insistence she resists the temptation at first. Roux is like an itinerant missionary. His impact on a village is limited. He questions their worldview and makes the village people feel uncomfortable, but he motivates no change in their behavior. Vianne, because of her commitment to the village, her preparedness to live in close proximity to them, and her compassion, ultimately transforms the village and reproduces herself in Josephine. This is how the missional-incarnational church thinks.

If I Could Do It All Again

One of the most subversive questions Alan asks when he is doing a church revitalization consultation with a local congregation is this: "If you could start again from scratch, would you do it the same way?" In his role as the director of mission and revitalization for the Churches of Christ in Australia, Alan was responsible for both mobilizing church planting (mission) and helping dying congregations to grow again (revitalization). When called into a church that was trying to rediscover its purpose for being in a particular community, he would begin with that question, and the usual answer was "No." If they could start over and begin doing church from scratch, they usually said they would not do it the way they were currently doing it. For Alan, then, it begged the response, "Then, why are you not changing it now?"

If you are digging a hole in one place and you realize you need to dig it elsewhere, you don't get there by digging in the same place, only deeper. And yet churches, when they realize that the old attractional mode isn't working, seem to believe that if they just do attractional church better, it will work. And, let's face it, so many of the church growth seminars and conferences are simply repackaging the traditional-attractional mode and promoting it to small, struggling, and dying churches as the only way to grow. There is a whole industry devoted to such conferences and the production of such materials that simply encourage struggling congregations to keep digging the same hole deeper. But to step out of the hole and begin digging elsewhere is a huge commitment for a local church to make. It is very hard to change the DNA of a church once it has a rhythm and life of its own. A template quickly develops. The shift from the attractional to the incarnational mode is enormous, we understand. And we don't commend it lightly. But as we've pointed out, the death of Christendom and emergence of postmodernism and the new global culture have highlighted the bankruptcy of the existing church and its inability to have a positive effect on Western society.

If we were doing it all again, what would we do differently? Here are some of our suggestions.

Listening to Your Patients

We've come to the conclusion that so much of what we do in church is "inorganic." It so often feels like an artificial experience. The communal life of many congregations doesn't reflect the rich complexity of their everyday experiences and beliefs, struggles and triumphs. If we were organic, we would be much more sensitive to the cultural forces, the patterns and structures and energies, of the people we were trying to reach. We would think like missionaries and spend more time listening to, eating with, and playing with the subculture or neighborhood we were trying to minister to. We would not assume to develop a model of church/community life until we had recognized and discerned the "natural" ways in which a given group gathers and assembles. In other words, we would seek to redeem the organic, existing culture rather than impose an alien model on it. We understand that many church planters these days spend considerable time interacting in a particular neighborhood or subculture before launching public church services, but we still find many church planters who, having done substantial "research" into a particular community, then go ahead and plant churches that look basically like every other church in the West, in a classic attractional mode. Instead, why not allow the rhythms and lifestyle patterns of the people we're trying to reach determine the shape our communal life and worship meetings take?

As missionaries, we need to ask, "What is good news to these people (What are the existential issues these people are grappling with before God?)?" and "What would the church look like for these people?" The answers will give us clues as to what element of the gospel we need to communicate first. The inventor of the stethoscope was noted as having said, "Listen to your patients. They're telling you how to heal them."

Instead of developing the rich myriad of intersecting friendships we spoke about in the last chapter, the Christendom-mode church is so infected by the spirit of "success" that real connection between people in church is usually quite rare. It then follows that the capacity for such connection with God is diminished. We need to ensure that there is close regular connection between our faith community and the not-yet-Christians we are trying to reach. That will definitely mean living in the same community, but it might also mean working in a local coffee shop, pumping gas in a local garage, setting up a medical practice in the local area, or coming over "to share a beer with me and see how I clip my roses." Slow it down, listen to your patients. As the poet Lao Tsu says,

> Go to the people,
> Live with them, learn from them,
> Love them.
> Start with what they know,
> Build with what they have,
> But with the best leaders, when the work is done, the task
> Accomplished,

The people will say,
We have done it ourselves.[1]

A term that missiologists use to describe this strong sense of affinity with a group of people is *interpathy*. It is not the same as sympathy or empathy. It describes that depth of relationship when an outsider to a particular host community develops a burden in her heart for that community. It refers to the capacity for an outsider to pick up a community's sense of values, what has hurt them and where they're headed as a people group. It's a form of identification so deep that the guest/missionary has almost become one of the host tribe.

Finding "Persons of Peace"

In Luke 10, Jesus, while touring the countryside and visiting many towns and communities, sent out an advance party of seventy-two disciples. In his commissioning address to them he instructs them to find a person of peace in each community: "When you enter a house, first say, 'Peace to this house.' If a man of peace is there, your peace will rest on him; if not, it will return to you. Stay in that house, eating and drinking whatever they give you, for the worker deserves his wages. Do not move around from house to house" (Luke 10:5–7). This was Jesus' church-planting strategy. He specifically instructed them not to go door knocking from house to house. He advocated against taking a blanket approach to evangelism. Rather, his advance party was to visit various families until they had found a "man of peace." Then they were to concentrate their friendship on this one household.

Missiologists like Charles Brock and George Patterson suggest that finding a "person of peace" is central to a healthy church-starting process. But few churches start this way. Many churches spend significant parts of their budget on advertising (print, electronic, letterbox), blanketing as many people as they can (in an attempt to get them to come to a church meeting). Finding a person of peace and basing our ministry there seems like a less effective method in the short term. But in the long term, a church-planting project that emerges out of the households of local, indigenous leaders will be much richer and more effective. Paul followed this model while in Corinth by focusing on the home of Priscilla and Aquila, the local tentmakers (Acts 18:1–4). People of peace are key people who are spiritually open, have good reputations, and have influence in the community. When they become believers, they then share their faith confidently with their networks of friendship and start new home-based

---

1. Quoted in Ashley Barker, *Collective Witness* (Melbourne: Urban Neighbours of Hope, 2000), 52.

churches. We suggest new-church planters take more seriously the effective role of the persons of peace, instead of trying a shotgun approach. It is radically different from putting on church programs in the church building and pulling occasional converts into the church culture, to hopefully one day send them back to reach out to others. Usually, in this approach, the new believers become instantly extracted from their rich social setting and disconnected from their net of friendships.

Using the person of peace/incarnational mode, the new believers stay in those networks and with training, nurture, and support can quickly lead friends to Christ, often starting a church "out there in the real world" (to use a terrible phrase). This mode is much more reproducible, sustainable, and contextualized.

Multiplication, Not Addition

In the incarnational mode we would be much more careful of "organized religion." We're increasingly convinced that bigger is not necessarily better. This is actually a modernist assumption. We have come to think smaller is better in the postmodern context as long as it is done with cultural vigor. Bigger means more programs; more programs means more organization and more control, i.e., less freedom! The missional-incarnational church thinks more in terms of multiplication rather than addition. Getting more and more people into the same room at the same time is not part of the incarnational agenda. This might have worked in the postwar US, where the 1950s American suburban culture was much more monochrome, where the world of the baby boom meant that a one-size-fits-all model of church was more likely to work. Now we are seeing such a dramatic fracturing of Western society into a range of subcultures, even in the suburbs, that one-size-fits-all is increasingly outmoded. This is called the *subculturization* or *tribalization* of the West. In fact, it could be argued that the megachurch in America thrives mostly in monochromatic baby boomer suburbs. Having said that, we recognize it is a great generalization, and we don't seek to explain the success of the megachurch phenomenon so simplistically. But we are forecasting what most Western social commentators are saying—that even the suburbs are now splintering into myriad subcultures. Churches, like missionaries, will need to understand subcultural mores and folkways and incarnate themselves into the rhythms of each specific people group or "tribe" to which they feel called.

Whenever one starts advocating smaller, targeted, incarnational communities, someone is sure to raise the charge that they are not evangelistic enough. But we are both strongly evangelistic in our outlook and practice. What we are advocating is an emphasis on multiplying incarnational congregations rather than the current emphasis on filling as many pews as possible. Jonathan Campbell's Baton church model has been inspirational to us in this regard. Using the image of a baton, Campbell claims the gospel and the biblical vision of church should be mobile, transferable, and contextual. He says,

> God's strategy for building his kingdom is through the growing and multiplication of missionary communities. Although the context and methods will change, the mission of the church is timeless. The church is to share the good news of Jesus Christ in the power of the Holy Spirit among all the social groupings and gather those who respond into disciple-making communities. New churches flow naturally out of disciple-making in the community context.[2]

So if a church is growing through disciple making (which assumes and includes evangelism), it will naturally be part of a cycle of growth and commissioning new congregations using persons of peace. Campbell believes this is the organic rhythm of a biblical church, as seen in the Acts of the Apostles (13:1–14:28) and summarized in the following diagram:

FIGURE 4

An existing church commissions church-planting team.

This team evangelizes strategic people.

With new disciples, the team establishes an indigenous church.

The indigenous church, in turn, commissions church-planting team.

This team evangelizes strategic people.

And on the cycle goes.

2. Jonathan Campbell, "The Way of Jesus: Patterns for Movement," in *The Baton: Rediscovering the Way of Jesus*, at http://www.geocities.com/g_westlake/BatonOview.html.

The missional-incarnational church then sees itself as part of an ongoing process, not as an end in itself. The days when churches would build monolithic church buildings and proudly proclaim that they've been here since 1861 (or whenever) are ending. Now churches will see themselves as strategic parts of an organic rhythm of witness. Some might exist for only a season, others might stay as an entity for generations, but the goal will be to reproduce, not just to sustain, itself. It is a send-gather-disciple-reproduce mode.[3] Thinking about church as a movement, rather than as an institution, will require a complete paradigm shift for current church leaders. But it is a shift long overdue. The church in the West needs to become a missionary movement in its own milieu.

Leadership Is Vital

If we could do church all over again, we would build clear leadership philosophy and vision, recognizing that imaginative, godly, biblical leadership is absolutely vital. It is the strategic area of leverage for change. We would focus on this first and keep focusing on it. It will be important in planting incarnational churches that the leaders select a team only on the basis of a clear, demonstrated commitment to stated philosophy and vision. We have found that some people who can cognitively agree with the philosophy of the incarnational-church mode still have great difficulty with it in practice. The attractional mode is so pervasive and so entrenched in the Western church that those who have grown up in it sometimes have a kind of default program in their imaginations. They can agree with the need for significant change, but they readily default back to standard practices in reality. It will be essential to take leadership teams through a process of recognizing the difference between what Brian McLaren calls church traditions and the Christian Tradition.[4] Leaders need to understand that church practices or traditions are culturally inherited. They are fully adaptable and flexible for the culture and must not be confused with biblical teaching that is not negotiable and not flexible.

The fourth section of this book deals with the issue of incarnational and apostolic biblical leadership, so we don't need to preempt what we will say later. However, we will put on the table our belief that the New Testament teaches a fivefold leadership matrix that implies a community of leadership made up of apostles, prophets, evangelists, shepherds, and teachers (Eph. 4:11–13). We think it is the legacy of the Christendom mode that sees Christian community in terms of a triangular hierarchy, with pastor-teachers at the pinnacle. In a post-Christendom world, the yearning for an egalitarian, gracious community

3. Ibid., 3.
4. Brian D. McLaren, *Reinventing Your Church* (Grand Rapids: Zondervan, 1998), 49–63.

of faith requires that leadership be egalitarian and cooperative as well. We cannot find the term *senior pastor* in the New Testament, but we can find Paul's desire for the church to be led by all five leadership giftings, acting in concert for a balanced biblical equipping of the saints. The church's current emphasis on pastors and teachers means that the cross-cultural missionary heart of the apostles and prophets is always quenched by the concerns for good teaching and pastoral care. So-called "good teaching" is not occurring in a church that has no heart for its community, since the purpose of teaching is to equip Christians for service.

This is not to say that the church should not be effectively shepherded by godly leaders ("elders" to be precise), but we see Christian leadership operating best as a community within a community. Any suggestion that there should be a distinct class of "priest" in the Christian church is clearly a contradiction of Pauline teaching. And this is not just a criticism to be leveled at the Episcopal churches. The evangelical and Pentecostal churches, with their hierarchies of pastors, are functioning with a priesthood in all but name. The New Testament radically reshapes the language of priesthood, presuming all believers to be priests, able to make their lives sacrifices, and able to gain personal access to the grace of God. There is no distinction in the New Testament between priest and laity, the sacred and the secular, the religious and the everyday. Only when all five functions of leadership are equally balanced do we have a leadership team worthy of Paul's vision in Ephesians. A new congregation should establish a full-fledged leadership matrix from the beginning. But as we said, more on that later.

Watch Your Use of Buildings

Michael attended a church once that had a sign out front that proudly announced: "Minister: The whole congregation!" Of course, as we've just mentioned, this is a very biblical way of looking at the church, with every believer involved actively in ministry. But upon entering the church it was apparent that a different message was operational. All the seating faced in one direction toward a high pulpit. The vicar wore a white surplice and a dog collar. During the service, he did about 90 percent of the talking. It might well have been that in the seven-days-a-week life of that congregation every member was involved in ministry, but their public church service sent some very clear signals that day. You can *say* that there is no distinction between clergy and laity in your church brochure or sign, but the medium is the message. In a later chapter on the medium being message we will address the various unspoken messages we send. But for now, while thinking about the shape of church, we can say that our church buildings and practices betray our refusal to embrace the radical biblical teaching on Christian community.

We advise church planters to watch for the problem of buildings. It seems most churches that don't have their own sanctuary building are devoted to getting one, but we're not so sure this is always necessary. Church planter Andrew Jones cleverly says, "Any church that cannot get by without buildings, finances and paid experts is not fully being church." Having a building, some shared money, and some paid staff doesn't preclude you from being an effective church, but if your church would be lost without them, there is a core problem. Where the church is thriving in Asia, Africa, and Latin and South America, many churches are meeting in homes, under trees, beside rivers, in cafés, and in public meeting halls. It's in the West, where the institutional church is slowly dying, that there seems to be such a reliance on church buildings. It's been called the church's *edifice complex*![5]

In his classic 1975 book, *The Problem of Wineskins*, Howard Snyder writes that church buildings attest to five facts about the Western church: its immobility, inflexibility, lack of fellowship, pride, and class divisions. "The gospel says 'Go,' but our church buildings say, 'Stay.' The gospel says, 'Seek the lost,' but our churches say, 'Let the lost seek the church.'"[6] The medium is the message. And more than that, once a building has been erected, the church program and budget are largely determined by it. In order to service the mortgage, the church has to keep the pews filled and the offerings up, and so the pattern of the attractional mode is reinforced and confirmed. Next time you attend a church service, listen to all the language that betrays a belief that we come into the church building to "meet" God. Subtly the building starts to direct the theology presented in it. We build a sanctuary in which to worship God, and then that building slowly enforces a sacred-versus-secular worldview upon us. What of God's words to King David?

> Would you build me a house to dwell in? I have not lived in a house since the day
> I brought up the people of Israel from Egypt to this day, but I have been moving
> about in a tent for my dwelling. In all places where I have moved with all the

5. We are not suggesting that traditional church buildings are unhelpful per se. In fact, we know of several inner-city churches that have incarnated themselves within trendy young urbanite communities and have found that meeting in a grand old cathedral-like building is very contextual. By lighting the Gothic-style building only in candles and making creative use of shadows and darkness, the echoing acoustic, and the artwork and sculpture, these churches see it as a contextualization issue. Communities made up of artists, filmmakers, and young people working in new media find the Gothic feel very stimulating. Missional considerations are driving such a choice of building, not faulty theological ones.

6. Howard Snyder, *The Problem of Wineskins* (Downers Grove, IL: InterVarsity, 1975), 69–73.

people of Israel, did I speak a word with any of the judges of Israel, whom I commanded to shepherd my people Israel, saying, "Why have you not built me a house of cedar?" (2 Sam. 7:5–7)

David, living in his own house of cedar, assumed that nothing less should be done for God. But the temple was not God's idea. Even though he accommodated human weakness and allowed David his temple, and the medieval church its cathedrals, and the modern church its sanctuaries, God does not need a home. As Stephen says at the moment of his martyrdom, "The Most High does not dwell in houses made by human hands" (Acts 7:48 NASB). Many ministers today would know these biblical verses and agree that God doesn't live in church buildings. But the arrangement of their buildings, the language used in worship services, the myriad unspoken messages that clergy send, belie an unconscious belief in the holiness of church buildings. It is not uncommon to see in older church buildings the following, oh-so-welcoming sign in the church foyer:

THIS IS THE HOUSE OF GOD
ENTER IT WITH REVERENCE AND QUIETNESS

And while we don't deny any church its preference for reverential and silent worship meetings, we take issue with the unspoken message that such churches send to their communities, that is, God lives here (and its underlying assumption, "and only here!").

Rob Warner, an English church leader, refers to this in his book *21st Century Church* as old temple thinking.[7] Such thinking consists of seven assumptions that we have slightly reworded to suit:

1. A vast number of cultures utilize religious buildings. Therefore, it is only natural that we Christians would refer to ours as the house of the Lord.
2. The prevailing assumption is that "proper" worship is only possible in certified religious buildings.
3. It stands to reason that, as the only certified place of worship, the church building must be a sacred place.
4. So, a proper church building is the only place for Christians to meet with God or to hear from him.
5. Church buildings stand out as a symbol of permanence and stability, like a beacon on a hill.

7. Warner, *21st Century Church*, 127–30.

6. In "Christian" countries, this *beacon* persona of church buildings is representative of the presence of God himself.
7. Since church buildings represent God they need to be more spectacular than buildings from other religions.

In effect, this is Christianity attempting to play by the rules of other human religions. There's a kind of keeping up with the religious Joneses going on here. But as French theologian Jacques Ellul points out, "For the Romans nascent Christianity was not at all a new religion. It was 'antireligion.' This view was well founded. What the first Christian generations were putting on trial was not just the imperial religion, as is often said, but every religion in the known world."[8] Christianity is antireligion, not just another religion competing with all other pretenders to the Way. Jesus and his earliest followers saw themselves as ushering in something much more radical than a new religion. Jesus called it the kingdom of God and referred to it in a manner that in no way resembles talk about a new institution or religion. Rob Warner writes,

> Christ is the new cornerstone, and in him we are the dwelling place of the Spirit and the spiritual temple, filled with the worship of God. There can be no good reason for us to ape the attitudes or building of other religious systems. Their dependence on holy buildings has been rendered obsolete. Their extravagant temples, whether sublime or grandiose, are surplus to requirements. We no longer have any good reason or need to conform to conventional religious instincts, for the living God established a rupture with religious conformity in bringing salvation to us. *In the death of Christ we are faced with the abolition of human religion.*[9]

And so even though Jesus and the early church completely revolutionized the idea of temple worship, the church has failed to sustain this revolution. For the early church, the home was the assumed meeting place. In fact, Robert Banks points out something interesting about the first purpose-built church buildings, "Not until the third century do we have evidence of special buildings being constructed for Christian gatherings and, even then, they were modeled on the room into which guests were received in the typical Roman and Greek household."[10] Even when the church was able to erect their own buildings, they modeled them on contemporary lounge rooms able to accommodate around thirty people. The medium is the message. A lounge room is a place of friendship, hospitality, and safety. It is a place where anyone can have his

8. Jacques Ellul, *The Subversion of Christianity* (Grand Rapids: Eerdmans, 1986), 55.
9. Warner, *21st Century Church*, 130.
10. Banks, *Paul's Idea of Community*, 41.

or her say. It is a place where food is shared and discussion can be frank. We do not want to limit church meetings to the home. We know of churches that meet in all sorts of environments (nightclubs, garages, wineries). We simply think it's important to remember what message we are sending by our physical environments. If we were doing it all again, we would watch the buildings and the programs. We would watch the subtle things we do—they communicate a great deal.[11]

To summarize the core differences between the attractional and the incarnational approaches to doing church, we turn to Carol Davis's diagram, which we have adapted in the list below. She refers to the attractional church as *extractional*. By that she means that the church extracts single converts, one at a time, from their world and incorporates them into the church. Davis prefers the term reproduction to incarnation. Nonetheless, the table is an extremely helpful summary of what we've been saying.[12]

Extraction/Single Convert/ "Growth" Model	Incarnational/ Reproduction Model
Church culture	**Mission culture**
Initial focus is on . . .	*Initial focus is on . . .*
Individual converts	Group conversions, e.g., households, networks
Believers' turf, e.g., church services	Unbelievers' turf
Recruiting Christians to come to services	Finding persons of peace
Begin in the church building	Begin in homes or Third Places
Large group meeting—celebration	Small groups—cell fellowship
Scripture taught as academic information	Scripture taught for practical application
Build programs and buildings	Build leaders
Leadership . . .	*Leadership . . .*
Pastor or lone-ranger	APEST (apostle, prophet, evangelist, shepherd, teacher) team
Imported professional clergy	Indigenous new disciples become leaders

11. This discussion might make us sound as though we don't accept that certain places might have particular spiritual significance for a person. That would be an inaccurate assumption. We fully appreciate that people might find a certain space, whether in their home or their church building or outdoors, to be helpful in their connection with God. But we are anxious that in our enjoyment of those spiritual places we not send a signal that we believe God "resides" in those places. It must remain part of our Christian spirituality that God is present in all places at all times, even though our imaginations are often more able to access God's presence at certain times and in certain places more than others.

12. Carol Davis, DAWN Report (June 2000).

Extraction/Single Convert/ "Growth" Model	Incarnational/ Reproduction Model
Leader of participatory audience at best	Equipper of emerging leaders and reproducers
Finances . . .	*Finances . . .*
Funded church planter	Bi-vocational church planter
Heavy financial investment	Minimal financial investment
Resources are imported	Resources are local
Structure . . .	*Structure . . .*
Needs of the church	Needs of the community
Clergy-centered/driven/dependent	Lay-centered/driven/dependent
For slow growth (leads to stagnation)	For rapid reproduction

Objective of Incarnational Mission

The four points mentioned above are simply some of the commitments we would make to ensure that our churches were incarnational in their orientation. This might seem obvious, given all that has gone before, but we want to make it even more explicit. In a previous point we indicated the necessity of listening to your patients. This implies an incarnational approach to ministry, but we have seen too many church planters who have done the research and then simply imported the standard model anyway. Christian ministry by definition is incarnational. We cannot just talk about the gospel from a safe distance outside a community. Doing so ignores the issues of credibility, relevance, and language differences (with the subculturization of Western society, don't for a minute think that different subcultures don't speak different dialects). A missionary needs to relate to those with whom he or she is communicating. Lobbing in "gospel grenades" from a distance only brings resentment. How can we listen and care from a distance?

We see there being four broad objectives of doing incarnational mission.

Real connection: The objective here is for not-yet-Christians to see that Jesus is "for" the host community. That is, Jesus has the host community's best interests at heart; he is on their side and is against anything that might cause them harm. In a world where many non-Christians assume God hates them (presumably because they gain the impression that God's people hate them) it is important to make one of the goals of incarnational church planting to help people connect with the God who is seeking them and desiring their friendship. To meet this objective we would use three fundamental strategies:

1. Presence (the missionary).
2. Partnerships. We believe that too much Christian ministry is a dupli-
   cation of projects and programs already being conducted by the community itself. An incarnational approach to ministry would see the
   Christian community partnering with local groups to assist in their
   work with families, the poor, youth, and single mothers. These partnerships would demonstrate that Jesus is pleased with the good works of
   not-yet-Christians and would provide a forum for the development of
   significant friendships. It's useful to regularly approach local community
   groups or projects and ask them three simple questions: (a) What are
   you most concerned about? (b) What are the causes of those concerns
   (the root of the problem)? and (c) What can we do together to help?
3. Inquiry groups (places to discover Christ). There needs to be the opportunity for Christians and those not-yet-Christians who want to explore
   the gospel further to gather together in a nonthreatening and respectful
   environment.

Real demonstration: The objective is to demonstrate that Jesus is "with" the
host community. Whereas a small team can meet the previous objective, this
second objective will require a critical mass, a church of some size. Being thoroughly loving and gracious within the host community will transform attitudes
toward Christ. The missional-incarnational church has to demonstrate God's
love in humility, mercy, and concern for justice. In a sense, the incarnational
church has to completely reframe the community's perceptions about Jesus and
the church. Many non-Christians in the West think the church is paternalistic,
manipulative, greedy, and controlling.

Real access: The objective here is to show that Jesus is "in" the host community. As the church community grows, the recognition that Jesus is in the
host community will be possible by noting several key indicators. First is the
paramount importance placed on having indigenous leadership development.
Whenever the church is led by "outsiders," no matter how incarnated they have
become, there will remain a suspicion that although Jesus has come into the
host community, he is not really part of that community. Indigenous leaders
are symbols of Christ's centrality in the culture. And so, second, and equally
important, is the need for imported or itinerant leaders to know when to move
on or to hand over complete leadership to local leaders. Third, it is important
to note that truly indigenous churches are ones that are self-theologizing. Christ
is in a community when it is able to develop its own theology using language,
symbols, and longings with local flavor and resonance. This sounds risky,

we know. But we are not suggesting that basic Christian doctrine be up for renegotiation. As indigenous churches grow, they must be people of the Word of God, but they need to express biblical theology in culturally relevant ways.

Real encounter: In this stage the host community comes to understand that Jesus is "of" their community. Only when two generations of leaders away from the initiating team emerge is it likely for Jesus to be "naturalized" among the host community.[13]

In Hobart, the most southerly city in Australia, a group of Christians calling itself Third Place Communities (TPC) has been attempting to engage in this process. The members have rented apartments within a two- or three-minute walk of a nearby pub. Some of the singles and childless couples live together in shared homes. Other couples live alone, but they all live in very close geographic proximity to one another. It is their practice to gather in the pub several times throughout the week simply to sit with and meet members of the local community. They refer to the pub and other similar meeting venues as third places. That is to suggest that the church is our place. The not-yet-Christian's home is their place, but a pub, club, café, or sporting team is a third place. It is shared space where Christians and not-yet-Christians can interact meaningfully and safely. TPC has established a business which seeks to foster similar experiments on the Australian island of Tasmania. By living so close to the pub, they are able to ask people they meet back to their homes for a meal, coffee, and further conversation. They are establishing real connection with the community.

One of their other projects is the establishment of a café/venue in downtown Hobart. They hold CD launches, live music, art exhibitions, and chill-out gatherings to engage the community in a relaxed third place. This is real demonstration. They are yet to offer real access or encounter, but they are well on their way. A group of young adults, the members of TPC are pioneering a new way of incarnating the gospel in an unchurched community. We have been greatly impressed by their energy, their creativity, and their devotion to Christ. Such projects are combusting right across the Western world. The question will not be about whether we should foster such experiments—they're going to keep happening anyway—but about how to provide nurture and encouragement to them.

13. We readily acknowledge the work of Ashley Barker, the director of Urban Neighbours of Hope in Melbourne, for these ideas. Ashley Barker has been a great inspiration to us both. He is a true missionary whose work among the urban poor has helped us to conceptualize the shape of the missional church.

Your Details

Order date: 03/03/2020
Order reference: WRDRY-55895286
Dispatch note: 2020030193680 1

Your Order

ISBN	Title	Quantity
9780801014918	The Shaping of Things to Come Innovat...	1

For returns information visit wordery.com/returns. Please keep this receipt for your records.

Thank you for your wordery.com order. We hope you enjoy your book #HappyReading

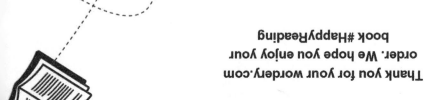

wordery
your online bookshop

2020030193680 1

5

The Contextualized Church

The church is described as belonging not to the people by whom it is constituted . . . nor to the district to which they belong . . . but rather to the one who has brought it into existence (that is, God) or the one through whom this has taken place (that is, Christ).

—Robert Banks, *Paul's Idea of Community*

Church 101

It is not uncommon for our students or interns to initially assume we are advocating some completely formless, unstructured approach to church. After giving a seminar on the future shape of the church, Michael went to dinner with some young men. At one point someone said, "I agree with you about the church. It needs a complete overhaul. I mean here we are, six guys eating together, talking about Jesus. We're a church now!" It's tempting, in our efforts to strip back the church from the empire created by Christendom, to overdo it and end up with the belief that any old bunch of believers sitting together in the same room is a church. But the six of us sitting around that table that night were not a church. We had made no mutual commitments, shared no long-term calling, were completely unaccountable to one another, and our purpose for gathering was mainly social. Of course, as Christians, our conversation centered on Christian things, and by the end of the evening we were encouraged in our faith and individual callings. We were doing *some* of the things a church might do, but our involvement was not permanent.

We don't think a church is just any old bunch of Christians who have bumped into each other. Neither do we think that a group of Christians who gather for a specific missional purpose is necessarily a church. Although it could be said that student bodies in theological seminaries, kids at Christian youth summer camps, and people on short-term mission trips create temporary forms of church, we believe it is the very impermanence of those communities that precludes us from identifying them as churches.[1] When we use the term church we are trying to do so in the same way the New Testament uses it. In Paul's writings he employed the term *ekklesia* (church) in a way that can only refer to an actual gathering of people, not to some ethereal theological concept. It is a regularly constituted meeting of God's people. However, he was mindful not to give the impression that the *ekklesia* was just another human association or club. Much of his language also spoke of the *ekklesia* as being a divinely appointed gathering. Robert Banks writes, "The church is described as belonging not to the people by whom it is constituted . . . nor to the district to which they belong . . . but rather to the one who has brought it into existence (that is, God) or the one through whom this has taken place (that is, Christ)."[2] So for Paul the church was the people gathered. As to what occurred in such a gathering, we think Acts 2:42–47 provides a neat snapshot. In this window into the regular gathering of the believers we see three broad elements, all of which should be held in tension:

FIGURE 5

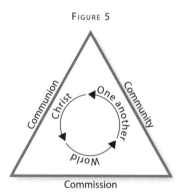

1. Many people find in a student body or in being part of a short-term mission team the very thing that ought to characterize being church: mission, passion, equipping, accountability, love, and respect. Sadly, they often report that their home churches are so lacking in these characteristics they'd rather stay part of such temporary communities than settle for what the institutional church has to offer.

2. Banks, *Paul's Idea of Community*, 37.

The first churches were concerned with balancing equal commitments to fostering their relationships with God, one another, and the world. Like an equilateral triangle, where all three sides must be the same size, the early church recognized the equal importance of all three broad commitments. In this respect, the essence of church is relationship and these three types of relationships interact so much that it is impossible to differentiate one from another. We show our love for God in our love for others. And we cannot be in a right relationship with the world if we are not living in a healthy relationship with God and his people. Some communities of Christians are chiefly concerned with *commission* (parachurch evangelistic organizations); others, *communion* (praise and worship conferences); and others still, with *community* (the house-church movement), but we believe the local gathering of believers must work hard to develop equal commitments to all three. Any emphasis on one at the expense of the others is folly. For a church to claim that it "specializes" in worship or teaching is to ignore the whole counsel of the New Testament. Worship that is in some way divorced from mission is counterfeit worship. And likewise, a missioning community that is not informed, inspired, and renewed through godly worship is a pale shadow of what church should be.

In fact, we have found that the separation between the missioning and the worshiping communities within the church has been one of the tragedies of Christianity. It might make sense for a large corporation to create departments that specialize in particular areas of the overall business, but the church is not a corporation. When the worshiping community of the church delegated the responsibility for mission to parachurch organizations and the missionary societies, it killed part of the church. Worship and mission and the development of Christian community must inform each other closely and regularly.

When we look at the snapshot of the first church in Acts 2, we see six features that seem to inform these three broad commitments:

Communion (in Relationship with Christ)

- God's word—The development of opportunities where the Christian community puts itself in places where it can hear God speak. "Everyone was filled with awe, and many wonders and miraculous signs were done by the apostles" (v. 43). This sense of awe and wonder was generated not only by the miraculous. (It seems that the early church sensed God's presence even more keenly in their gathering than at other times. From the rest of the book of Acts it is obvious that the first Christians sensed

God and heard him speak in all manner of situations, but the gathered community did seem to expect a communal sense of God's presence in their meetings.) It was generated also by the apostles' teaching and the breaking of bread (v. 42).

- Worship—For the first Christians, worship was the opportunity for them to respond to God. Whether it was in homes or the temple courts (v. 46), they took opportunities to praise God and apparently did so in such a way as to find favor with the broader community. There was also a strong sense of the immediacy with God in Christ.

Community (in Relationship with One Another)

- Learning—Often in the modernist church the emphasis is on teaching, but we find that the emphasis for the first Christians was on learning, that is, the formation of individuals and the Christian community as a whole into the likeness of Christ. This was centered on the apostles' teaching, the community of fellow learners, and the Christian love feast (vv. 42 and 46).
- Fellowship/friendship—This is the church as antireligion. There seems to have been no differing echelons of involvement. "All the believers were together and had everything in common" (v. 44). Rather than instituting offices of priests, scribes, teachers, deacons, and so on, the first Christians unraveled traditional human religion by refusing to build sacred sites, by not having altars, and by not ordaining people to a holy office. It was a genuine community of friends. From the beginning it seems that this idea of the church being an organic network or web of friendship was assumed.

Commission (in Relationship with the World)

- Serving/giving—"Selling their possessions and goods, they gave to anyone as he had need" (v. 45). Generosity and hospitality were hallmarks of the Christian movement from the start. And this took the form of costly and radical sharing. As worthwhile as food drives and Christmas baskets might be, much of the church's generosity is not terribly costly for the believers. Selfless, humble, and gracious hospitality will mark the church as a unique source of salt and light in the community. Clearly the early church, centered as it was on the apostles' teaching about Jesus, saw generosity as an obvious expression of Christlikeness.
- Gospel telling/sharing—There is no mention in this passage that the believers were "preaching" the gospel as such. But obviously their presence

in the temple courts, their worship of God, their acts of service, and their commonality had significant impact. Together with the public proclamation of the gospel by the apostles (v. 38) it reaped a great harvest: "And the Lord added to their number daily those who were being saved" (v. 47). This is the very model we have been advocating. The webs of friendship developed by socializing, sharing, and hospitality, together with prayer (v. 42) and the teaching of the apostles creates a potent community, fully incarnated and totally missional in its orientation.

This might sound like Church 101 because it is so basic, but our experience has been that many people accept church as it currently happens because they assume their local church service is somewhere prescribed in the pages of Holy Writ. As long as these three Cs are present and being maintained, any group of Christians can legitimately be considered a church in any place. While we said that any old group of Christians who occasionally have dinner together might not be a church, as such, if they embraced the six features above and met as regularly as was required to fulfill them, they could call themselves "church."

- Do you need to meet in a church building? Not necessarily.
- Do you need to meet weekly? Not necessarily. The first Christians met every day. A church can meet as often as it needs in order to fulfill the above commitments.
- Do you need a minister? Not necessarily. The New Testament is clear on the need for accountability, admonishment, and learning. It does speak about leaders (elders) exercising humble and loving care for a community. But you don't need an ordained minister for that.
- Do you need to sing hymns? Not necessarily. There is mention in the New Testament of the value of singing spiritual songs. But if the goal is that worship and learning occur when you meet, you can use as few (none?) or as many songs as you need.
- Does someone have to bring a sermon? Not necessarily. As long as people have an opportunity to hear from God, through his Word and other means, it doesn't matter whether one person speaks for thirty minutes or thirty people contribute a minute each. Learning, worship, and the opportunity for God's Word are essential. How they play out is entirely open to experimentation.

Ask yourself, "If we could start church all over again from scratch, would we do it the way it's currently being done?" Then ask yourself, "What is essential

for the church to retain and what is optional?" Jonathan Campbell's Baton
churches have developed the following grid that might help you:

Sphere of Authority	Description	Degree of Flexibility
Christ's Commands (the core)	Jesus is our ultimate authority. His commands are unquestioned.	No adaptation possible, nonnegotiable.
Biblical Principles (the substance)	These are cross-cultural principles drawn from apostolic biblical teaching.	The essence is unchanging. Adapt only to maintain dynamic equivalent.
Apostolic Patterns (the application)	Behaviors, practices, lifestyles of the first-century church.	Interpret or contextualize to fit the culture.
Church Practices (the expression)	Established ways of thinking about and doing church.	Fully adaptable and flexible for the culture.

We are advocating that all church planters take the considerable time required to untangle what we do because it is commanded by Christ, what we do because it was taught by the apostles or modeled by the early church, and what are relatively recent church traditions. Hold fast to the core but experiment like wild with the expression. The missional-incarnational church is entirely open to innovation, experimentation, and creativity. It doesn't, by its very nature, see itself as the opening of a new franchise of the church, like a McDonald's where every burger tastes the same no matter which culture it is sold in. As an incarnational community it is concerned about reflecting local flavors, spices, and textures and developing an ambience and a communal spirit that is sensitive and hospitable to local culture. As a missional community it is careful not to abandon the truth of the gospel nor to water down its implications. This is called the process of *critical contextualization,* and it will be important to turn our attention to that process now.

Thinking Mission

"Don't think church, think mission!" We don't know how many times we've used that phrase in our lectures as part of the Forge Mission Training Network. Forge is based in Melbourne, Australia, and is a year-long internship for radical church planters interested in developing missional churches. It is designed to assist young leaders to stop thinking conventionally about how to do church and to start thinking like missionaries to their own contexts. We have found it terribly difficult to get people to think in a missions-to-the-First-World kind of way, but those who can have felt liberated to dream creatively about new approaches to doing and being church. It seems as though everyone is only now getting used to the idea that the church in the West must become a missionary church in its own milieu if the church is to survive. Institutionally, of course, this is a massive paradigm shift from our standard ministry focus. The seemingly steadfast refusal or resistance by the church to seriously contextualize the gospel is one of its greatest mistakes and will sadly hasten its declining influence on Western society. It is not taking standard cross-cultural mission principles seriously and is therefore not taking the gospel seriously.

We have strongly advocated the need for an incarnational mode of church to emerge in the West. Associated with the emergence of such a mode is a whole new set of skills and assumptions not normally made in the attractional-style church. This includes new ways of thinking about Christian spirituality and leadership, which we will look at in due course. But it also means skills like contextualization will come to the fore. The missional-incarnational church must contextualize its language, worship, symbols, rituals, and communal life in such ways as to be sensitive to and impactful in a particular cultural context.

Knocking on the Wrong Doors

When the first British missionaries arrived in what was then called Rhodesia in southern Africa to preach the good news about Jesus, they came with all the trappings of the colonial era. Bound up with their preaching were certain assumptions and inherent belief systems that they thought to be Christian, but which we now see as simply reflecting the culture of Victorian England. For example, when the Zanaki people along the shores of Lake Victoria first converted to Christianity, they were encouraged to wear Western-style clothing, since Victorian modesty was supposed to be a Christian virtue. When the Zanaki were baptized, they were given "Christian" names like James, William, and Charles.

We could talk at length about the mistakes of the colonial-style missionaries. They have been portrayed in popular fiction by such books as James A. Michener's *Hawaii*, Peter Matthiessen's *At Play in the Fields of the Lord*, and Barbara Kingsolver's *The Poisonwood Bible*, where the American Baptist missionary to the Congo insists on holding baptismal services in a nearby river. When no one chooses to be baptized, he sees it as faithlessness. But unbeknown to him it has more to do with the fact that the river is infested with crocodiles! The inability by many missionaries to understand and respect the cultures in which they were working is now infamous. But one telling example will suffice. When the British preachers evangelized the Zanaki people of what is now called Zimbabwe, they did so by quoting Revelation 3:20, "Here I am! I stand at the door and knock. If anyone hears my voice and opens the door, I will come in and eat with him, and he with me." This verse and its use by the preachers is a very helpful case study in what is called poor contextualization, which is an inability to communicate the gospel in a form that makes sense within a particular context. Allow us to explain.

In polite and proper British culture, when one visited someone else's home, the door would be closed and probably locked and the inhabitants would be privately and securely ensconced inside. Therefore you knocked loudly on the front door to gain entry. In Zanaki culture homes have no doors. To enter the home of a friend in your village, you would call out loudly at the doorway. In a small community your voice would be immediately recognized, and you would be invited to enter. The only people who knocked were thieves. They did not wish to be identified. Having knocked surreptitiously, if the thieves heard stirring inside the house, they would sneak away. If you knew this about Zanaki culture when you came to preach Revelation 3:20, in which Jesus talks of himself both knocking and calling out, which would you emphasize? Because the British missionaries had no knowledge of Zanaki customs, they blithely preached that Jesus was knocking on the door. And by doing so they inadvertently made him out to be a sneaky thief! This is an example of noncontextualized Christian ministry. The message is still true—Jesus desires to have a relationship with you if you would only open your life to him. The context in which that truth was presented required a different use of metaphor and language for it to make sense.

We're not simply making a play for "relevant" preaching. We are advocating a total recalibration and a radical rethink about the symbols, language, metaphors, vernacular, and idioms we employ when presenting Christ to our world. The church can no longer make excuses for non-contextualized mission. In fact, the only worthwhile Christian ministry is culturally contextualized mission. It is truth ministry, but it is also understandable, believable, and accessible truth. As David Bosch says, "The missionary nature of the Church does not just depend on the situation in which it finds itself at a given moment, but is grounded in the Gospel itself."

Contextualization: A Working Definition

For certain reasons contextualization has had a shaky reception by the more conservative or moderate sections of the church. Some conservatives claim that "if we just preach the gospel," the West will be transformed by the power of God's Word. We've had more than one noted evangelical leader tell us, "You can examine culture and understand contemporary trends if you like. As for me I'll just preach the Bible." This is usually said with the kind of flourish that betrays their assumption that they are making a high and noble claim. But in many cases where we ignore principles of contextualization our preaching of the Bible may well have as much impact as preaching in Swahili to English speakers.

In 1972 a document called *Ministry in Context* sought to wrestle with the difficult issue of how best to respect and value the cultural context in which any ministry takes place. Its chief concern seemed to be with those churches and denominations that were not equipping their leadership to relate effectively to the needs, concerns, and interests (material, political, and otherwise) of the people to whom they were ministering.

In that document is one of the first attempted definitions of a then very new missiological term: *contextualization*. This term can only be understood if we can first agree on some presuppositions. First, as proponents of contextualization, we believe that the core of the gospel is valid for all cultures and times. Second, however, we recognize that such a gospel must be clothed in time-specific cultural forms in order for it to be communicated and understood. Contextualization, then, can be defined as the dynamic process whereby the constant message of the gospel interacts with specific, relative human situations. It involves an examination of the gospel in the light of the respondent's worldview and then adapting the message, encoding it in such a way that it can become meaningful to the respondent. Contextualization attempts to communicate the gospel in word and deed and to establish churches in ways that make sense to people within their local cultural context. It is primarily concerned with presenting Christianity in such a way that it meets people's deepest needs and penetrates their worldviews, thus allowing them to follow Christ and remain in their own cultures. Cross-cultural missionaries are noted for using the expression, "Contextualization is when the gospel presented and the response called for, offends for the right reasons and not for the wrong ones." Latin American theologian René Padilla says,

> To contextualize the gospel is so to translate it that the Lordship of Jesus Christ is not an abstract principle or a mere doctrine, but the determining factor of life in all its dimensions and the basic criterion in relation to which all the cultural values that form the very substance of human life are evaluated. Without contextualization the gospel will become tangential or even entirely irrelevant.[3]

Because the gospel is always God's good news to humankind, it cannot be defined without reference to the human context. So although the gospel is unchanging, the contexts in which it must be related will be regularly changing. It must be communicable for it to be *news*.

---

3. René Padilla, *Mission Between the Times* (Grand Rapids: Eerdmans, 1985), 93.

When we give thought to a contextualized approach to evangelism in the West, we are not supposing some simple, cosmetic reworking of church symbols or language. We yearn for something richer and more complex, more daring and dangerous. As we have already noted, the one-size-fits-all approach to church mission and evangelism must be abandoned. This wouldn't seem to be such a radical statement, but churches throughout the West seem to be more eager than ever to embrace formularized, "successful," prepackaged models of evangelism. Fewer and fewer churches, from our experience, seem to be developing evangelistic ministries specifically contextualized to the geographic area or subculture in which they are living. No matter the socioeconomic, ethnic, or age group, the gospel must relate to the whole human context, including both the situational and the experiential.

By *situational* we mean all that is true of people in their given situation, comprising their past, present, and future—their lot in life, including their culture, nationality, language, and the laws that affect them. It also includes their situation as God sees it—their fallenness and their beauty. But the gospel must also relate to the *experiential* context of people—the subjective experiences of humans arising out of, but also creating, their situational context, such as feelings of insecurity, hopes, and fears. The totality of context is obviously very wide and fluid. This makes the concept of contextualization an ongoing, dynamic process wherever the gospel is being preached and lived.

This is not merely the dilemma of missionaries who are ministering cross-culturally. Following Lesslie Newbigin we can therefore say that it is necessary for the church to rethink its stance entirely and to become a missionary church within the West.

Why Contextualize?

It might seem obvious from all we've said so far that if the church is prepared to adopt an incarnational stance, it should take seriously the issue of contextualization. Let us outline some fundamental reasons for the necessity of contextualized mission. For this list we are indebted to friend and missionary, Robert Lutton.

Christ Did It!

The classic example of someone from outside another culture becoming immersed in it while retaining his or her own identity is Jesus himself. Oft-quoted Philippians 2:5–11 makes this point: though he was in very nature God, he put his right to a heavenly world aside and, entering a fallen world, at great cost to himself, became one of us. Further, his lifestyle was marked by his preferential involvement in the lives of ordinary people, rather than pious religious people. He partied with Matthew and his friends; he played with children; he fried fish for breakfast with Peter; he provided wine for a wedding in Cana.

The First Christians Practiced It

Any study of the preaching styles and content of the sermons in Acts will reveal that the gospel message was presented in differing ways depending on whom it was presented to. To those in the synagogue, the gospel was presented as the fulfillment of Old Testament prophecy, and Jesus was seen as a rightful descendant of David (see Peter's sermons in Acts 2:14–40; 3:11–26; Stephen's speech in Acts 7; and Paul's at Antioch in Acts 13). Compare this with Paul's approach in Acts 17:16–34, where Paul, schooled as he was in Greek thought, made strategic use of the idol to the unknown god to pry open the minds of those at the Areopagus. It's interesting to make a comparison of two of Paul's sermons to see the contextualizing process at work. At Antioch, Paul was speaking to the Jewish community, and in Athens, to a Gentile audience. It can be illustrated in the following way:

Topic	Antioch	Athens
God	Covenant Lord of Israel	Transcendent/Immanent Creator
Humanity	Has rejected the promised Son of David	Has wrongly depicted the Creator by a portion of creation
Jesus	Son of David/Son of God	The risen Judge
Response	Welcome the gospel	Turn from worship of idols
Promise	Forgiveness of sin	Escape the coming wrath

It just makes sense, doesn't it? But when churches in the West talk about contextualization, they are often meaning nothing more than a simple change in the style of music or the introduction of drums or new seating to replace the pews. To contextualize is to understand the language, longings, lifestyle patterns, and worldview of the host community and to adjust our practices accordingly without compromising the gospel. Many churches change the style of their Sunday services without any research into the host community. We often change things because *we* want the change, not because of a heart for cross-cultural mission in our own context.

A *billabong* is an Australian term for a pond or lake that was once part of the bend of a river or creek but which has been cut off from the flow as the river slowly changed direction. Many second- or third-generation Christians find themselves in a church billabong. Where once their parents or grandparents were part of a church that was like a flowing stream, now they are trapped in a stagnant backwater. Growing up Christian, they have adopted a middle-class perspective and embraced a certain way of doing church. Their motivation for staying in the church is no longer to fulfill Christ's mission in this world, but to have their own needs met. If the church doesn't work through the process of contextualization, this generation of Christians will become the "New Colonials," as it adds to the gospel according to its own tastes. Just as many colonial-era missionaries added Western democracy, capitalism, pews, pulpits, formal clothing on Sundays, and Western organizational systems and rules to the gospel, those second- (or more) generation Christians today can add their own spin to the essence of Christ's gospel.

The church ought to be more like a tidal pool than a billabong. In the deep rock pools formed by the ever-swirling surf of the ocean, whole ecosystems can develop, filled with weed, rock crabs, mollusks, etc. If left untouched by the ocean, the pools would overheat in the sun and become stagnant as the sea life dies. What a tidal pool needs is the regular flushing of the ocean as the tide rises and falls sweeping the pool clean each day. Any church that doesn't engage in the work of contextualization, motivated by a heart for local mission, overheats and becomes stagnant. It's in the engagement with not-yet-Christians that we regularly adjust our language and its idioms, our practices, our emphases, and our worship life. We need to be regularly swept by incoming new Christians.

Because It Works!

We don't advocate that the church simply embrace strategies because they work. This kind of pragmatism has done untold damage to the Western church. But our experience and observation have been that when the Western church engages in the biblical process of contextualization, it's not only being true to its heritage, but it is much more effective in its host community. Incredible movements of God are happening around the world as new radicals are contextualizing the gospel. We believe that when we incarnate ourselves into a host community of not-yet-Christians and contextualize our message and our practices to engage that community, we honor God because we demonstrate that we love his message and the people to whom we minister so much that we will do all we can to communicate it effectively.

The Essential Link of Gospel and Context

Charles Kraft, an evangelical scholar, rightly states the obvious when he says that human beings are as immersed in culture as fish are in water; that culture constitutes the most fundamental aspect of human beings' context.[4] There seems to be general agreement among evangelical scholars that in an important sense the gospel is supra-cultural, inasmuch as it originates in the mind of God who is outside the context of all human culture. Yet, as we've noted, the gospel is good news for humankind who cannot access truth outside of their cultural context. Kraft and others therefore operate from within the fundamental premise that God is above culture but has chosen to work within it to achieve his purposes.

Orlando Costas argues that the gospel cannot be defined at all without reference to context, since the context is the stage where all comprehension takes place. "It is the reality that ties together and therefore shapes, all knowledge. . . . We participate in it, actively or passive. Not one of us can claim to stand outside it. The question is whether or not we can consciously and critically incorporate it into our efforts to interpret and communicate the gospel. This is what we do in contextualization."[5] At the same time the coming of the gospel from outside the cultural context gives it the ability to affirm those aspects of every culture that agree with God's purposes and that predispose members of that culture to comprehend the gospel. But the gospel also comes to judge the evil elements in every society that are contrary to God's will. The creation of humankind in God's image means that there is no culture that lacks virtuous elements in terms of which the gospel can be expressed. At the same time the fall of humankind from grace means that no culture is completely virtuous. It was this sin of ethnocentrism (assuming Western culture was virtuous and Christian) that made many colonial-era missionaries impose Western culture on the Two-Thirds-World nations as the standard expression of Christianity.

The gospel message as we find it in Scripture is for all peoples, all nations, and all subcultures. Yet it is expressed in terms of the Jewish and the Greco-Roman cultural contexts of the first century. Therefore, for God's message to cross from that context into ours, or from our context to others in evangelistic ministry, there has to be the complex work of contextualization.

Biblical Examples of Contextualization

Finding biblical examples of contextualization is not difficult, since it could be argued that the whole Bible is an example of divine contextualization. To claim that an eternal, omnipotent Spirit God, who is above all human culture, has spoken to us in human language, using human imagery, tapping into

4. Charles Kraft, *Christianity in Culture* (Maryknoll, NY: Orbis, 1979), 46.
5. Orlando Costas, *Christ Outside the Gate: Mission Beyond Christendom* (Maryknoll, NY: Orbis, 1982), 5.

human longings and fears is to claim God is the ultimate contextualizer. Says Orlando Costas, "When we take a close look at its pages . . . we note that the Scriptures are contextual from beginning to end."[6]

Charles Kraft presents four principles for seeing the place of contextualization in the Bible. They are:

1. The Bible goes considerably beyond revealing merely intellectual truth or information. It demonstrates how truth is conveyed. Says Kraft, "Our God . . . is mainly a God of dialogue who interacts with us, not simply a God of monologue who makes pronouncements above us."[7]
2. God's communication with humanity is depicted in the Bible as coming to humans in familiar, expected ways (though the message itself was often unexpected).
3. God's method of self-disclosure is demonstrated to be participatory.
4. We observe God's revelatory activity in the Scriptures to be situation-specific.

If we adopt these principles, we are logically drawn to recognize the biblical writers' role in contextualizing the divinely revealed truth they present. In other words, the contextualizing process is as keenly recorded in Scripture as is the message itself. Sometimes God reveals himself and his will through a thunderous visitation at Mount Sinai, and at other times through the systematic argumentation of Saint Paul. Not only is the information revealed on those occasions recorded, but the very process of their transmission is also revealed.

Clearly, the most profound example of contextual self-revelation by God is the Incarnation. If we believe that in the Incarnation God's true self has been ultimately revealed and, as Karl Barth states, the true identity of humankind is also revealed, then two things follow: first, men and women discover their authentic humanness in Jesus; and second, they come to know the true God through him. Let us put it another way: the Incarnation makes the study of God and the study of anthropology a christological issue. It therefore makes contextualization an essential and inevitable process for a proper communication of the Christian message. Contextualization becomes a theological necessity in the sense that it is simply not possible to understand God or humanity without understanding the person and work of Jesus. We cannot remove God from the picture and examine him under a microscope as it were, in some clinical, abstract way. He can only ever be fully known in context and

6. Ibid.
7. Kraft, *Christianity in Culture*, 24.

that context is Christ. Evangelism, then, is a missiological enterprise. It is about using contextual methods to point people to a God who has revealed himself contextually. This will demand a rigorous devotion to the centrality of Christ and to the ongoing examination of human culture.

How will this work itself out in cross-cultural ministry? Allow us to repeat ourselves here: we believe that *all* ministry in the West is cross-cultural or should take cross-cultural contextualization seriously. So, if contextualization is so important, then we need to explore its process.

In 1987 missiologist Paul Hiebert proposed a framework for the *critical* contextualization of the gospel in un-Christian contexts. His model has been embraced around the world by those involved in cross-cultural mission. It is a four-step method that is transferable to a variety of contexts including Western subcultures.

Critical Contextualization

Hiebert's model attempts to build safeguards that minimize the risk and limit the possibility of syncretism or a betrayal of the gospel. First, he encourages the church to engage seriously with an examination of the host culture, as we've been advocating. Second, he strongly recommends a clear commitment to biblical authority. A missional church ought to be filled with students of the Word of God. He says,

> This step is crucial, for if the people do not clearly grasp the biblical message as originally intended, they will have a distorted view of the gospel. This is where the pastor or missionary . . . has the most to offer in an understanding of biblical truth and in making it known in other cultures. While the people must be involved in the study of Scripture so that they grow in their own abilities to discern truth, the leader must have the meta-cultural grids that enable him or her to move between cultures.[8]

So the role of missional church leadership includes the examination of the community it is trying to reach and the teaching of biblical truth to a local congregation. The third step "is for the people corporately to evaluate critically their own past customs in the light of their new biblical understandings, and to make decisions regarding their response to their new-found truths."[9] Hiebert's next step sounds easy, but is in fact very demanding. After emphasizing the importance of

8. Paul G. Hiebert, "Critical Contextualization," *International Bulletin of Missionary Research*, 2 (3):104–10.
9. Ibid.

the expertise of the evangelist/missionary in the second step, he now turns the process back to the people. This is an important feature of his model; it is congregationally based. It is not reliant on "experts." It validates the contribution of new converts and longer-term committed Christians. Only at the stage of Bible teaching does he emphasize the role of the leadership. He says, "(The gospel) is a message to which people must respond. . . . It is not enough that the leaders be convinced about changes that may be needed. Leaders may share their personal convictions and point out the consequences of various decisions, but they must allow the people to make the final decision in evaluating their past customs."[10] His assumption is that the new converts understand their culture better than do those of us who examine it from without. If we teach the Bible effectively, and if we have examined the culture creatively, then we must trust the Christian community to evaluate the changes in language, customs, practices, and beliefs that need to be embraced in order to critically contextualize the gospel.

This is where Hiebert is at his most radical. He wants leaders to trust the congregation, something that clergy have been notoriously poor at doing in the past. If the process is guided effectively, he suggests a number of ways a congregation might respond to old beliefs and customs.

Keep That Which Is Not Unbiblical

Many cultural practices are neither Christian nor non-Christian. They are neither sanctioned nor condemned in the Bible, and therefore Christians can be ambivalent about them. Hanging certain kinds of art in the church building might be an example. In keeping such practices the church can reaffirm its own cultural identity and heritage.

Reject That Which Is Unbecoming for Christians

Sometimes we might be surprised by what is rejected because we don't understand the significance of the rejection of certain songs, customs, beliefs, and so forth. On other occasions to help the congregation remain aware of any cultural blind spots, the evangelist will need to probe why certain customs have not been rejected.

Modify Practices to Give Them Explicitly Christian Meaning

Hiebert mentions Charles Wesley's use of popular pub songs to which he set Christian lyrics and the fact that the early Christians used the synagogue form of

10. Ibid.

worship, but modified it to fit their beliefs. In our context, if we were trying to reach young people, we might reject "moshing" as an aggressive form of dancing that emphasizes individuality and includes a lot of pushing, shoving, and jumping. Or we might validate it, but modify it to express togetherness, community, and vitality. Hiebert suggests three other ways of doing such modification:

Reject Current Unbiblical Practices and Replace Them

People who are living together when they become Christians would be encouraged either to get married or to live separately. The close relationship is not rejected; it is simply replaced with a structure that is more in keeping with Christian morality.

Adopt Rites Drawn from the Christian Heritage

Naturally the adoption of the Lord's Supper and baptism connects any congregation with their new history as Christians. Culturally sensitive expressions of the communion feast and the rite of entry through baptism need to be thoroughly and biblically contextualized by the church.

Create New Symbols and Rituals

Finally, develop new, fresh expressions of the Christian experience. The Jesus Movement of the late 1960s and early 1970s—forms of which experienced a revival in the 1990s—developed a series of hand signals, sayings, slogans, and even jewelry to communicate Christian beliefs. Today the five colored beads are still popular among younger Christians as is other pop paraphernalia and artifacts.

After the arduous but important process outlined above, the congregation, under the leadership of the missionary team, will seek to arrange the practices they have chosen, modified, and created into a new set of rituals that contextually expresses Christian meaning. What that looks like will be different for each context. Our desire is not to present a new template for churches in the West, but to inform the missional-incarnational church movement and to celebrate the many forms it takes around the world.

One of the great pioneering thinkers about and practitioners of critical contextualization is Phil Parshall, an American missionary to Muslim communities in Asia for over forty years. Parshall's radical incarnation of the gospel within a Muslim worldview earned him a worldwide reputation as a leading thinker in the area of contextualization. While some thought he had gone too far in establishing communities of "messianic Muslims," others were inspired by his example and began going even further by encouraging Muslims to continue worshiping at mosques as secret or underground believers. In response to both his detractors and to those who thought he had not gone far enough, Parshall's associate, John Travis, developed a spectrum for thinking about the different possible levels of contextualization.[11] While thinking about new contextualized practices, it will serve our purposes to reproduce that spectrum below. It is a practical tool for defining six types of Christ-centered communities currently found in the Muslim context. The six types can easily be applied to any context in the West also. In fact, all six types are presently found in some part of the US.

Travis refers to the six types as C1 to C6, the "C" standing for "Christ-centered communities." His references to insiders and outsiders refer to Muslims and non-Muslims respectively. We could use the terms in the West to refer to local indigenous members of the host community and missionaries/church planters respectively.

C1—Traditional Church Using Outsider Language

This is where the church reflects Western culture in an Asian Muslim context. It uses non-indigenous language (English) and imported symbols. A huge cultural chasm often exists between the church and the surrounding community. C1 believers call themselves "Christians."

C2—Traditional Church Using Insider Language

This is essentially the same as C1 except for language. Says Travis, "Though insider language is used, religious vocabulary is probably non-Islamic (distinctively Christian)."[12] The cultural gap between host community and missionary church is still large. However, Travis points out that the majority of churches located in the Muslim world are C1 or C2. C2 believers also call themselves "Christians." C2 music style and meeting place are Western.

C3—Contextualized Christ-Centered Communities Using Insider Language and Religiously Neutral Insider Cultural Forms

Religiously neutral forms may include folk music, ethnic dress, artwork, etc. The aim of C3 contextualization is to reduce the foreignness of the

11. John Travis is a pseudonym for a church planter to Muslim communities in Asia. His C1 to C6 spectrum appeared in Phil Parshall's article "Going Too Far?" in the *Evangelical Missions Quarterly* 34:3 (Oct. 1998). See also Travis's article "Must All Muslims Leave Islam to Follow Jesus?" in the same issue.
12. Ibid., 3.

gospel by contextualizing to biblically permissible cultural forms. C3 churches sometimes meet in a religiously neutral location. C3 believers call themselves "Christians."

C4—Contextualized Christ-Centered Communities Using Insider Language and Biblically Permissible Cultural and Islamic Forms

This is similar to C3, though biblically acceptable Islamic forms are also introduced (e.g., praying with raised hands; keeping the fast; avoiding pork, alcohol, and dogs as pets; using Islamic terms and dress; and so forth). Meetings are never held in a traditional Christian church building. "C4 believers, though highly contextualized, are usually not seen as Muslims by the Muslim community. C4 believers identify themselves as 'followers of Isa the Messiah' (or something similar)."[13]

C5—Christ-Centered Communities of "Messianic Muslims" Who Have Accepted Jesus as Lord and Savior

According to Travis, believers in the C5 group maintain their full legal and social status within the Islamic community. Elements of Islamic theology precluded by the Bible are rejected or, if possible, reinterpreted. Members of this group often participate in corporate Islamic worship in some way, though C5 believers also meet regularly with each other and share their faith with unsaved Muslims. Travis notes, "Unsaved Muslims may see C5 believers as theologically deviant and may actually expel them from the community of Islam. Where entire villages accept Christ, C5 may result in 'Messianic mosques.' C5 believers are viewed as Muslims by the Muslim community and refer to themselves as Muslims who follow Isa the Messiah."[14]

C6—Small Christ-Centered Communities of Secret/ Underground Believers

C6 believers are Muslims who have chosen to worship Christ in secret. They may have been converted through evangelism while abroad, radio broadcasts, tracts, dreams, visions, miracles, or their own reading of the Bible. They are usually silent about their faith and often worship alone (though infrequently they may gather in small groups). Though followers of Jesus, they are perceived as Muslims by their community and identify themselves as Muslims.

13. Ibid.
14. Ibid.

Just as the majority of Christian churches in Islamic communities are operating at C1 or C2, we feel drawn to the same conclusion about churches in post-Christian Western communities. It's not unusual to find C3 churches in the West either. But it is rare to encounter churches attempting C4 or C5 levels of contextualization. Currently in a number of Muslim nations, cross-cultural missionaries are attempting radical incarnation with C5 levels of contextualization. The believers are not necessarily identified as Christians, but as Muslims who follow Isa the Messiah. At first glance, the members of the church are seen as no different in appearance from the Muslims around them. In some countries, C5 contextualized churches are seeing literally thousands of Muslims come to Christ. How can the church in the West, while recognizing it is now operating within a post-Christian mission field, not take steps to move toward deeper levels of critical contextualization! Since the church in the West is likewise operating in a post-Christian mission field, we need to work toward something between C4 and C5 levels of critical contextualization.

Risky Negotiation

In Australia a handful of missionaries-to-the-West have fully embraced Parshall's teaching on contextualization, going so far as to incarnate themselves into such traditionally no-go zones as the Muslim communities of suburban Melbourne and the urban rave/dance party scene in Brisbane. By adopting Muslim or rave clothing, names, language, and customs, these daring missioners have entered fully into each community to be Christ in their midst. Calling themselves Frontier Servants, they have been uncompromisingly cross-cultural in their practice. The rave party team has become so accepted they are often called upon to be DJs at dance parties. Their approach is to fully embrace the host culture in every way, but without sinning. In Melbourne, the "Muslim" Frontier Servants attend the local mosque for worship and share about the way Isa the Messiah has set them free from sin and guilt.

The above process is a difficult and painful one. It invites us to do what the Jews in exile in Babylon were forced to do: be the people of God in a foreign land. But the mission imperative placed upon us as Christians is even more urgent because of Christ's injunction for us to make disciples. It is risky because we run into the ever-real possibility of compromising the gospel in our attempts to be contextually appropriate. Missiologists refer to such compromise—putting the context over the gospel—as syncretism. John Travis, while commending C5 contextualization, understands the possibility of syncretism and builds in checks against it.[15] The four-step method outlined by Hiebert has several checks against syncretism built into it also. Hiebert says that critical contextualization:

- Takes the Bible seriously;
- Recognizes the work of the Holy Spirit in the lives of all believers;
- Sees the church as a hermeneutical community;
- Sees each church operating within a global network, thus ensuring a broader international perspective.

So we will be well advised to recover the idea of the church as a missions movement in a hostile and unreceptive empire. We are exiles, in a sense, from a world that mocks our symbols and disregards our God. The only way forward is to finally be honest about our situation and to thoroughly contextualize the gospel within the culture and subcultures to which Christ has called us.

15. While specific to Muslim mission, Travis's guidelines for avoiding syncretism in a C5 movement are helpful to note. Travis says, "Those working with new believers should emphasize at least the following in the discipleship process:
    1. Jesus is Lord and Savior; there is no salvation outside of him.
    2. New believers are baptized, meet regularly with other believers (this may need to be done with great discretion), and take communion.
    3. New believers study the Injil (and Torah plus Zabur if available).
    4. New believers renounce and are delivered from occultism and harmful folk Islamic practices (i.e., Shamanism, prayers to saints, use of charms, curses, incantations, etc.).
    5. Muslim practices and traditions (e.g., fasting, alms, circumcision, attending the mosque, wearing the head covering, refraining from pork and alcohol, etc.) are done as expressions of love for God and/or respect for neighbors, rather than as acts necessary to receive forgiveness of sins.
    6. The Qur'an, Muhammad, and traditional Muslim theology are examined, judged, and reinterpreted (where necessary) in light of biblical truth. Biblically acceptable Muslim beliefs and practices are maintained, others modified, and some must be rejected.
    7. New believers show evidence of the new birth and growth in grace (e.g., the fruit of the Spirit, increased love, etc.) and a desire to reach the lost (e.g., verbal witness and intercession)." Travis, *"Must Muslims Leave Islam?,"* 3.

6

Whispering to the Soul

The church has sought to guide the spiritual lives of its members in very practical, reasonable ways. That sounds like a compliment. It's not. Contrary to Western thought, spirituality is anything but reasonable and practical.

—Jeff Woods

The Shared Journey

There has been much talk around these days about how so-called postmodern people are awfully spiritual and that they don't want to hear propositions about God, they want a direct experience of God. What is also clear is that when people face some existential angst, traditional Christianity is often the last place they turn to for spirituality. As Barry McWaters writes in his book, *Conscious Evolution*, "We are listening for messages of guidance from every possible source; tuning in our astroradios, talking to dolphins, and listening more and more attentively to the words of those among us with psychic abilities. Is there help out there? Is there guidance in here? Will anyone respond?"[1] What follows are two testimonies that we found in mainstream publications of people searching for help out there. In both cases, the writer faced some kind of painful experience that activated a search for peace. In both cases, their pain

1. Barry McWaters, *Conscious Evolution* (Los Angeles: New Age, 1981), 111–12.

was eased by a spiritual encounter. In neither case was the traditional Christian church involved. First, journalist Ruth Ostrow describes such an experience:

> I've just lost a loved one to cancer. Like a child, I am in some dazed state, searching for someone who can tell me where she's really gone. Going to see rabbis, gurus, reduced to the vulnerability and intellect of a five-year-old whose dog has just died. "You'll grow up one day," sighs my mother sarcastically. "There is nothing after life, dear. Nothing. Just accept it. No one has ever come back to prove otherwise," she says.

Ostrow's experience (the death of a relative) is common to us all, as is her reaction (existential searching). As she continues her spiritual search, she remains uncomforted by the so-called sensible answer and does not accept her mother's cynicism and down-to-earth practicality. Her quest goes on:

> At night, in the darkness, I swear I see a sliver of light, perhaps a soul coming to say goodbye. In the days after my beloved aunt's death, I feel strange energies around me. I dream of dead relatives who come to me with messages. "She's okay. She's with us. You will see her again one day." I wake up with my cheeks stained with tears. I hear words in the whispering of trees, signs in the way a spate of leaves arrange themselves on the ground. A message in the presence of a strange black bird that has mysteriously perched on my window sill.[2]

In her column, she confesses to finding hope and a sense of community with fellow searchers at a Metaphysical Mastery seminar conducted by New Age gurus Louise Hay, Wayne Dwyer, and Deepak Chopra. Her newfound belief in karma and reincarnation help her to chart a way forward through her pain. Our concern here is not necessarily to consider the religious longing in many non-Christian people, but to ask why Ostrow didn't attend a church service to help find answers. We can barely imagine how a traditional church leader or minister might respond if Ruth Ostrow ended up in their office for counseling. Some logical-thinking person might conclude that Ostrow is just experiencing the kind of desperate grief-induced search for hope we all feel after the death of a loved one. Would that satisfy her longing for answers to life's deepest questions? If the traditional-attractional mode of church gives no credence to "unchurched spirituality," it will have no answer to the very deep yearnings of a grieving woman like Ostrow, something someone like Ostrow might already suspect. We're not suggesting the church doesn't have an answer for the question about what happens to people after death. Our fear is that many traditional church leaders don't have an incarnational

2. Ruth Ostrow, "Call Me Cosmic Any Day," *Weekend Australian* (21 August 1999), 30.

response to Ostrow's experience of the wind, the leaves, her dreams, and the strange black bird.

Another example of similar journalistic confession was written for *Time* magazine by screenwriter and film producer Marty Kaplan. He discloses that he was suffering from chronic stress and that the attendant tooth grinding was ruining his teeth. In order to relieve the stress he attended meditation classes (which he read about in a Deepak Chopra book—that man again!) and got more than just mind-body medicine. He got religion:

> What attracted me to meditation was its apparent religious neutrality. You don't have to believe in anything; all you have to do is do it. I was worried that reaping its benefits would require some faith I could only fake, but I was happy to learn that 90% of meditation was about showing up. The spirituality of it ambushed me. Unwittingly, I was engaging in a practice that has been at the heart of religious mysticism for millenniums. To separate 20 minutes from the day with silence and intention is to worship, whether you call it that or not. To be awakened to the miracle of existence—to experience Being not only in roses and sunsets but right now, as something not out there but in here—this is the road less traveled, the path of the pilgrim, the quest. The God I have found is common to Moses and Muhammad, Buddha and Jesus. It is known to every mystic tradition. In mine it is the Tetragammaton, the name so holy that those who know it dare not say it. It is what the Cabala calls Ayin, Nothingness, No-thingness. It is Spirit, Being, the All.[3]

The encounters of both Ostrow and Kaplan confirm what most of us know intuitively—that "spiritual growth" often takes place in contexts of pain, struggle, doubt, and the unknown. In these times, neat, "off the shelf" answers don't suffice. Any yearning for spiritual wholeness will not be satisfied with formulae, programs, or doctrine. It takes time for the spiritual to find its touch point in each individual life. It's only through a shared pilgrimage that Christian and not-yet-Christian can come to a place of encountering the Holy in the midst of the storm. We shudder to think of Ostrow or Kaplan in the pastor's office being fed predigested bits of Christian doctrine. As we've mentioned before, people these days don't want to learn from experts or higher authorities, but from others who share the same life context and have found a way forward. The success of the twelve-step programs attests to this. Self-help television shows like *Oprah* offered the viewer a parade of ordinary people who have beaten depression or self-doubt, obesity or grief, and have lived to tell the tale. For many people, practical, earthy spirituality is best found on a shared journey.

3. Marty Kaplan, "Ambushed by Spirituality," *Time* (24 June 1996).

Whispering to Our Souls

Some years ago we came across the story of Monty Roberts, called the *Man Who Listens to Horses* (after his bestselling book). Though loosely the basis of the book and film, *The Horse Whisperer* (starring Robert Redford), Monty's story doesn't quite resemble the film's melodrama and romance. His is the simple story of a man's affinity with animals, in particular the wild mustangs of Montana's mountains. Monty grew up on a ranch with his family of horse traders. For generations the Robertses had ridden out into the rugged mountains to round up the wild horses that they would then break and sell to other Montana ranchers. The magnificent untamed beasts that roamed the mountains were all sinew and muscle, all wild instinct and sheer physical power. Breaking them was no mean feat. Once Monty's grandfather, father, uncles, or brothers had captured a mustang and confined it to a corral, they then had to break its magnificent spirit. This could mean weeks of work, as these most spirited of animals were often very difficult to tame. Monty says that some horses were so wild that one of their fetlocks had to be tied with rope around their necks. The wildest, most powerful animals could finally be broken only after much blood, sweat, and suffering.

Even as a young boy, Monty Roberts suspected that there had to be a better way to befriend these mustangs than to break their spirits so cruelly. Then, during his adolescence, while riding up in the Montana high country, he noticed that whenever a beast was separated from the herd and left to wander alone in the mountains it often became sick, even to the point of near-death. This got him thinking. If these were such herd animals with such a powerful, innate instinct for connection with other creatures, then maybe that instinct could be used for taming them. He began experimenting on a different way of "breaking" wild mustangs, until in his early adulthood he developed a whole new method. Now, he travels the world demonstrating this approach.

During a *60 Minutes* program, Monty Roberts taught the world his method of horse whispering. It involves his getting into the corral with the untamed mustang and staying as far from the animal as possible, without leaving the enclosure. He also refuses to allow any eye contact between him and the horse. By moving slowly, but surely, away from the horse and by keeping his head averted from the animal's gaze, Monty slowly draws the horse to himself. Even though the beast is pounding the earth with his hoof and snorting and circling the corral with great speed, Monty keeps steadily moving away from the horse. He won't look at it. He won't approach it. As astounding as it sounds, within an hour, Monty can have a wild mustang saddled and carrying a rider quite happily. When asked his secret, he says, "These animals need contact with

others so much, they would rather befriend their enemy than be left alone."
When he discovered this method of "whispering" into the horse's deepest
longing, he told his weather-beaten father and uncles and brothers that there
was no longer any need to crush the mustang's spirit. He demonstrated his
new method, but to this day, in spite of the evidence that it works, Montana
ranchmen still use the traditional approach.

Monty's story reminds us of the church. Even though he has discovered an
effective way of *listening* to horses (his own term), the old Montana horsemen
won't budge. They've been breaking horses their way for generations. Why
should they change now? To return to the earlier examples of Ruth Ostrow
and Marty Kaplan, the church might say, we've been "breaking" sinners like
them for generations. Leave them to us. But the old method of crushing the
spirits of seekers who don't fit the conventional, stereotypical church testimony
won't be effective any longer. Ostrow, Kaplan, and an army of *Oprah* viewers
are avoiding the church like the plague. It's time for us to develop a spirituality
of engagement with not-yet-Christians. That will involve true listening and
genuine presence.

The traditional method of reaching not-yet-Christians has been to bludgeon
them into a recognition of how broken they are. To crush their spirit. To tear
them down and bring them to their knees (we're sure we've heard evangelists
actually speak like this!). It's like Gene Greitenbach's analogy about Charley
and Sara. They hang out together, but Charley sees too many of Sara's faults
to be romantically interested in her. Then one day it dawns on him:

> The way to help Sara is to date her. If we were to go out, my strengths would
> rub off on her, and she would be far better off for it. It will require sacrifice on
> my part, but it's the least I can do.
>   Charley marches up to Sara's door with a book entitled *100 Things Sara Needs
> to Change in Order to Become a Real Person*. He rings the doorbell. When she
> answers, he shoves the book in her face and states, "I've decided it would be best
> for you if we date. When you finish reading this, I'll be waiting in my truck!"[4]

Greitenbach says that Charley is his metaphor for the traditional approach
to evangelism. There's very little genuine friendship happening. When churches
do befriend unbelievers it's often *so that* they might become Christians. And it's
assumed that the way to become Christian is for them to see how truly bad they
are. Surely, not-yet-Christians see how disingenuous this is. True friendship is
God's calling, in and of itself. If people find friendship with Jesus through our

---

4. Quoted in Leonard Sweet, *Postmodern Pilgrims* (Nashville: Broadman & Holman, 2000),
4, from J. Mack Stiles, *Speaking of Jesus* (Downers Grove, IL: InterVarsity, 1995), 120.

friendship with them, that is the work of the Holy Spirit. Instead of having such a combative, manipulative spirituality of engagement with others, we believe the church needs to recover a spirituality of engagement that whispers into the souls of not-yet-Christians. As Monty Roberts appeals to his wild mustangs' deepest longings, we need to develop an ear for listening to such longings in our friends and engaging them with respect, grace, and compassion.

The Skills of the Whisperer

How can we whisper into the deepest longings of not-yet-Christians today? As we have already mentioned, listening is an essential element. As is the need to recognize that people are much more likely to come to faith gradually than through some cataclysmic Damascus-road experience. In 1992 an exhaustive study of over five hundred Britons who had come to faith in the previous twelve months found that 69 percent described their conversion as gradual. It was not terribly different (63 percent) in the strongly evangelical churches where dramatic conversions are anticipated. Overall, only 20 percent of converts described their experiences as dramatic or radical. The report suggested:

> The gradual process is the way in which the majority of people discover God and the average time taken is about four years: models of evangelism which can help people along the pathway are needed.[5]

We don't ever want to rule out the possibility of God's breaking into the consciousness of an individual and bringing about a dramatic, overnight turnaround in his or her life. But we have to be cognizant of the facts: most people are whispered into the kingdom slowly and graciously. Holding so many evangelistic rallies or revivals simply reinforces our belief that people *only* come to faith like Paul on his way to Damascus. What are the features of a ministry that is undergirded by a spirituality of engagement? How can we whisper people toward Jesus? Allow us to suggest a few ways:[6]

Excite Curiosity through Storytelling

Jesus' stories contained no references to the law of Moses. In his parables he didn't seek to explain the words of previous prophets or teachers. There was often no reference to Yahweh. What kind of biblical teaching was this! Stories about a father who welcomes his wayward son back, a woman who

5. John Finney, *Finding Faith Today* (London: Bible Society, 1992), 25.
6. Once again we are indebted to Chris Harding from Youth for Christ, Sydney, for these ideas.

turns her home upside down looking for a lost coin, references to shrewd business managers, foolish farmers, and wise investors. The parables were very surprising forms of religious communication indeed. So surprising were they, in fact, that their meaning was often lost on many, especially those schooled in traditional religious speech. In Matthew 13, his disciples approached Jesus after he had told a story about sowing seed. They asked him, not the meaning of the story, but why he used these quaint stories at all. Jesus replied, "This is why I speak to them in parables: 'Though seeing, they do not see; though hearing they do not hear or understand'" (Matt. 13:13). In other words, he used parables to *veil* his meaning, not to make it clearer!

Jesus understood that his ministry was fulfilling the prophesy of Isaiah 6:9 that foretold of a time when Israel's heart would be calloused and her ears clogged and her eyes closed to the truth of God's grace. Jesus' teaching ministry was purposefully cryptic, allowing those who sought answers, rather than those who "had all the answers," to access the surprising truth of grace. So then he went on to explain the parable of the seed and the sower. By outlining the different types of soil that the seed fell on (the path, the rocky places, the thorny soil, the good soil) he demonstrated something about the different ways people would access his stories. Some would openly dismiss them as silly children's stories (particularly the Pharisees and scribes), others would be slightly interested for a while, and still others would be tantalized by these strange but wonderful tales. They would be so intrigued that they would have to enquire further. And as Jesus had already told his disciples earlier, it was this kind of genuine enquiry he was seeking to evoke: "Ask and it will be given to you; seek and you will find; knock and the door will be opened to you" (Matt. 7:7).

In our attempts to make the gospel clear, we have often squeezed all the life out of it. Jesus' parables were intriguing, open to interpretation, playful, interesting. They provoked people to search further for the truth. Elie Wiesel tells about an editor who once told him, "If you want to hold the reader's attention, your sentence must be clear enough to be understood and enigmatic enough to pique curiosity. A good piece combines style and substance. It must not say everything—never say everything—while nevertheless suggesting there is an everything."[7] Parables, stories, will be more likely to excite curiosity than propositionally presented outlines of the gospel. In *Faith in a Changing Culture*, John Drane outlines the importance of storytelling in this day and age. He proposes the importance of using three kinds of stories. First, God's story. He claims that God is present and actively involved in our world and we should be prepared to tell such stories about him. By this, we take him to mean

7. Elie Wiesel, *All Rivers Run to the Sea* (London: HarperCollins, 1996), 164.

God's prevenient grace. Tell your friends about a film you've seen where God's truth was revealed in a particular scene or character. Tell your friends about sunsets, items in the newspaper, and so-called coincidences. As Drane says,

> The Bible unhesitatingly affirms that God is constantly at work in the world in many ways, times and places. Evangelism is not about Christians working on God's behalf because God is powerless without them. Effective evangelism must start with recognizing where God is already at work, and getting alongside God in what is going on there. God's story, not ours, is the authentic starting point.[8]

Second, Drane recommends the use of Bible stories. This might sound like the ultimate conversation stopper, but we have found that at the right time and place, within the context of a strong friendship, the retelling of an ancient biblical story can evoke a great deal of curiosity. And third, he advocates the use of personal stories on the basis of 1 Peter 3:15, "Be prepared to give an answer . . . for the hope that you have." While propositions about Jesus are words on a page, stories are events in a life. Drane puts it well:

> Telling stories demands personal honesty, accepting our weaknesses as well as our strengths. It is only when we reveal ourselves as weak and vulnerable that others will readily identify with us and be able to hear the invitation to join us in following Jesus.[9]

Too often, Christian proclamation sounds like a patronizing sermon, in which we, the Christians, are the experts and all others are ignorant. As Karl Barth put it, "When we speak of our virtues we are competitors, when we confess our sins we become brothers." Drane says that if you think of the three kinds of stories as three overlapping circles, their point of intersection, where God's story, our story, and the biblical stories overlap, is where effective evangelism takes place.

Provoke a Sense of Wonder and Awe

Michael and his family once spent a week in a beach house on Ocean Isle Beach, North Carolina. Astride the house were windswept sand dunes and heavily leaning picket fences. The beach was clean and covered with sand dollars and seashells. The Atlantic Ocean lapping incessantly on the shore was a deep, gray-green. The previous tenants had left a copy of Rachel Carson's *Silent Spring* on the table on the back veranda. Having heard of this seminal

8. John Drane, *Faith in a Changing Culture* (London: Marshall Pickering, 1997), 63.
9. Ibid., 67.

work, but never having read it, Michael took the battered, old, original 1962 copy onto the wooden staircase that ran down to the sand and began to read. Carson's love of nature and her capacity to describe in such richness the beauty and wonder of the sea and its shore swept him away as it has swept away generations of Americans. Her rage at the injustice of the human degradation of the earth's ecosystem was powerful and motivating. When his eyes left the pages of the book and looked again at the fragile environment of the barrier islands of the eastern seaboard of the United States, he did so with wonder and awe. And he felt closer to God.

We have seen people silenced by astonishment in such places as the Cathedral of Notre Dame in Paris, the Grand Canyon in Arizona, and the rim of the Great Rift Valley in Kenya. It is difficult to encounter sheer majesty and beauty and not be drawn into a quest for the author of all beauty. The experience of wonder naturally draws us toward God. In fact, Paul says, "For since the creation of the world God's invisible qualities—his eternal power and divine nature—have been clearly seen, being understood from what has been made" (Rom. 1:20). Everyone from Saint Francis of Assisi to John Calvin has made this point. The sparks or traces of the glory of God can be found in every spot in the universe (to paraphrase Calvin). But, given the fury and the busyness of life in most Western cities, the capacity to stop and be overwhelmed by astonishment or wonder is increasingly rare. As G. K. Chesterton said, "The world will never starve for wonders, but only for the want of wonder." To whisper into the souls of not-yet-Christians, we need to lie in the grass under a starry sky with them. We need to wander with them through an art gallery. We need to take them camping, hiking, or for dinner at a seaside or mountaintop restaurant. The universe is a wonderful testimony to the glory of God. It's possible to awaken not-yet-Christians by our own wonder and appreciation of its complexity and mystery. And beyond expressing wonder at God's magnificent creation, we should demonstrate what it is to be astonished by beautiful food, children's laughter, film, literature, sadness, grief, weddings, picnics, parties and thunderstorms, Cezanne's apples and Pollack's splatters. Writes Eugene Peterson,

> In the presence of the beautiful we intuitively respond in delight, wanting to be involved, getting near, entering in—tapping our feet, humming along, touching, kissing, meditating, contemplating, imitating, believing, praying. Painted prayers; sung prayers; danced prayers. It's the very nature of our senses to pull us into whatever is there—scent, rhythm, texture, vision . . . (and most) exquisitely beauty that finds its fulfillment in the human face.[10]

10. Eugene Peterson, *Leap Over A Wall* (San Francisco: HarperSanFrancisco, 1997), 85–86.

It is our view that Christian worship also ought to evoke a sense of beauty and wonder. In our attempts to communicate clearly with non-Christians, the church has embraced the idea of the seeker service, a service devoid of overtly religious language so as to make nonchurchgoers feel more comfortable. We appreciate the need for Christian worship to at least make sense to not-yet-Christians, but to strip it of the evocative or mysterious is a grave mistake. It seems to us that the rich, wonderful corporate worship life of the first Christians was part of their strange attraction. And in an increasingly postmodern environment, a focus on logic instead of the full experience in worship could be seen as bland and tasteless. At Vaux, an alternative worship gathering in the Vauxhall area of London, worship is choreographed to take the participants' breath away. A Vaux service could involve writing prayers on pages that are then folded into origami dragon boats and floated across a large swimming pool placed in the middle of the church sanctuary. It will involve many screens placed around the church on which there is a constant stream of images playing. Candles, incense, ambient music, water, chanting, food, wine, dancing. It is a sensual feast designed to evoke a sense of awe and wonder.

In cities around the world like Auckland, New Zealand (CitySide Baptist Church), Glasgow, Scotland (the Late, Late Service), Waco, Texas (University Baptist Church), Hobart, Australia (TPC), Chesterfield, England (Fuzzy), London, England (Grace), and Pomona, California (Ichthus), local churches are experimenting with sensual, experiential liturgies. The use of ancient buildings, the interplay between light and dark, the importance of visual imagery, and influence of Celtic symbols and practices is melding into an exciting new movement in worship. Many postmodern people will find this alternative worship experience more valuable for tapping into their desire for the mysterious, the Other, than guitar-based bands and long sermons. Leonard Sweet has developed an acrostic to describe where the worship experience is going in the future. He says postmodern culture yearns for corporate worship that is E.P.I.C.: experiential, participatory, image-driven, and communal.[11]

Be Extraordinarily Loving

Another way to whisper into the hearts of non-Christians in order to activate a search for God is by being, like Christ, extraordinarily loving. The unrelenting kindness and grace of one person toward another is infused with the potential for transformation. When we live holy, gracious lives under the noses of our friends, neighbors, and associates, we commend an alternative

11. Leonard Sweet, *Soul Tsunami* (Grand Rapids: Zondervan, 1999). For a briefer treatment see his book *Postmodern Pilgrims* (Nashville: Broadman & Holman, 2000).

reality to the one they live with every day. We don't commend a holier-than-thou attitude. Rather, we believe if we live like Christ, we whisper into the souls of not-yet-Christians.

Some years ago, Michael was at an evangelistic rally in Sydney. After the evangelist had addressed the audience, he agreed to take questions from anyone who had any queries about the Christian faith. The audience was asked to scribble their questions on the back of feedback cards and hand them to an usher to be delivered to the evangelist on the stage. While a good number of the inquiries were typical of the questions asked at these forums, one of the feedback cards created quite a stir that night. The speaker stood to one side of the platform while a convenor read the questions from the other side. Her voice was clear but hesitant as she read, "Where was God when I was raped?" You could hear a pin drop.

The evangelist paused, then attempted to reply. All his other answers had been smoothly recited without a note of hesitancy. This time he was clearly shaken. Each time he leaned toward the microphone to answer, he couldn't bring himself to speak. Then big salty tears began to stream down his face. He couldn't speak because of the lump in his throat. He wept openly on the platform that night. Michael can't remember any of his other answers that night, no matter how clever or well presented they had been. Only one answer stood out—the evangelist's compassion for the member of his audience who had been raped. When later he had composed himself, he raged against a patriarchal society that gives men the assumed permission to see women as objects. Where was God when I was raped? He was epitomized in those salty tears and that anger at violence and oppression.

In the second century, Diognetus wrote of the fledgling Christian community in the following way:

> They dwell in their country, but simply as sojourners. As citizens, they share in all things as if foreigners. Every foreign land is to them as their native country and every country of their birth as a land of strangers. They marry, as do all others; they beget children; but they do not destroy their offspring. They have a common table, but not a common bed. They are in the flesh, but do not live after the flesh. They pass their days on earth, but they are citizens of heaven. They obey the prescribed laws, and at the same time surpass the laws by their lives. They love all men, and are persecuted by all. They are unknown and condemned; they are put to death and restored to life. They are poor, yet make many rich; they are in lack of all things and yet abound in all; they are dishonored and yet in their very dishonor are glorified. They are evil spoken of, and yet are justified; they are reviled and bless; they are insulted, and repay the insult with honor; they do good, yet are punished as evil-doers. When punished, they

rejoice as if quickened into life; they are assailed by the Jews as foreigners and are persecuted by the Greeks; yet those who hate them are unable to assign any reason for their hatred.[12]

Even those who don't share our faith will be impressed with so loving and gracious a community.

Explore How God Is Working

Chris Harding is a youth evangelist in Sydney, working with Youth for Christ. We've been inspired by his ability to activate a search for God in the imaginations of young people who would otherwise never attend an attractional church. Harding says,

> It's possible to learn to recognize the myriad ways that God touches us outside of that which is openly spiritual and we can share these moments with others. God touches us through painful growth experiences of loss and grief, through moments of creative and athletic excellence, through moments of victory over our problems and through the tenderness of relationships. God's grace falls on the just and the unjust alike. All humanity experiences God's hand. These moments when we touch something eternal and noble and good are God's footprints in our lives—His prevenient grace. People need to realize that the God they feel they do not know has, in fact, been at work already in their lives in many ways.[13]

By pointing out these ways to people, it's possible to energize them in their quest to encounter God. The authors have both been touched in dramatic and transformational ways by God. He has invaded our lives with purpose and brought healing, freshness, vigor, and growth to us. At times that has occurred through something we have read or seen, through philosophy or art. At other times it has come through a supernatural inbreaking of the Spirit of God. By frankly declaring what has happened to us, we offer hope to others that the God they desire to know is not very far away.

Focus on Jesus

Above all, the church must focus on Jesus if it is to tantalize an emerging generation into searching for God. Jesus, when presented without all the churchy trappings, still has great currency today. But in order to really understand him without all the embellishments Christendom has added to him, we

12. Quoted by Robert Webber in Mike Yaconelli, ed., *The Door Interviews* (Grand Rapids: Zondervan, 1989), 212–13.
13. Chris Harding, unpublished policy paper, Youth for Christ Australia.

need to "go back, way back, and picture Jesus as a first-century Jew with a phylactery on his wrist and Palestinian dust on his sandals."[14]

There is a now-legendary story about the Spanish artist, Bartholomew Murillo. As a young boy he already showed considerable promise in the visual arts, but was yet to find a patron or any real source of encouragement. In his childhood home there hung a picture of Jesus as a deadly serious shepherd boy. It portrayed him, in the style of the time, standing bolt upright, his shepherd's crook like a sentinel's bayonet. About his head shone an obligatory halo. Young Murillo detested the picture. So one day when his family was out of the house, he impetuously took the painting down from the wall and went to work on it with his paintbox. In his youthful brilliance he was able to create a new richer image of Jesus.

Upon their return home, the Murillos were aghast to see their Lord had been defaced. The stern unflinching face now had a lively grin, his eyes alive with mischief. The halo had become a battered straw hat and the plastered-down hair had been tousled into an unruly mess. His crook had been transformed into a gnarled walking stick and the limp and sad looking lamb at Jesus' feet was now a troublesome puppy. The shepherd boy had become a lively, excited hiker in search of adventure.

After his father had beaten him to within an inch of his life, young Bartholomew was forced to carry the sacrilegious picture throughout the town as penance. The offending work was spied by a local artist, who saw Murillo's obvious talent and offered himself as the boy's patron. And the rest, as they say, is history.[15]

We tell this story because Bartholomew Murillo did for Jesus what we seek to do also. He stripped Jesus of the trappings and paraphernalia bestowed upon him by the Christendom era church and tried to recover something of the humanity of the incarnated Christ. Is there any wonder that the Christendom church cannot embrace an incarnational ecclesiology when it cannot fully embrace the incarnation of Christ? The church seems more comfortable with the Transfiguration, the Resurrection, and the Ascension than it does with the Jesus who plays with children, smells the lilies, and eats with shady businessmen.

14. Philip Yancey, *The Jesus I Never Knew* (Grand Rapids: Zondervan, 1995), 50.

15. This story first appeared in Michael Frost's *Jesus the Fool* (Sydney: Albatross, 1994), 19. In fact, the book itself sought to deal with the surprising, subversive, unconventional manner that Jesus reframed the worldview of those around him. The provocative title offended many Christians and some Christian bookstores refused to stock it. Nonetheless, many secular and New Age bookstores snapped it up, illustrating our point that Jesus, if shed of conventional churchy garb, still holds great fascination for many nonchurchgoers.

As a Jew, Jesus' approach to life was essentially Hebraic. Nowhere do we find him speculating on the nature of being, and abstracting "essential" truths from historical events. He makes no philosophical formulas or introduces no abstracted ideas of God. His religion was relational and not philosophical. His "ethic," if he had one at all in the way we mean it, was action oriented and always pointed to concrete situations. He found God in the world, not apart from it. There is no hint of the dualism that later plagued Christendom throughout the ages. His way is the way of wisdom—an earthy, life-affirming wisdom that people could relate to.

In terms of his discipleship ethic, he called for *followers,* not just *believers.* It wasn't good enough to confess that he was "very God of very God"; he called people to an active trust in his rather dangerous promises (Matt. 8:18–22). In fact he sent people away on precisely this basis. He nowhere asks us to commit to a creed but calls us to trust in God and what he is doing. In his teaching, he used common relational metaphors—for example, Father-Son—to express his relationship with God, and other daily metaphors (sheep, gates, houses, and so on) to express other great truths of faith. He constantly used subversive parables that reflected ordinary life to confer profound spiritual meaning. His teaching style was definitely nonacademic: he discipled his followers into a lifestyle (called the Way) rather than send them to an academy to learn about God divorced from the context of life and mission.

His love of life was infectious. His form of holiness was not the alienating form so often associated with religious types. It was thoroughly redemptive. We have often pondered what kind of holiness was present in Jesus that ordinary people—broken, sinful, marginalized people—loved to hang around him. They didn't feel condemned by him. Sadly, these same types don't ordinarily like to hang around church people today. What's the difference? Jesus was even accused by religious types of being a bit of a drunkard and a glutton and of fraternizing with all the wrong kinds of people. He was certainly not afraid of pleasure but oriented it toward God. His is an *all of life* religion, with no separation of the private and the public. He should be the church's hero, the one we all aspire to become like. Instead we have so emphasized his divinity over his humanity that Jesus seems otherworldly, nonhuman, inaccessible.

Theologian Harvey Cox once told of speaking at a conference for Christian healers and therapists. The audience was full of pastors, doctors, nurses, counselors, and psychologists, all committed to bringing healing as an intrinsic part of their Christian faith. Cox says he retold his audience the story of Jesus raising Jairus's daughter from the dead and how along the way he healed the hemorrhaging woman. This story occurs in Luke 8:40–56 and is a wonderful episode that shows Jesus' compassion for both the religious leader, Jairus, and the scorned woman. Having recounted the story, Cox then asked his listeners to identify which character in the story they related most strongly to. Was it the bleeding woman, abandoned, suffering, and defeated? Or Jairus, anxious and grief-stricken? Or even perhaps the disciples who observed these fantastic miracles in wonderment and awe? Sections of the audience identified with different characters. Then Cox asked them how many identified with Christ. Six out of six hundred raised their hands.

When confronted with a story about Jesus the healer, only 1 percent of an audience full of *healers* related to Christ himself. How many teachers relate to Jesus the teacher? How many of us identify with Jesus as a person we aspire to become like? Of course, he is divine as well as human, and therefore we can never hope to fully emulate him. But we are called to live Christlike lives. We need to recapture our focus on Jesus and live like him, adore him, befriend him again.

Martin Buber once made the claim that "we Jews know [Jesus] in a way—in the impulses and emotions of his essential Jewishness—that remains inaccessible to . . . Gentiles."[16] This is not made as an arrogant statement, as Buber himself was a remarkably humble and gentle man. Rather he was highlighting the fact that to truly know Jesus, one must learn to look at him from the perspective of his Jewishness. If we fail to do this, we cannot hope to truly comprehend him correctly.

16. Quoted in Yancey, *The Jesus I Never Knew*, 50.

MESSIANIC SPIRITUALITY

7

The God of Israel and the Renewal of Christianity

The Bible of Judaism . . . makes one contribution to Christian faith. It is the profound conviction of these ancient rabbis, whom Jews revere and call "our sages, of blessed memory," that Scripture forms a commentary on everyday life—as much as everyday life brings with it fresh understandings of Scripture.

—Jacob Neusner

Toward a Messianic Spirituality

An incarnational ministry draws not-yet-Christians toward God by exciting curiosity through storytelling, by provoking a sense of wonder and awe, by showing extraordinary love, by exploring how God has touched our lives, and by focusing on Jesus.[1]

Can we ever expect to truly incarnate Christ within host cultures unless we can come to terms with Jesus, his life and teaching? We need to recover the kind of worldview that can awaken our deepest passions and give us a redemptive framework and fund an inner meaning for our activities in the world on God's

---

1. We have subsequently written a whole book exploring the defining role and ongoing significance of Jesus in the life of the church. See Hirsch and Frost, *ReJesus: A Wild Messiah for a Missional Church* (Grand Rapids: Baker, 2008).

behalf. It won't be good enough merely to get better techniques and methods. Even incarnation and contextualization won't suffice unless we can find the spiritual framework and resources for real and lasting engagement. In fact, what is required is a spirituality of engagement, as modeled for us in Christ. Such incarnation cannot occur without a sustaining and energizing spirituality. Spirituality has for so long been the domain of a type of mysticism that has sought God apart from a real engagement with the world. It has been assumed that God can only be related to by either negating the world or bypassing it. So many influential Christian spiritual writers have developed their ideas and written their books on spirituality from monasteries, seminaries, or from churches that identify their prime task as pastoral care rather than the making of disciples or of mission.[2] Even a cursory reading of many of the Western mystics and spiritual writers indicates that so much of their writings have been infused with an otherworldly dualism that, as we have seen, is a hindrance to organic spiritual growth in real life. At its worst such otherworldliness has led people away from missional interaction in the world to a view that God is best served far away from people and things.

Furthermore, so many of the people hailed by the church as saints have been extreme ascetics. Not many in Christendom articulated a robust life-affirming spirituality of engagement. The Celts, who were wonderfully missional, seemed to get the closest, but Patrick, Aiden, and Cuthbert, for instance, were given to extreme ascetic practices. Even Francis of Assisi, one of Christendom's greatest flowers, could not conceive of love for God without punishing his body very harshly. He refused to wear shoes, refused to bathe, froze his naked body in the snow to drive away temptation, and refused to own anything. Whatever we may say in praise of Francis, and he was truly a great man who accomplished much for God, his particular expression of spirituality was a far cry from the life-affirming religion of Jesus. For that reason we must return to Jesus himself to see what missional-messianic spirituality will look like. We need to explore in what way, and how, our actions extend the logic of Jesus' mission and how they act redemptively in the world.

Defined by Our Relation to Jesus the Messiah

We have used the term *messianic* in a very deliberate way. What we mean by it is that which has traditionally been called Christology must of necessity define missiology. This, combined with the idea that God's people operate

2. If this seems overly harsh, all we ask is that you look at the books on your shelf and ask yourself about the contexts of their writing and the effect of their ministry on non-Christian people. You will be surprised.

messianically in the world, refers back to the person and work of Jesus as witnessed to in the Gospels.

In effect, Jesus is our primary model of mission, and the Gospels are our primary texts. This might sound somewhat prosaic, but it is actually a massive paradigm shift from the way the church has generally viewed Christology in the Christendom mode. Jesus has generally been read through dogmatic ontological frames (as in the creeds) or through the structures of Paulinism (as in the Reformation), both we believe obscuring the primary historical portrait of Jesus as found in the Gospels. The Christendom-era church has tended to load so much into the historic debates about the nature of Christ in his being that it has obscured the fact that Christ was a historic person who represents *the* principal model for mission, ministry, and discipleship, and *the* focal point of an authentic New Testament faith.

We evangelicals have for too long read Jesus through predominantly what have been called Pauline eyes. We doubt the Apostle Paul read Jesus this way himself. But by reading the gospel *through* the Epistles, a disturbing distortion develops. Effectively, the Gospels are not taken seriously as prescriptive texts for life, mission, and discipleship. Now let it be said that we affirm the Pauline view of Jesus. But our perspectives of Jesus can be so weighted by and filtered through the Pauline interpretation of the Messiah that we are unable to see him without hearing the Pauline formulas in our heads. Actually the problem is not Paul at all, the problem lies in Paulin-*ism*. Like always, the *ism* is the problem. It is worth being reminded that Paul himself was very keen to ensure that we focus on Jesus and not on him (1 Cor. 1:11–17) and he encouraged us to follow him only insofar as he followed Messiah (1 Cor. 11:1). Paul always pointed us to Jesus, and we need to take his advice again now as we find ourselves in a missional setting remarkably similar to the one Paul was in.

To be sure, we need Paul as an indispensable (and divinely inspired) guide but not as the *only* guide. Rather we should read all the writers in Scripture through the perspective of the Gospels, including Paul. Jesus is my Lord and Savior, not Paul. If ever there was a time to rediscover Jesus the Messiah, it is now. In widespread public opinion surveys Jesus ranks very high and always gets a good rap. There is real missional currency to be found in presenting Jesus to a needy world. And why should this surprise us? He has always been the most alluring and fascinating person in the history of the world. But our reasons are not only "market driven," but rather based on the belief that it is Christ who defines Christianity and that in order to birth a new mode in the church, the missional-messianic mode, we need to recover the centrality of Jesus the Messiah to all aspects of the life and faith of his disciples, including mission.

Jesus defines us totally. And so it was meant to be. Our primary relationship with God is through the mediation of Jesus the Messiah, and so he
remains the central person in Christian consciousness. Our connection with
the Trinity is through its Second Person. This has many implications, but
for one it means that we can never get beyond the fact that we are disciples
and therefore people directly connected to the messianic purposes in the
world. We can never remove Jesus from the foremost place in our thinking,
adoring, and actions.

Dietrich Bonhoeffer put it this way:

> Discipleship means adherence to Christ and, because Christ is the object of
> that adherence, it must take the form of discipleship. An abstract theology, a
> doctrinal system, a general religious knowledge of the subject of grace or the
> forgiveness of sins, render discipleship superfluous, and in fact exclude any idea
> of discipleship whatsoever, and are essentially inimical to the whole concep-
> tion of following Christ. . . . Christianity without the living Christ is inevitably
> Christianity without discipleship, and Christianity without discipleship is always
> Christianity without Christ.[3]

Christianity is not a doctrine but a person to whom I entrust myself without reserve. If Christianity were merely a doctrine, its leader would be just
as superfluous as the teachers of any other sort of religious or philosophical
system. The focus would be on truth claims, which are learned and then ap-
propriated independently of the instructor. Since, however, Christianity is
not simply a set of beliefs but is inseparably connected to the *person* of the
Messiah, it stands or falls with him. Christianity's principles, moreover, can
never be understood independently of the person of Christ. Consequently,
to understand Christ's words "by themselves"—that is, as doctrine—is to
discount the element from which they receive their basic meaning, the divinity of their speaker. For the true believer, it is blasphemy to say that Christ's
words are merely wise or profound, for that puts them on a par with human
philosophies and takes away the transcendence of him who proclaimed them.
Our histories as well as our destinies are caught up inextricably with the person
of Jesus the Messiah. We are embroiled in messianic destiny.

Not only does our connection with Messiah mean that we are tied inextricably to him, but it also means that we must affirm, as do the Scriptures, that
Jesus is the only way to salvation. It is a given to say that in the ideological/
cultural climate of the emerging global culture, this aspect of the Christian
claim is under serious threat, and it is not getting any better. When Jesus said

---

3. Dietrich Bonhoeffer, *The Cost of Discipleship* (New York: Touchstone, 1959), 59.

in John 14:6, "I am the way and the truth and the life. No one comes to the Father except through me," then once again we must realize that our identities, as well as our mission, are tied to the Messiah. We agree with Peter's confession, "Lord, to whom shall we go? You have the words of eternal life" (John 6:68). We either deny him or we confess him, but we cannot avoid him. And neither can our spirituality avoid the messianic (Christocentric) nature of the New Testament faith. We sink or swim with Jesus.

So much reflection on Jesus portrays a man who is overly serious, who wrung his hands a lot, who was way too intense and deep, and had an unusual penchant for suffering. And while there are certainly dimensions of Jesus' personality that fit this description (who doesn't do these things at times?), we feel that the dominance of this image is the result of our historical life-suppressing perspective on life, faith, and God. There is an entirely different way to read Jesus.

We have already mentioned that the kind of holiness he exuded was the kind that didn't repulse normal "sinners." Rather, his was a very attractive spirituality. And yet he was not your ordinary evangelical guy. He was notorious (yes, that's the right word) for hanging out with the wrong types. In contrast with today, when so much of our Christianity is being with the right people in the right places at the right times, Jesus was always in the wrong places, with the wrong people, at the wrong times, according to the religious establishment. We want to say that this is the Jesus we must rediscover to balance our excessively sober images of our Lord. We need his model of holy laughter, of his sheer love of life, of his infectious holiness, of his common people's religion, for our day. We want to say that being Christlike is not only hard work, it is also a load of fun—you get to do what Jesus did and hang out with the interesting people. This is our eternal destiny, to be conformed to the image of Jesus (Rom. 8:29) and this must now become a vital dimension of our messianic mission in the world. Being Christlike gives us a positive model of engagement, and this is why we need to imitate Jesus as our primary model for mission and evangelism.

Our Actions, Redemptive Significance

We are called to do more than simply act in the manner that Jesus acted. There is, in some mysterious way, a link between our very actions and the purposes of God in and through Jesus. Without weighing in on the tired old Christendom debates between Arminianism and Calvinism, we need to be willing to re-approach the Scriptures with a renewed post-Jesus Jewish mysticism perspective to see if there is a way forward for the missional church in all this.[4] We Protestants have generally struggled to affirm our place in God's plan of redemption for fear of developing a salvation by works. In our efforts to ensure that God's sovereignty remains unsullied, we have tended to downplay the vital part that God has set for humanity in the redemption of the world. We have tended to make a formula of "all of God" and "we are nothing." Not only is this highly questionable theologically, loaded as it is with dualistic self-hatred, but it has not necessarily brought God any glory. In actual fact it might actually have served to diminish the sheer value of the investment he has made in human freedom and the preciousness of his image that he has placed in the human being. Perhaps the central idea of the post-Jesus Jewish mysticism perspective is this ability, indeed the destiny of humanity, to play a central role in the life of God. Hegel suggests that world history is God's autobiography. We disagree: world history is God's biography as written by God and people; God supplies the letters and people write the sentence.

We partner with God in the redemption of the world. This is not just an issue of theology or of spirituality; it is an issue of a thoroughly reorienting missiology. It will provide God's people with a new sense of purpose, a divine connection to daily actions. We need to grasp the fact that in God's economy our actions do have an eternal impact. We do extend the kingdom of God in daily affairs and activities and actions done in the name of Jesus. We live in an unredeemed world. But out of each human life that is given over to God and committed to his creation, a seed of redemption falls into the world, and the harvest is God's!

Going Back to Our Roots

It is essential to a revolutionary new approach to church that there be a fundamental shift in our collective thinking. Essentially we need to recover the missional genius of the early church, which was modeled on Jesus. The problem the church faces today is that it is seeking to recover that genius from a viewpoint of two thousand years of Christianity in the West, much of it deeply grounded and indelibly shaped in the Christendom paradigm. To recover a primal sense of who Jesus was and how he engaged people missionally will require a fresh look at the central person of the faith.

We believe that an alternative, missional approach to being and doing church is best supported by an alternative approach to Christian spirituality. Too

4. The issue of salvation by works or by grace will be dealt with in the chapter on action as a sacrament. Suffice to say here that the authors fully affirm salvation by grace alone. All we are saying is that our actions do have intrinsic, but not salvific, value as well as redemptive significance.

much Christendom spirituality has been concerned with retreat and reflection. While we acknowledge the value of a rich interior life, as well as the value of solitude in interiority, we believe that retreat and reflection should be embraced as part of a broader spirituality that values engagement and action. We need to find a renewed framework and basis for understanding everyday life and our actions as a vital source of experience of God. We believe in the need for the recovery of a *messianic* spirituality, one rooted primarily in the life and teaching of Jesus himself.

However, developing such a messianic spirituality requires a good deal of digging. Much of our Christology in the Western tradition was highly influenced by concerns relating to the Hellenistic-Roman contexts of Christendom with its focus on ontology. Ontology is the philosophical concern with the nature of "being" (*ontos*). As a result, it is more concerned with metaphysics (a reality above or in back of the physical world) rather than physics and is therefore highly speculative by nature. Ontological Christology, therefore, focused on the nature of Christ's humanity in relation to his deity. It also focused on the preexistent role of the Logos in the Godhead, something the Bible only vaguely hints at.

What we want to do in this chapter is lay the groundwork for a Christology from behind or within, rather than from above, and then we want to look at its implications on our faith and praxis. What we mean by this is that Jesus must be comprehended first and foremost through his national and religious history to be understood at all. Jesus' first followers understood him and his teaching through Jewish eyes. Our undertaking will involve asking how Jesus' Jewishness defined him. It will also require us to consider how his cultural and ideological Jewishness affect the way his teachings are to be understood. Are they only understood from within his worldview? And if so, do we need to recover something of the Hebraic worldview, its structures of plausibility, to really reinvoke the missional church, canted as it is on Jesus and not on massive, complicated creeds associated with Christendom?

We start by confessing a great (and increasing) sense of personal disquiet about the spiritual health and viability of the Western spiritual and theological tradition. It is a tradition that has carried us to this point in history and left us more than a little spiritually bankrupt and with no real success in the grand mission of God. As we have indicated, the Christendom project has succeeded in basically inoculating the Western cultures to that raw, unadulterated gospel that alone can save us. This idea of inoculation is one worth considering at this point. If you were to go to the doctor to be inoculated against a certain disease, the doctor would inject you with a form of the bacteria/virus, not enough to cause harm, but enough to stimulate your immune system to create antibodies so that your body will recognize the really harmful version and be able to fight it. It is our contention that this is exactly what Christendom has done to our missional contexts, wherever it has manifested itself.

In fact, it has created as many problems for us as it has solved. After seventeen centuries of Christianity in the West, we still have not done the task; and where we have managed to establish Christianity nationally, we have not always brought good news to the people. One look at the history of South Africa, the American South, the conquest of Latin America, or at "Christian" Europe will quash any doubts you might have about the above comment. Europe, in spite of those seventeen centuries of the faith, still can't seem to resist genocidal tendencies! Witness the Balkans; it was those raised in the Orthodox confession (which recently celebrated a millennium in the area!) that led the charge in killing people en masse. The history of Europe has been one of horrifying bloodshed and cruelty, culminating in the holocaust. It was T. S. Eliot, himself very much a European, who once noted, "After two thousand years of Christian mass, we've come as far as poison gas."

Now, we don't say this to be cynical or frivolous. We just want to point out the primary disquiet that has led us in a search to find new soil, new roots, a new basis, for our following of Jesus into the strange places that his mission will take us. We feel that, in all integrity, we can no longer offer to the world what we believe is becoming bankrupt. We can only apologize for it.

This sense of dis-ease has taken us on a journey, one that for different reasons has led us to the Hebrew spiritual tradition. For Alan, a Jew who has found redemption in Jesus, this was something of a natural place to look, a kind of return—one that has been at times lonely but joyful and has brought out of him a deep love of God. It has enriched his life and renewed his experience of, and focus on, Jesus. It has also led to a deeper appreciation of the divine gift placed by God in the Jewish people. For Michael, originally raised as a Catholic, it began as a journey into Benedictine thinking on the sacralizing of the everyday culminating in his previous book, *Seeing God in the Ordinary*. During that pilgrimage, he encountered the works of Martin Buber and Abraham Heschel and returned again to rediscover a worldview at the same time more primitive and more sophisticated than the Benedictines—that of the Hebrews. But for both of us, it has been a wonderful surprise to find that in so many ways Judaism, particularly as articulated by Buber, Heschel, Elie Wiesel, and rabbis of the early Hasidic movement, is an amazingly rich tradition. It is one that on some points resonates more deeply with the Scriptures, including the New Testament teachings, than Christendom, its historical counterpart and persecutor.

Recovering a Messianic Spirituality

This spiritual resonance should not surprise us, as the Jewish heritage is the primordial matrix out of which Christianity was birthed, and which we would argue is the only matrix out of which it could be organically understood in its fullness. Except for Luke's writings (he was in all likelihood a proselyte of Judaism), the New Testament is a document written by Jews. Therefore biblical Christianity's "genetic" code, its kinships, its plausibility structures, its genius, are all Hebraic to the core and back. This is not to say that the coming of the Messiah and the advent of Christianity did not in a fundamental way redefine Judaism. It did. The messianic element of Christianity reshaped and recentered the theocentric nature of Judaism in a profound way. If Jesus was God's anointed deliverer, the fulfillment of Israel's identity, destiny, and purpose, then he has the right to redirect its energies to the world mission that was at the heart of Israel's vocation. Even if early Christianity reshaped Judaism, it worked with basic Hebraic ideas and elements and retained its essentially Jewish structure and religious patterning. It was a redefinition "within the family," so to speak.[5]

The fundamental problems later associated with the Western/Christendom tradition were seeded into Christianity as it traveled farther and farther from its homeland and took root in Hellenistic-Roman culture. Many benefits ensued from the gospel's taking root in the Roman Empire, but one of the most damaging results was the destruction of the primary Hebraic worldview, which both birthed and sustained the key biblical ideas. As it moved farther away from Israel geographically, and Judaism politically and socially, the gospel began to define itself over against Judaism, and even began to become shamefully anti-Semitic.

This was a tragic historical blunder because it was only out of the Hebraic matrix that a true understanding of the faith of the Scriptures, including the New Testament, could be maintained *over the long haul*. As a result, the elemental biblical worldview was replaced by, at best, a syncretistic blend of the Hebraic and the Hellenistic, and at worst, an outright rejection of the Hebraic in favor of the Hellenistic (witness Marcion and the Marcionite leanings in the later church).[6] This move away from the matrix that gave New Testament

---

5. This is not to say that the expanding church was not concerned with, or influenced by, Hellenistic-Roman ideas and forms; only that the fundamental core, the DNA, was Hebraic.

6. Marcion was a representation, albeit an extreme one, of the basic anti-Judaic, dualistic, Docetic, deeply Hellenistic, nature of the sub-apostolic church. His influence is still felt today. In fact the great church historian, Adolf von Harnack, was himself a self-confessed Marcionite. The same tendency led the Nazi theologians (Gerhard Kittel, Otto Weber, et al.) to their attempts to de-Judaize the faith, which could be called a kind of theological "final solution."

Christianity its inner meaning and vigor has deeply infected the church's understandings of God, Jesus, his people, the mission of the people of God, our ethics, and our way of living with unbiblical, sometimes outright pagan, understandings and assumptions. This "infection" has taken place more on the subconscious level of assumptions, presuppositions, and worldview than on the conscious level, and for that reason it has been much more insidious.

Now before we continue, we wish to make it clear that many of the Hellenistic perspectives on life and being have added much insight into our understanding of faith in general—insights that could not have come from the Hebraic worldview. This highlights the wonderful fact that each nation or culture has a depository of truth and has something to bring to the text of Scripture. All we wish to say here is that such a perspective was not the original and organic one, and as it began to dominate theological reflection, it pushed out the Hebraic approach and fundamentally distorted its own handle on the truth. This shift set the future church on a distorted theological and spiritual trajectory.

In order to embrace the emerging missional paradigm for the church, it will be important for us to understand the core differences between Jerusalem and Athens and their implications for our understanding of God, Jesus, and mission today. Only by understanding those differences can the church recover a messianic spirituality of engagement with the world and culture.

Hebraic Spirit or Hellenistic Consciousness?

Much study has been done to compare the differences between Hellenistic and Hebraic consciousness, between Jerusalem and Athens, so to speak. The differences are great, but can be summarized under two broad categories.

Concrete/Historical versus Speculative/Theoretical

First, it should be noted that Hellenistic thinking is speculative in nature, whereas the Hebraic spirit is much more concrete. A mere perusal of the early Greek theologians and philosophers will give a person a feel for Hellenistic thinking. Much is about the nature of being in itself, the metaphysical basis of existence, the nature of spirit, substance, procession, interpenetration, stasis, and so forth. One of the most startling discoveries is that the kind of metaphysical language so fundamental to the speculative world is almost

---

This could be so because the basic rejection of the Hebraic worldview took place back then. The infection, it seems, is still with us.

entirely lacking in the Scriptures. Nowhere will you find anything that even gets close to a philosophical discussion on ontology.[7] Perhaps the closest one gets is the prologue of John's gospel in its teaching of the *Logos*, the Word.

We'll get back to this when we reflect on biblical monotheism, but in order to highlight how much early Christianity was to be intoxicated by ontology, just compare for a moment Christendom's fascination with speculative ideas and abstract notions about God and faith. You have to look no further than the creeds. The focus of the early Christian creeds, such as the Apostles' Creed, is on the nature of God-in-himself and on the relationship between the persons of the Trinity. This is all good and well, but nothing at all is said about ethics, discipleship, life, and mission, the very elements that are stressed in the Scriptures. Again we don't want to be read as not affirming the essential truths of the creeds; we do. All we want to point out is that they are skewed in a certain direction. This skewing was to continue until the present day.

The creeds focus primarily on the doctrines of God and Christ. They say little more about anything. The church gets a mention, but it is scant indeed. And where the creeds do try to define the boundaries of speculative Christology, there is no mention at all of Jesus the revolutionary, the subversive, the activist. It is all speculation on his divine/human nature. The primary focus is on *theo*-logy, and theology of a distinctly speculative kind—one that takes basic phrases and ideas in Scripture and works them into a systematic and philosophically consistent whole. For instance, the Latin and Greek theologians who worked on the doctrine of the Trinity took the unadorned phrases of Scripture—mostly mysterious hints about something of a oneness/threeness thing in God's nature—and worked it into a full-fledged systematic doctrine. So refined was their work that they ventured to define the eternal interrelationship between the three in the Godhead itself to a fine degree, as if we could really know that detail from a few verses of Scripture. This analysis included determining that the one interpenetrates the other without losing distinct identity within the oneness; and that the Son is coeternal with the

---

7. The Bible never self-consciously talks about that oneness on the metaphysical level. It assumes it. Or as Buber has put it, "God makes no philosophical statements about Himself and speaks in no formulas" (Martin Buber, *On Judaism* [New York: Schocken, 1967], 91). Says Heschel, " 'The God of Israel' is a name, not a notion, and the difference between the two is perhaps the difference between Jerusalem and Athens. A notion applies to all objects of similar properties; a name applies to an individual. The name 'God of Israel' applies to the one and only God of all men. A notion describes; a name evokes. A notion is attained through generalization; a name is learned through acquaintance. A notion is conceived; a name is called. Indeed, the terms 'notion' and 'the God of Israel' are profoundly incompatible. . . . The God of Israel is a devouring fire (Deut. 4:24), not an object of abstraction and generalization." *Moral Grandeur and Spiritual Audacity* (New York: Noonday, 1996), 268.

Father but proceeds in eternal generation from the Father; and that the Holy Spirit eternally proceeds from the Son.[8] And soon—hopefully you get the idea. Again we wish to affirm the truth of God as Trinity—all we are saying is that whatever affirmations we wish to make about the eternal nature of God as Trinity must be done with a great sense of mystery and humility as the information is sparse and the topic too great for us to truly comprehend. As Philip Yancey says in his remarkable book *The Jesus I Never Knew*, "In church we affirmed Jesus as 'the only begotten Son of God, begotten of his Father before all worlds . . . Very God of Very God' . . . .[But] These creedal statements are light years removed from the Gospels' accounts of Jesus growing up in a Jewish family in the agricultural town of Nazareth."[9] It is our contention that by focusing on development of the speculative doctrines, the early church lost the vital focus on the historical and practical implications of the faith. Mission and discipleship as such became marginal to theological correctness. Orthopraxy gave way to orthodoxy.

The problem is that nowhere in Scripture do you find anything that even gets close to an ontological discussion on the notion of God, let alone a discussion of the interpenetration of the three persons of the Godhead. We are not denying the creeds or Trinitarian theology at all, but we do seek to seriously question the overly speculative/theoretical nature of the Hellenistic worldview. It has led to the situation where differences on barely remembered doctrines like Monophysitism and the *processio* have resulted in sometimes-violent debate and costly councils.

What is more interesting is that none of the creeds get to talk at all on right *living*, the very topic the Bible itself cannot seem to talk enough about. In its Hellenistic bent, doctrine shifted from right *acting* to right *thinking*. This has been referred to as the distinction between ortho*praxy* and ortho*doxy*. Orthopraxy is a system that believes that right living provides the context for us to embrace right thinking. Note the Pauline Epistles and Paul's constant references to righteous Christian living as the framework for Christian theologizing. The reverse is called orthodoxy. It assumes that if we change a person's thinking, we will change the way he or she lives. But there is too much evidence to the contrary. Many great theologians have "thought" rightly about Christian teaching, but their lives have not necessarily

8. Because of this minor, barely discernable "teaching of Scripture" came the later schism between the Western and Eastern churches into that of Roman Catholicism and Eastern Orthodoxy. What kind of mentality is it that would split the apparent unity of the churches on a marginal philosophical-speculative idea of the nature of God in himself? It is precisely this fussiness with minutiae of doctrine that exposes the mindset of Christendom in its Hellenistic expression.

9. Yancey, *The Jesus I Never Knew*, 49.

mirrored their beliefs. This bent toward orthodoxy can be seen in Christian seminaries around the Western world. Seminarians' minds are filled with propositional truth for up to four years and then they are sent to practical ministry in local churches. And while many have found that the shift from Christian living to Christian belief is a natural one, the opposite shift from belief to action isn't quite so natural. We wish to affirm that seminaries that are adding a practicum or supervised ministry element to their programs are taking a small step in the right direction. The more our educational institutions embrace a balance between orthodoxy and orthopraxy, the more biblical they will become. The embracing of a balance between orthodoxy and orthopraxy is one of the correctives we must take in order to become more truly biblical, where the focus is definitely on right acting rather than merely on right thinking. We have to recover a sense of the ultimate meaning of our actions if we are going to become a truly missional-incarnational church.

History as the Vehicle of Revelation in Biblical Faith

Second, the Hebraic spirit is a religion of time. One of the unique aspects of the Hebrew Bible is that it describes the first (and possibly the only) religious system that posits history as the primary source of revelation of God and God's will for the world. And while at first this might not take your breath away, it is nonetheless a very important aspect of the Hebraic worldview, one that opens up many possibilities in engaging life and doing mission.

Any look at history, with all its wars, loves, adulteries, highs, and lows will tell us that life is a mess. Life as we know it, what C. S. Lewis called an "astonishing cataract of bears, babies, and bananas; this immoderate deluge of atoms, orchids, oranges, cancers, canaries, fleas, gases, tornadoes, and toads" is the place where God chooses to reveal himself to us.[10] When the biblical faith affirms that God actually uses history to reveal himself to us, it is saying that God is to be found in that immoderate deluge. God is involved in the mess; and even more remarkable, the mess can actually constitute revelation.

A cursory reading of the Bible will reveal that its "saints" are real people who sin and pray, love and hate. They can be bigoted, deceptive, and fearful, and yet God uses them as vehicles of revelation of himself to lost humanity. This should give us great hope, because when we look at our own lives, they don't look all that different. The most marvelous expression of this God-in-the-mess activity is found in the Incarnation when he came to us as a

10. Quoted in Gilbert Meilaender, *The Taste for the Other: The Social and Ethical Thought of C. S. Lewis* (Grand Rapids: Eerdmans, 1978), 22.

five-and-one-half-foot-tall (or so) Jewish peasant who was possessed of all the same bodily functions we have. He ate and cried and celebrated like any other human. The Creator of the universe had come to town, and no one even had a clue that God was in their neighborhood. Not only is humanity dignified in the Incarnation, but we were redeemed by Jesus' life and work in all the nitty-gritty of dusty Judea two thousand years ago.

The humanity of Jesus was problematic to Hellenists, who held the presuppositional belief that matter and spirit were diametrically opposed to each other. This *dualism* held that spirit is good, and matter resists spirit and is therefore evil. If anything, dualism is *the* defining idea of the Hellenistic spirit. When applied to history, it takes on a distinctive form, trying to "cleanse" God of the filth of history, with all its death and destruction, loves and hates. Its intention is to preserve an idea of the goodness of God, but in the end it leaves us in self-loathing despair because we are matter, and we are the stuff of which filthy history is made.

In the emerging Christendom church (post AD 300) dualism came to the fore in a number of contexts. The church rejected the most exaggerated forms of dualism because they challenged fundamental truths of the biblical faith. Marcion, who has been mentioned, felt that the god of the Old Testament was actually an evil demiurge or subordinate god who created matter in the first place. So Marcion rejected the Old Testament faith as a base and evil religion. But he didn't stop there. He identified certain ideas as being painted with the Judaic brush, and so he began cutting out elements of New Testament teaching as well. All he was left with once he was finished were some of Paul's writings and the Gospel of Luke.

The other main form of theological dualism was fought over the issue of whether Jesus was really a man or if he only seemed to be one. The word for this heresy was Docetism (drawing on the Greek word "to seem"), and it had severe problems with God's becoming a man. It was rejected, because it was rightly concluded that if true, then our redemption could not take place through Jesus' life and work. Especially not through the cross.

These doctrines seem strange to us, but they are still very much part of Christendom in various forms. Marcionite and Docetist assumptions abound in more subtle forms and in many ways. So many Christians struggle with the humanity of Jesus. For them Jesus was above humanity; he simply could not have had to go to the toilet and undergo the same humbling task of daily defecation. He couldn't have any sexual stirrings at all, and therefore had never experienced sexual desires. But the end result is that this sort of thinking leaves us with a Jesus who walked two inches above the ground and never sullied his hands with "ordinary" humanity. The Bible is quite clear about this—such a being is useless to us in terms of redemption.

One of us recently had a conversation with a minister whose predominant theological paradigm was that of liberation theology. He was impressed by its central emphasis on the liberation of slaves from Egypt in the exodus. When we engaged him in the topic, he could not affirm that the exodus actually took place in history because that would have involved God in actually killing countless Egyptians and in being part of the conquest and colonization of Canaan. He preferred to think of it as a spiritual metaphor for how God works with us. This totally de-historicized freeing of slaves becomes thereby a bloodless event that speaks of spiritual freeing for all peoples from political oppression. But what is the result of that act of de-historicizing the faith? Is it not the same end as Marcion and the Docetists reached? Where do you stop? By what principle does one discern the historicity of any event? If an event didn't happen, can it be true? And worst of all, in trying to ensure that God's name is not muddied by human involvement, do we remove all of God's involvement from history and find ourselves left alone in our sin and despair?

If we are to be a truly biblical people then we *must* affirm that God is here with us and has always been. He's not afraid to get his hands dirty in the horrors of human freedom that is called history. Even war can be used for his purpose. He *is* involved. The structure of Hebraic faith that affirms that history is the means of revelation and that God uses ordinary people to bring his kingdom to the world, keeps us from making the terrible mistake that Marcion and others have made throughout history.

What has this got to do with mission and the emergence of the missional-incarnational church? Everything. History is where we must do our work to advance the kingdom. If we assume that God is involved in the slums of India, then we should be as well. If God doesn't shrink back from trying to redeem the horrors of Rwanda, then neither should we. If he is deeply involved in the mess of history and doesn't shirk from a deep involvement in human affairs, then neither should we.

The Redemption of the Everyday

One of the great strengths of the Jewish people throughout history has been their sheer love of life. *L'chaim* ("to life!") has been a defining catch cry of this ancient people even in the midst of unrelenting historic suffering throughout their long existence. What exactly is it that has allowed them to sustain an amazing cultural vigor, an optimistic, life-affirming, and vital faith in the face of opposition that would have crushed so many other cultures? We believe it is found in the post-Jesus Jewish mysticism perspective based on their view of God and the world.

Much to this point has been a critique of some of the prevailing Hellenisms that have led to a malaise in the missional impulse of God's people in the West. What we want to do now is to try and construct a missional perspective based on a positive reading of the Hebraic worldview. What we are suggesting here is that the reader be willing to learn from Judaism how a Hebraic worldview might be engaged missionally and be willing to adjust one's thinking and practice as a result. It is our opinion that by doing this we can discover a deeper, more passionate experience of God in Messiah and certainly a more engaged and missional faith. In order to make sense of the Hebraic spirit and its relation to the missional church, we will look at seven salient features.

The Redemption of Pleasure and the Missional Task

In its more severe forms, dualistic religion actively suppresses and denies matter and therefore relegates the body to being seen as a disgusting thing. It follows then that pleasure, too, is seen as evil and destructive and "of the devil." This is so because there exists no framework to connect pleasure with God. One doesn't have to search long to discover this distortion in Christendom's conduct and ideas in relation to sex, food, and other forms of pleasure.

It is our belief that the skewed ascetic perspective fueled by dualism has deeply alienated the average person from Christianity by failing to help integrate one's body and associated physical life into a spiritual experience of God. We cannot underestimate the damage that this life suppression has done to the way we are perceived by the average non-Christian, not to mention the fact that it represents a distortion of the biblical view of the world. It also highlights the need to recover a redemptive framework for pleasure *as a missional asset.* Can people meet with God in and through their experience of, and love for, life itself? To this question we want to say a wholehearted yes! In fact, if the church fails to actually construct this bridge, it will fail to have any real impact in the postmodern world that we inhabit.[11] The materials for this missional bridge-building exercise can be found in the Hebrew tradition with its affirmation of life in all its manifestations.

11. While this might seem to be an overstatement, we call the reader's attention to the fact that according to religious theory, paganism has a tendency to celebrate the physical without constraint. Many observers have rightly noticed the similarities of postmodern culture to paganism with its focus on the body and on pleasure. While historically Christianity has suppressed the physical, Judaism has tried to hallow it. This now becomes our task.

Furthermore, with reference to pleasure, the tragedy consists in the fact that to define faith negatively (that is, by what we should not do) is the wrong place to draw the line of the gospel. The impression given to non-churchgoers is that the church suppresses life. The line is drawn on the issue of *apparently sinful* pleasure, and as such it is drawn in precisely the wrong place. How is it that the church now embodies a Christianity noted for a denial of pleasure and the nullification of life? And how much damage has this done to the cause of Christ through the ages?[12]

A few years ago Alan conducted a wedding where he spoke about the fact it was God who invented the orgasm and who structures life and marriage. He ended with an open invitation to come and meet the incredible Person who designed the orgasm. Ironically, many Christians had never heard the words *God* and *orgasm* mentioned in the same sentence and were somewhat offended. But the effect on the not-yet-Christians present at the event was remarkable. In a discussion with the best man after the ceremony the question was asked, "You mean the God behind the message of the church was the same one who designed one of the most profound pleasures known to mankind? Was all pleasure made by God?" Who wouldn't want to meet with such a person if one had the chance?

Films like *Babette's Feast* and *Chocolat* are potent parables of the power of pleasure to redeem and reconcile. It is not for nothing that most of the covenants (new and old) were sealed in full meals, replete with four glasses of wine. Pleasure can be a greater motivator for God than pain or threats. It is *unredeemed* or *undirected* pleasure that destroys life and wastes human effort. Missionaries and leaders do well to learn that people are motivated by their deepest pleasures, and if we can connect these to God, we will have established a vital bridge into the lives of ordinary people. And whereas Christendom has failed to integrate pleasure, the post-Jesus Jewish mysticism worldview gives permission for all this to the glory of God. Clearly the Scriptures teach us that God not only made the orgasm and the tastebuds and the spices and garlic but that we should enjoy what he has given us within the framework of his moral will revealed in the same Scripture.[13]

12. "I have no doubt at all that pleasure is in itself a good and pain in itself an evil; if not, then the whole Christian tradition about heaven and hell and the passion of our Lord seems to have no meaning. Pleasure, then, is good; a 'sinful' pleasure means a good offered, and accepted, under conditions which involve a breach of the moral law." C. S. Lewis, "Christianity and Culture," *Christian Reflections* (Grand Rapids: Eerdmans, 1995), 21. For an excellent analysis of C. S. Lewis's wonderful perspective on pleasure see Meilaender, *The Taste for the Other*, 8–31.

13. To say it in another way, a biblical doctrine of creation begins with the primary affirmation that life, the world, humanity, was made by God and is, in essence, good. The secondary truth, one that qualifies the primary truth, is that all of it is fallen/broken and in some ways dangerous

It reminds one of the old rabbinical saying that one day we will all stand before God and he will judge us for all the possible pleasures he gave us to enjoy, but we failed to enjoy.

The Daily Connections between Heaven and Earth

The Hebrew word *Torah* has traditionally been interpreted as "law," that is, a set of rules or legal codes. This is a somewhat misleading interpretation as it implies the rigid approach to life that distorts the inner intention of the idea of Torah.[14] A truer translation is that of "instruction" or simply "teaching." A better way of looking at it is to see the Torah as an orientation course in the ways of God. Torah is the training that Israel needed to learn about her covenantal God. The instruction aims at the harnessing and directing of the community's resources toward a redemptive end.

When reading the Pentateuch, one is immediately struck by the radical nonlinear logic associated with it. One verse deals with the Israelites' approach to God in the temple. The very next verse deals with what one does when one's donkey falls into a pit. The next might well deal with the mildew in the kitchen, the next with the female menstrual cycle. It seems to be radically discontinuous and generally lacks the sequential reason that we look for in a text. What is going on here? How can we comprehend the meaning of this?

We suggest that there is indeed a rather profound logic going on in the Torah, a logic that attempts to relate *all aspects* of life to God. Therefore, everything—one's work, one's domestic life, one's health, one's worship—has the same significance to God. He is concerned with every aspect of the believer's life. Not even the mildew is insignificant. While in the Western spiritual tradition we have tended to see the "religious" as one category of life among many, the Hebrew mind incorporated "religious" existence into all of life. As such there is no distinction whatsoever between the secular and the sacred in the Hebrew worldview. All of life is sacred when it is placed in relationship to the living God. The Hebraic mind can draw a direct line from any and every aspect of life to the eternal purposes of God—this is the logic of the Torah.

Following the Torah means to submit to the complete shaping of a God-oriented communal life in all its dimensions, not just the "religious." It implies the acceptance that all things relate to God and that God is concerned with all

to the soul. Sin has so qualified the world that it has made it precarious and ambiguous, but it has not obscured God's hand and his love.

14. While there is no question of a tendency for legalism in Judaism, it is equally clear it is not limited to Judaism. Christianity has produced at least as much legalism over the centuries. There is much that can be learned about a truer biblical perspective from Judaism, but we need to overcome the stereotype and caricature of Judaism in order to do that.

of life, not just a disembodied spiritual dimension unrelated to other aspects of life. Here again is one of the sources of the Hebrew love of life. This is an entirely different view of the law than the caricature that is generally cultivated in Christendom circles.[15] At the very least we should recognize that the Torah does not imply a legalism in the heart of God, but rather an attempt to orient human religion to concrete expressions of life, something we have generally failed to do.

Practical Monotheism

Under the influence of the speculative/abstractive Hellenizing bent in Christendom, even the biblical teaching about God's unity/oneness becomes a matter of philosophical speculation. But such biblical passages as Deuteronomy 6:4 are not merely a description of the pure nature of God in his eternal Being. They are in fact actually far more concrete and practical than that. The Shema ("Hear, O Israel . . .") in Deuteronomy 6:4 is the claim of Yahweh over against the competing claim of the many other gods in the polytheistic religious environment of the day. It is a call for the loyalty of the people. This statement is therefore an attack on heathen religious polytheism rather than just a statement about so-called "ethical monotheism" of the later speculative theologians.[16] The claim has direct and concrete implications: It is a call for the Israelites to live their lives under the Lordship of one God and not under the tyranny of the many gods. In other words, it is a practical call not to live one's life as if there were a different god for every sphere of life—a god of the field, a god of the river, a god of fertility, a god of the sun, and so forth.

Judaism loudly proclaims that there is only one God and he is Lord of every aspect of life. Again, here the concrete and practical nature of Hebraic thinking comes to the fore. Polytheists can compartmentalize life and distribute it among many powers. But as Maurice Friedman rightly says, "The man in the Israelite world who has faith is not distinguished from the 'heathen' by a mere spiritual view of the Godhead, but by the exclusiveness of his relationship to God, and by his reference of all things to him."[17] Monotheists (really *biblical* believers) have only *one* reference point. This is the biblical mode of

15. That the law can "save" should get an unambiguous Pauline "no." That the law is "good" and useful for orientation to God should get an equally unambiguous Pauline "yes."
16. We are not saying that these verses (the Shema) have no indirect implications for our understanding of the nature of God, but in Deuteronomy 6:4, in their original context, they constitute more a statement against the prevailing way people saw and experienced God than what theologians have called the "Eternal Being of God."
17. Maurice Friedman, *Martin Buber: The Life of Dialogue*, 242, quoted in Roy Oliver, *The Wanderer and the Way* (London: East & West Library, 1968), 13.

thinking—concrete and practical, as opposed to theoretical and speculative. The implications are far reaching, not as simple theology, but as practical missiology. A re-Hebraizing of Christianity is so vital for the emergence of the missional-incarnational church.

This claim to unify our lives under the one God (called *yichud* by the rabbis) has truly radical implications for us today as we struggle to find new ground on which to base our discipleship. Biblical monotheism means that we cannot live like there is one "god" for the church and another for politics and another in economic life or still another for the home. No, all of life, every aspect of it, *every dimension*, is to be brought under and unified under the ONE God, Yahweh. Seen in this light, the Shema is a claim of God's exclusivity and a direct challenge from God about the role of idols in the believer's life. In the first, and original, instance it has nothing to do with the Eternal Being of God.

This is a radical teaching that, if applied, unites all the dimensions of life under Jesus. For one, it "liberates" God from being a prisoner of the stained glass prison of the church. It obliterates the deeply *un*biblical, Hellenistic schism between sacred and secular so fundamental to Christendom modes of thinking. It frees us to perceive life as ministry, work as mission, play as worship. If all are embraced under the impulse of the unification of life under God, then life itself becomes missional worship. Life in all its forms opens itself up to the radically spiritual.

Releasing the Glory of God

One of the most wonderful metaphors in Jewish mysticism is the rabbinical teaching on the *Shekinah* ("God's glory"). In the typically playful way Jewish theology was presented, the Shekinah gains a personality and usually takes the form of a woman. She is metaphorically portrayed as God's wife, but she is in exile, i.e., God and his glory have been tragically separated through the fall. The separation is one of a cosmic crash in which God's glory was scattered into myriad sparks and caught up in all created matter. The holy sparks are now imprisoned in all things. Even the lowest of created things have the holy sparks in them.

The remarkable aspect of this Jewish teaching is the view that it is our holy actions—that is, actions filled with holy intent and directed toward God—that actually free the holy sparks ensnared in all things allowing the exiled Shekinah to journey back to her Husband, namely, God. God and his glory are joined together again when people *act* in holiness. Says Martin Buber, "The *Shekinah* is banished into concealment; it lies, tied, at the bottom of every thing, and is redeemed in every thing by man, who, by his own vision or his deed, liberates the thing's soul."[18] Isaac Bashevis Singer, the Nobel laureate who wrote marvelous novels exploring aspects of Jewish mysticism, said that "when man chooses virtue, he strengthens all the dimensions of life. Angels . . . look forward to a man doing a good deed, since this brings joy and strength to the entire world. A good deed helps God and the Divine Presence to unite. A sin, on the other hand, evokes gloom in all the world."[19]

Now, without taking the teaching as literal truth (most of the rabbis don't!), this is a very helpful way of viewing the mission of God's people in the world. When we act redemptively and in holiness, we fan into flames the creational purpose that lies at the heart of all things in God's world—we liberate God's glory that lies in it. And in so doing we bring God glory. Again the post-Jesus Jewish mysticism perspective brings the focus of faithfulness to the whole of life in all its concreteness—the very element missing in so much Christendom proclamation and action. All things have elements of the sacred in them and should be respected—people, animals, the environment, even our technologies. The founder of Hasidism, Rabbi Israel Baal Shem Tov, said that "one should even have mercy on his tools and all he possesses because one should have mercy on the holy sparks."[20]

There's a story told about a certain Rabbi Jacob, a deeply godly and zealous but somewhat ascetic man. One day he has a vision where he meets a woman who symbolizes the exiled glory of God, trying to make her way back to God. The woman is covered from head to ankles in a long black veil. Only her feet are bare and they are caked with dust and blood from long traveling on harsh roads in her exile.

The woman addresses the rabbi, saying, "I am weary unto death, for people have hunted me down. I am sick unto death, for they have tormented me. I am ashamed, for they have denied me. *You,* [you humans] are the tyrants who keep me in exile. When you are hostile to one another, you hunt me down. When you plot evil against each other, you torment me. When you slander each other, you deny me. In doing these things you send your fellow human into exile and so you send me into exile. And for you Rabbi Jacob, do you realize that while you intend to follow me with your religious rituals you in actual fact estrange yourself from me all the more? One cannot love me [the *Shekinah*] and abandon people."

18. Buber, *On Judaism*, 106. Or if this sounds much too foreign to our evangelical ears, then we need only to turn to C. S. Lewis who has a strikingly similar view of things in his essay "The Weight of Glory" in *The Weight of Glory and Other Addresses* (Grand Rapids: Eerdmans, 1965), 4.

19. Isaac Bashevis Singer, *Love And Exile* (Garden City, NY: Doubleday, 1984), 19.

20. Martin Buber, *Tales of the Hasidim*, Vol. 1, *The Early Masters* (New York: Schocken, 1955), xi.

And she concludes, "Dream not that my forehead radiates heavenly beams. And has haloes all around it. My face is that of the created being."

She then raises her veil from her face, and he recognizes the face as that of a neighbor.

The Heart of the Matter and the Matter of the Heart

In Judaism, there is a distinct activity called *kavanah*. It is cultivated in order to maximize the inwardness of our actions.[21] It means to pay attention, to direct the mind and heart in order to maximize the levels of intentionality in our actions. This applies to actions/deeds as it does to the study of Scripture and to prayer but goes beyond these activities themselves to the notion of attentiveness to God himself. It is not primarily an awareness of being commanded by God, but an awareness of the God who commands. The focus in *kavanah* shifts from the deed itself to its inner meaning, the goal being to find access to the sacred in the deed itself. It is finding the essence of the task, to partake of its inspiration, to be made equal to the task of fulfilling holy commands. Abraham Heschel says that "*kavanah* is direction to God and requires the involvement and redirection of the whole person. It is the act of bringing together the scattered forces of the self; it means the participation of heart and soul, not only of will and mind."[22]

Martin Buber, one of the most influential interpreters of Judaism for the twentieth century, quotes a Hasidic anecdote and points out the interrelation between direction and redemption:

> Enoch was a cobbler, and with every stitch of his awl that drew together the top and bottom of the leather, he joined God and the Shekinah. . . . Man exerts

21. Much more will be said later about the idea of developing holy intention as an exercise in spiritual attentiveness to God. What we will note here is the element of intention that gives actions their inner meaning.

22. See the remarkable book by Abraham Heschel, *God in Search of Man: A Philosophy of Judaism* (New York: Harper & Row, 1955), 316. Pages 314–18 deal with this intriguing topic. Maurice Friedman, in his definitive biography of Martin Buber, notes that "*Kavanah* (in its Kabbalistic form) represents the deliberate concentration of will, an inner attitude which is far more effective than the particular nature of the action being performed." *Martin Buber, A Life of Dialogue*, 18. In its Hasidic form it is transformed from a magical intention into a general consecration or inner dedication, which people bring to all their actions. The Hasidic *kavanah* "signifies less an effort of the will centered on the attainment of a definite end than the purposeful direction of the whole being in accordance with some feeling springing up in the depths of one's nature. Without *kavanah* no service of God (*abodah*) has any value, for right (moral) action is dependent on the intensity of inner religious feeling. Thus Hasidism does not recognize any division between religion and ethics—between the direct relation to God and one's relations to one's fellows, nor is its ethics limited to any prescribed and peculiar action" (ibid., 21).

influence on the eternal, and this is not done by any special works, but by the intention with which he does all his works. This is the teaching of the hallowing of the everyday. The issue is not to attain to a new type of acting which, owing to its object, would be sacred or mystical; the issue is to do the one appointed task, the common, obvious tasks of daily life, according to their truth and according to their meaning.[23]

Buber goes further, "He who does a good deed with complete kavanah, that is, completes an act in such a way that his whole existence is gathered in it and directed in it towards God, he works on the redemption of the world, on its conquest for God."[24] Buber says elsewhere,

What matters is not what is being done, but the fact that every act is filled with sanctity—that is, with God-oriented intent—is a road to the heart of the world. There is nothing that is evil in itself; every passion can become a virtue, every inclination a "vehicle of God." It is not the matter of the act that is decisive, but its sanctification. Every act is hallowed if it is directed towards salvation. The soul of the doer alone determines the character of the deed. With this, the deed does in truth become the life center of religiosity.[25]

This is a very useful and thoroughly biblical idea. Biblical ethics has always highlighted the element of motive and intentionality in the teachings of the New Testament, but seldom have we made this so accessible and meaningful to Christian life and mission. Furthermore, we lack the theological framework to affirm so directly the impact of our everyday actions on the task of redemption. But as we will affirm in a later chapter, the reclamation of the deed as a means of grace is vital if we wish to sustain a vigorous missional engagement in our respective contexts.

A word must be said here on the Jewish teaching on the two inclinations: the good inclination and the evil inclination. The good inclination is that which leads us to God. It is the directed forces of the soul. The evil inclination, on the other hand, is those passions left undirected. They are not evil in themselves, but are evil because if left without holy direction, they will inevitably lead us away from God. The belief is that we can, and indeed must, worship God with the evil inclination. This is not as startling as it first appears. It simply means that we must serve God with *all our passions*. Nothing is to be left out of the redemptive direction of the heart toward God. Says Buber, "The Mishnah interprets the phrase 'Thou shall love the Lord your God with all thy heart' to

23. Martin Buber, *Mamre* (Melbourne: Melbourne University Press, 1946), 78.
24. Ibid., 173.
25. Ibid., 48.

mean; with both your inclinations, the 'good' and the 'evil'; that is, with and by your decision, so that the ardor of passion is converted and enters into the unified deed with all its strength. For no inclination is evil in itself; it is made evil by man when he surrenders to it instead of controlling it."[26]

What humankind certainly knows about passion is that it can overwhelm us. Essentially the doctrine of the two inclinations tells us that a lower passion can only be overcome by a greater passion. It takes an act of holy passion to redeem our evil impulses. Paul Ramsay points out, "If a man does not love the Lord with all his mind he does not thereby become a pure reason with no loves; he simply loves something else with all his heart, soul, strength and mind. One's loves are always deeper than his reason; and reason is always in the employment of some love."[27]

Passion is only evil when it remains in the directionless state, when it refuses to be subject to holy direction, when it will not accept the direction that leads toward God. In Judaism there occurs again and again the insight that passion (the "evil urge") is simply the elemental force that is the sole origin of great human works, the holy included. Buber claims, "Of all the works of creation, it is passion which is the very good, without which man cannot serve God, or truly live."[28]

The issue is about the *direction* of our actions. Once again C. S. Lewis has grasped the importance of direction when he notes in *The Great Divorce* that "there is but one good; that is God. Everything else is good when it looks to Him and bad when it turns from Him."[29] It's the direction that in some way determines the nature of the act; it is the passion that determines its energy.

Again, we believe this is very suggestive in the reframing of a missional faith. Because of its innate dualism, Western Christianity has generally struggled to

26. Ibid., 82. Maurice Friedman notes, "Passion means that one does not suppress one's humanity before bringing oneself into relation with others, but, on the contrary, directs one's 'evil' urge into that relationship in such a way that, without losing its force, it ceases to be evil." *Religion and Psychology: A Dialogical Approach* (New York: Paragon, 1992), 23.
27. Paul Ramsay, *Christianity and Society* (1943 viii): 31.
28. Martin Buber, *Israel and the World: Essays in a Time of Crisis* (New York: Schocken, 1963), 18.
29. C. S. Lewis, *The Great Divorce* (New York: Collins, 1946), 97–98. Christianity is not without people who have recognized the necessity for directing our actions to God. In his poem *Ascent of Mt. Carmel*, Saint John of the Cross says, "The strength of the soul comprises of the faculties, passions, and appetites. All this strength is ruled by the will. When the will directs these faculties, passions, and appetites towards God, turning away from all that is not God, the soul presents its strength for God, and comes to love Him with all its might." *The Collected Works of Saint John of the Cross*, translated by Kieran Kavanaugh and Otilio Rodriguez (Washington: ICS, 1991), 292. The general difference is that in Western Christianity it is usually spiritual actions and not everyday ones that require direction. The everyday deeds generally have little meaning for religious purposes in the saints.

integrate pleasure, passion, and instinctive drives into the faith. As a result, it has tended to focus on the soul and has left bodily drives outside of Christ's redemptive work. This leaves people to struggle to make sense of these drives. Human sexuality is a classic case in point. But the Hebraic spirit seeks to harness the forces of our sexuality in their intended creational purpose. The problem is that if we fail to integrate our sexuality, then we are doomed to experience it as a dark, even satanic, force that operates against faith and contrary to God. A missional faith must be far more spirited than that and should seek nothing less than to bring all aspects of the self under God, including, and perhaps especially, our sexuality. Nothing is to be left undirected. It is *toward* him that we complete our lives. This, coupled with holy passion, makes for a very vigorous faithfulness in the world.

Hallowing the Everyday

Directly related to the idea of direction-intention (*kavanah*) is the idea of the hallowing of the everyday. Once again we see the focus on the concrete that is so typical of the post-Jesus Jewish mysticism worldview. This concept of the hallowing of the everyday has already been highlighted in the quotes of Buber given above but deserves further clarification in a section of its own.

At core it is built on the Hebraic understanding that there are effectively only two realities in the world: the *holy* and the *not-yet-holy*, and that the missional task of God's people is to make the not-yet-holy into that which is holy. This is done by the directing of the deed *toward* God (and not away from him) and by the level of intentionality and holiness with which we perform our daily tasks. It is important to note that any and every deed, no matter how seemingly profane or trivial, can become a place of holiness when performed with the right intention and with the appropriate holy direction.[30]

The post-Jesus Jewish mysticism maintains a wonderfully positive view of holiness. In contrast, so much of Christendom's view of holiness can be defined as holiness by negation or holiness by avoidance; a faith defined more by what we shouldn't do than by what we should. The life orientation inherent in the post-Jesus Jewish mysticism perspectives leads to a much more life-affirming stance vis-à-vis holiness. Holiness is primarily defined not by what we don't do, but rather by what we do in our hallowing of the everyday. All things, all

---

30. "If you explore the life of things and of conditioned being you come to the unfathomable. If you deny the life of things and of conditioned being you stand before nothingness. If you hallow this life you meet the living God." Martin Buber, *I and Thou*, trans. R. G. Smith (New York: Collier, 1958), 79.

events, all activities, can be occasions of hallowing if one brings to them the direction and intent of true *kavanah*.

> One should, and one must, truly live with all people and things, but one must live with all these in holiness, one must hallow all which one does in one's natural life. No renunciation is commanded. When one eats in holiness, when one tastes the flavor of the food in holiness, then the table becomes an altar. When one works in holiness, he raises up the sparks that hide themselves in all tools. When one walks in holiness across the field, then the soft songs of all herbs, which they voice to God, enter into the song of our soul. When one drinks in holiness to each other with one's companions, it is as if one read together in the Torah. When one dances the roundelay in holiness, brightness shines over the gathering. When a husband is united with his wife in holiness, then the Shekinah rests over them.[31]

A positive post-Jesus Jewish mysticism holiness is active in the world. It is a missional holiness. It moves to change the world, to sanctify it. This is not an ephemeral thing; it is active in *every sphere of life* and does not shirk back from the redemption of dark things. Holiness partners with God in the redemption of the world. "True holiness is when God's hallowing of the world and our hallowing of the world meet."[32]

Faith and Faithfulness

There is one more theme of the post-Jesus Jewish mysticism that needs to be explored. And that is the difference between the Hebraic and the Hellenistic definitions and assumptions about the nature of faith. It must be mentioned here because of its reorienting significance and its usefulness for us in becoming a truly missional people of God.

The difference between the two worldviews is summed up in the two words used for "faith" by the two language groups—these being the Hebrew *emunah* and the Greek *pistis*. Essentially the meaning of the word *emunah* is that of active faith, better rendered by the word "faith-*fulness*" or "active trust." It is a typically Hebraic word in that it focuses on concrete actions and relationships. It has strong existential tones and is thus life-oriented. The Hellenistic idea of *pistis*, on the other hand, focuses on the intellectual content of faith, its propositional base. Faith is thus a kind of knowledge or belief. Essentially, therefore, the focus of the Hellenistic concept of faith is on its *creedal* nature while the Hebraic is on its *existential* character.

31. Buber, *Mamre*, 178.
32. A statement by Martin Buber, source unknown.

The trajectory of Western Christianity, however, has been dominated by the Hellenistic concept over the Hebraic, even though elements of the Hebraic have remained all along. Witness Luther's recovery of the Hebrew idea of faith in the Reformation, a recovery that was easily obscured by the fussy theological arguments that were associated with the Reformation and the Counter-Reformation. Creed soon dominated trust, and it is our contention that this is still the case. We believe that this must be reversed if we are to have a more engaging, missional faith. Creed is important, but it ought not to be dominant. As a missional church we can no longer afford the debates regarding subtle points of doctrine (a form of *gnosis*?). Rather, we do need to recover a sense of existential trust in God in spite of our circumstances. Our evangelism in the emerging global culture needs to offer a real *encounter* with Jesus, and not merely a doctrine of Jesus. To be sure, it must be an experience that is biblically accurate, but it must be experience nonetheless. We need to get over our addictions to *gnosis* and need to find a more biblical way of expressing our faith through active trust in him. This is precisely what a messianic spirituality does for us.

8

Action as Sacrament

Christians have often disputed as to whether what leads the Christian home is good actions or Faith in Christ. . . . It does seem to
me like asking which blade in a pair of scissors is most necessary.
A serious moral effort is the only thing that will bring you to the
point where you throw in the towel. Faith in Christ is the only thing
to save you from despair at that point: and out of the Faith in Him
good actions must inevitably come.

—C. S. Lewis

Reaching Emerging Generations

Earlier we argued that the new global culture holds to a worldview that is holistic in its outlook. It sees a need for a greater integration between spirit and
matter. Its perspective on spirituality is more incarnational and immanental
than dualistic. In fact, its worldview is closer to the classic Judaistic spirit
than to Hellenistic consciousness. With the collapse of both Christendom and
modernism, a postmodern sensibility has emerged that relates more powerfully
to the hallowing of the everyday and the pursuit of sensuality. The very things
we have been outlining, if incorporated into a Christ-centered Christianity,
are likely to provide many more portals for postmodern people to access the
Christian message than ever before.

Today, contemporary people are searching for an inclusive community that is democratic, nonpatriarchal, and compassionate. Their preference for a group is that it be raw, not refined; earthy, not sophisticated; concerned with action, not just theory. They articulate a strong interest in the environment, politics, and ethics, not directed by pure ideology but all approached from a concern for human wholeness. It is obvious that the various elements of a Hebrew worldview that we've outlined are likely to provide plenty of connections for postmodern people. By Hebraizing the Christian movement and recovering a messianic spirituality as lived by Jesus, Paul, and the first Christians, we believe the church is in a much better position to recalibrate itself to reach an emerging generation.

Let Your Light Shine

We're certain that we can whisper into the souls of postmodern people in order to activate a search for God. But we don't believe that sermons or church services will have the same impact they have had in the past to create that hunger for God. Rather it is simple, meat-and-potatoes things like sharing our own story or being loving. This leads us to a question we are often asked about the relationship between proclamation and good works. In some quarters of the church, the emphasis is very much on the former. They train their congregations to share the gospel with their friends, and they hold many outreach or evangelistic events at which the clear preaching of the gospel is expounded. Other churches emphasize good works. They'll often quote Saint Francis's axiom, "Preach the gospel at all times and if necessary use words." In these churches, social ministries and care for the community constitute mission.

Why is it that there has traditionally been such a dichotomy between proclamation and mercy ministries? While we recognize that there are some notable exceptions, like Soul Survivor in Manchester, we are concerned by this separation of preaching from action. In our model for the missional church, we want to continue to impress the need for a contextualized proclamation of the claims of Christ. But we cannot see how such proclamation has any impact if it does not issue from a loving, hospitable, generous community of faith. In some sectors of the traditional evangelical church there has been a minimizing of the efficacy of good works. It is assumed that because good works cannot save us, we should not be encouraged to perform them as a central part of gospel ministry. This is an overreaction. We agree that good works cannot save us. That is the work of God's grace in Christ. But we insist on seeing godly action as having a sacramental effect.

The recovery of a messianic spirituality that hallows the everyday is essential to the missional church because it is in the everyday that the missional church exists. If we are an incarnational community, the church must recover the ability to see God in the so-called ordinary world of action. We propose that the church needs to be able to find more innate meaning and purpose in its actions as God's people if we are to become truly missional with an enlarged perspective on life. In other words, we need to be able to redeem both the primacy and the value of the deed done in the furtherance of God's cause in the world. Our spirituality must move from primarily a passive/receptive mode, to an *actional* mode. This again is paradigmatically different from the way spirituality has generally been conceptualized in Western contexts. The church must rediscover the ability and inclination to find God in the place of action so that others might find him there as well.

Viewed as such, action itself is a sacrament of grace, not only to the recipient of the gracious act, but to the actor as well. We are advocating a kind of missional action that, when done in the name of Jesus, is *the* primary sacrament of the missional church. We are proposing an activist understanding of church. By activist we mean that the church must recover its understanding of the holy deed done in God's name, which we find reflected in so much of the Old Testament. Martin Buber is right when he says that "something infinite flows into a (holy) deed of a man; something infinite flows from it . . . the fullness of the world's destiny, namelessly interwoven, passes through his hands."[1] Just as the Lord's Supper and baptism are sacraments in and through which God's grace is made visible and apparent, so is the holy deed of a godly person. If we take Buber at his word, then we can truly embrace our missional task to communicate the gospel and grace with a great sense of God's nearness in what we do. This is why the missional action is a supreme source of spiritual insight and experience. The rabbis say that no one is lonely when doing a good deed, for this is where God and human meet.

A messianic spirituality has a redemptive approach to all aspects of life. This theme has much to offer us in the construction of a courageous missional spirituality because it gives us a framework to (re)conceptualize our actions in the world. If God acts redemptively, then it is all right for us to act in precisely the same mode.

One of the great themes of Scripture is that God is a redeemer. Redemptive action may take two forms, (a) a redemption by power, whereby people are released from slavery through an act of violence, or (b) redemption by purchase where a kinsman-redeemer pays the price to free a person sold into

---

1. Buber, *On Judaism*, 86.

servitude. God acts in both ways in Scripture (the Cross has both ideas to it), and these can become metaphors for missional action in the world. In other words, God is the redeemer, and in that mode he provides a model for how we can act in the world. To redeem is to buy back that which is lost, clean it up, and put it back to its original intended use.

There is virtually nothing in human existence or culture that cannot be redeemed and made into worship, including action. If we take C. S. Lewis's point that all vices are virtues gone wrong, then we can take a different look at humanity and associated culture. We must be active in all dimensions of human life, especially at the cultural level, because culture is the sphere where people and societies share common meaning. As part of the redemption of all aspects of life we should be actively interpreting movies, literature, pop-culture, experiences, new religious movements, and the like. They can be redeemed and directed to the glory of God. It is precisely these things that have the elements of human searching and yearning in them that must be correlated to the mind and heart of God if they are to be redeemed. This is exactly what Paul was doing in Acts 17 in his speech on Mars Hill. He was highlighting to the Greek philosophers that the search going on in their own writings was a legitimate one. He then directed them to the resurrection of Jesus. We have to be able to name the name of Jesus in the midst of the search going on in our day—it is our missional responsibility! If we don't, who will? Or do we believe that we have nothing to say about art, culture, and the search for meaning? Acting redemptively will require that we are in the midst of it all trying to buy back some of the lostness in the name of Jesus.

In saying this we are affirming that our actions, or more particularly our missional deeds, actually confer grace. In fact, this could be the case even more so than the standard (somewhat abstracted) sacraments of the Christendom church. Humans have the freedom to protest against human suffering by *acting* to alleviate it. An alleviation of suffering in the name of Jesus bestows something of the grace of God through his people. Such an action pulls a person away from his own self-involved concerns and directs him missionally toward other human beings in such a way that they, the persons acted upon *and* the person acting, find God in a new way. Elie Wiesel, winner of the Nobel prize for peace and luminous Jewish writer, has a character in one of his books affirm the sacramental value of the human, and humanizing, deed in the following passage from *Twilight*:

> If you could have seen yourself, framed in the doorway [Pedro once said to Michael], you would have believed in the richness of existence—as I do—in the possibility of having it and sharing it. It's so simple! You see a musician in

the street; you give him a thousand francs instead of ten; he'll believe in God. You see a woman weeping, smile at her tenderly, even if you don't know her; she'll believe in you. You see a forsaken old man; open your heart to him, and he'll believe in himself. You will have surprised them. Thanks to you, they will have trembled, and everything around them will vibrate. Blessed is he capable of surprising and of being surprised.[2]

As such, deeds are not only sacramental, but they are themselves revelatory, that is, they reveal God in his goodness. There is a Talmudic saying that may be interpreted as meaning that revelation resides within the deed itself: "From within his own deed, man as well as nation hears the voice of God."[3] The New Testament writers are entirely comfortable with this typically Hebraic mode of thinking. The following are examples:

In the same way, let your light shine before men, that they may see your good deeds and praise your Father in heaven. (Matt. 5:16)

Live such good lives among the pagans that, though they accuse you of doing wrong, they may see your good deeds and glorify God on the day he visits us. (1 Pet. 2:12)

If anyone speaks, he should do it as one speaking the very words of God. If anyone serves, he should do it with the strength God provides, so that in all things God may be praised through Jesus Christ. To him be the glory and the power for ever and ever. Amen. (1 Pet. 4:11)

The sacred deed is full of God's glory. If we take verses like these seriously, then we must acknowledge that God is found more in acts of kindness than in the mountains and forests. It is more biblical for us to believe in the immanence of God in holy deeds than in the immanence of God in nature.

For us there are such exciting possibilities in the belief that our deeds and actions are both sacramental and revelatory. This is not only so because of the missional effect on people around about us, but also because of its effect on us. In the action we can find God where we could not find him before—in the streets, at work, in the marketplaces, at play. In fact, we can find him anywhere where we can act in holiness and so become a conduit of God's grace to the world. When Paul says, "For we are God's workmanship, created in Christ Jesus to do good works, which God prepared in advance for us to do" (Eph. 2:10), he was expressing something profound about our creational purpose

2. Elie Wiesel, *Twilight* (Suffolk: Viking, 1988), 69.
3. Buber, *On Judaism*, 112.

"in the Messiah." Our actions are part of God's plan for us. No one can therefore say that our spirituality has nothing to do with our good works. It has everything to do with them. It's time to reclaim the deed.

Salvation by Good Works?

All this talk about deeds and action raises the specter of salvation by good works—something the Reformers rightly fought against at all cost. Justification by grace through faith alone is a central theme of Paul's writings. When Paul was struggling to find the source of justification, he insisted that it is from God (his grace) and it is through faith (not works). What we are presenting here will not take away at all from this essential, nonnegotiable doctrine of New Testament faith.

What we are trying to do here is affirm the inherent value of deeds themselves. Will they save us? No! Are they still inherently valuable? Absolutely, yes. They are in fact fundamental to our communal and personal missions, as well as our personal piety. If one is given to questioning this stand, then answer this: Why are we (redeemed people) judged by our deeds before God at the final judgment (see 1 Cor. 3:10–15; Matt. 12:36–37; Rev. 20; John 5:27–30)? If they are not intrinsically valuable, why then do they follow us to the heavenly court? Why does God seem to take them so seriously? Does goodness reside only in the heart's intent or in the deed? Or only in God and not in humanity? Well, if goodness does not lie in redeemed humanity, we cannot be responsible for lack of it.

We need to seriously get over Christendom's theological cringe factor regarding the value of human goodness (dualism again?). We don't have to denigrate genuine goodness in order to glorify God. James says that all good things come from God and have their source in God (1:17) and so it does not denigrate God when we say that some human acts are *good*. If someone sacrifices his or her life or possessions to help someone else, then we must affirm that it is in itself a good act. It has *intrinsic* value. Will that act bring that person salvation? No, a person can be saved only through active trust in God's saving work in the Messiah Jesus.[4] We are not altering the basis of our evangelical faith, only its missional focus—we are reclaiming our actions as a place of grace and blessing, a place to meet with God.

---

4. Do we, the authors, represent new forms of the Judaizers? Only in the same way that Paul himself was a Judaizer. Paul was a profoundly religious Jew, deeply rooted in the Hebraic worldview, who was commissioned to take the Jewish religion with its message about the Jewish Messiah and make it accessible to a non-Jewish world. What we want to do is place the message back in its original context and let it come alive for our day.

In his book *The Crooked Shall Be Made Straight*, Israeli writer S. Y. Agnon tells the story of a simple, godly man named Menashe.[5] He runs a grocery store that slowly goes broke because, being so generous a man, Menashe cannot bear to ask for money from customers who cannot afford to pay. His ruthless competitors eventually run him out of business, and he has to resort to traveling from town to town begging. The village rabbi takes pity on poor, decent Menashe and gives him a letter commending him as a good and honest man who is deserving of charity.

Menashe begs for over a year, eventually collecting enough to restart his business. On his last night on the road, before returning home to begin his life again, he lodges at an inn and happens upon a local con man. This man is as vile and contemptible as Menashe is good and upright. When he sees Menashe's letter of commendation from the rabbi, his eyes light up. "If I had a letter like that I would never have to work another day in my life," he glowers, and then offers Menashe a substantial amount of money to purchase the letter. Tempted by the opportunity to virtually double his money and knowing that he no longer needs the rabbi's letter, Menashe sells the document. Then, with more money than he's ever seen before, he decides to celebrate his good fortune. Perhaps motivated also by shame at having sold the honorable rabbi's letter, Menashe gets horribly drunk and in his stupor is robbed of everything he has, even his prayer shawl. With not enough money to get home, Menashe is reduced to begging again.

In the meantime, the liar and con man is set upon by robbers and murdered. His body is mutilated beyond recognition, so that when his corpse is found with Menashe's letter in the pocket, it is immediately assumed that it is in fact Menashe who has been murdered. His wife is notified of her husband's death. Some months later she remarries, and a year later she gives birth to a son just as the destitute Menashe finally drags himself home. He arrives in town just as his wife and her husband are celebrating the circumcision of their child.

Menashe, the decent man, is in a terrible dilemma. If he reveals his identity, he will effectively end his wife's new marriage by revealing it to be illegal. He will also brand her child as illegitimate, causing him to be an outcast in the Jewish community. Unable to destroy the lives of those he loves, he retreats to the cemetery outside the town. There he confides in the custodian by telling him his tale of woe. The custodian takes pity on this sad, godly man and keeps his secret and supplies him with food and shelter. When Menashe dies

5. Agnon's book, written in 1912, has never been translated into English. We came across a retelling of his famous story in Rabbi Harold Kushner's *How Good Do I Have To Be?* (Boston: Little, Brown & Co., 1996), 171.

shortly after, the custodian has him buried in the very plot his wife had arranged when she thought him dead two years previously.

What does this story mean? It is a parable about losing one's name and finding it. When Menashe was a decent, kind man, his good name was his passport, as symbolized by the rabbi's letter. When he sold the letter, he was acting out of character by doing something for a quick dishonest buck. By selling the letter, he literally gave away his name. It was as if the real Menashe ceased to exist. Only later, when he performs his immense act of self-sacrifice, does he receive his name and therefore his identity again. By being buried under his own gravestone, his name is restored. Menashe is alive again (ironically at the point of his death).

Our actions are a representation of our name, our integrity or identity. When we abandon the high calling to live like Christ, we abandon our Christian identity. We are not saved by our actions, but we are known by them. Jesus told his own disciples that they would be known (identified as followers of Jesus) by how much they loved each other. Their actions typified their name.

In and Out

We have already highlighted the vital importance of intention and direction in our discussion on *kavanah* in the previous chapter. Intentionality is of absolute and vital importance if we are going to act meaningfully in our missional tasks. A deed done will benefit others, but without the inner devotion of the heart to God, it will not benefit the doer. But the God of the Bible is interested not only in right thinking or right motives or right action but also in *right living*. Again it is the whole that counts. Right living should occur in all of our life, not just in the part of it in the realm or theater of the holy. The world needs more than the secret holiness of individual inwardness. It needs more than sacred sentiments and good intentions. God asks for our bodies because he needs our lives. It is by the church living in conformity with God's will that the world will be reclaimed for God (Rom. 12:1–2).

Obedience takes place on two levels. First, it is an act of the soul—an act that involves developing the right intention, that is, inward obedience. Second, it is an act of the body. It involves putting right intentions into actions—outward obedience. The following silly joke highlights the difference between inner and outer obedience. Mom asks little Johnny to sit at the table and eat his supper. Like many children at mealtime, little Johnny refuses to eat. Mom says, "Johnny, sit down and eat your dinner!" Again Johnny refuses. Eventually Mom prevails by pushing him down into the chair and threatening the removal of privileges. Defiant to the end, little Johnny says, "I may be sitting down on the outside, but I'm standing up on the inside!"

Both inner and outer obedience is necessary to fulfill holy commandments. Without inwardness our actions are incomplete. An external act calls for inner acknowledgment—*participation*. Abraham Heschel asks, "Is it the artist's inner vision, or his wrestling with the stone that brings forth a sculpture?" Right living, he suggests, "is like a work of art, the product of both an inner vision and a wrestling with concrete situations."[6] Our actions are incomplete if they do not contain both dimensions—inner vision and outer action. We turn to Heschel again: "No religious act is properly fulfilled unless it is done with a willing heart and a craving soul. You cannot worship God with your body if you do not know how to worship Him with your soul."[7] We suggest that the main reason for God's calling us to obedience is not for an imposition of discipline for discipline's sake. Rather it is to keep us spiritually perceptive, open to God, attentive to his voice.

Just Do It!

At the risk of being accused of pure activism, we wish to reiterate that we are not encouraging a blind drivenness here. The whole aspect of intentionality emphasized in *kavanah* keeps one from a meaningless activism. What we are attempting to do is to redress the imbalance in the way we mature as disciples of Jesus. Growing in faith is not just about disciplines of study and withdrawal, as vital as these are. Certainly there need to be disciplines of passive receptivity to hear from God and to know him in prayerful stillness. But there must also be rhythms of activity if we are to be mature followers of the Messiah. Jesus was a real revolutionary, but there doesn't seem to be a lot of revolution going on at the moment. There tends to be a whole lot of talk about mission and postmodernism and not a whole lot of direct missional action. While there is a proliferation of books telling us all how to do it, there don't seem to be many working models showing us how to do it. This must change. There needs to be a whole lot more action, and we believe that only in actually doing it will the church discover God in a new way. As someone once said, "The best way to predict the future is to invent it." This doesn't mean we believe that the future is in our hands completely. It is God who directs this process, but it's in action and invention that we can discover God's will for the future. The Bible records God's mighty acts in history. What we

6. Heschel, *God in Search of Man*, 296.
7. Ibid., 306.

overlook is that on every page of the same Bible we come upon God's hoping and waiting for his people's mighty acts.

Buber says, "To do the good deed is to fill the world with God; to serve God in truth is to draw Him into life."[8] It is characteristic of biblical faith that the Christian cannot be content with truth as mere idea or with truth as aesthetics, neither with the truth of a philosophical theorem nor with the truth of a work of art. Said Bernard of Clairvaux (1090–1153):

> There are those who seek knowledge for the sake of knowledge; That is curios-ity. There are those who seek knowledge to be known by others; That is vanity. There are those who seek knowledge in order to serve; That is love.

Truth must issue forth as action. Any quest for the truth must result in good deeds. This was C. S. Lewis's take on good works. The good deed both leads you to Christ and issues forth from a relationship with Christ. He believed that a genuine effort to live a truly moral life would eventually exasperate you and lead you to the source of true justification: Jesus. He also recognized that those who had already put their faith in Christ would express that faith in good actions. Our goal is *truth as deed*, and the striving toward this truth is its meaning and lasting significance. Messianic faith is imbued with the will to fashion the true community on earth. Its longing for God is the longing to prepare a place for him in the true community.

Heschel puts it succinctly when he says, "Action *is* truth." He goes on to say, "The deed is the elucidation of existence, expressing thirst for God with body and soul. The Jewish *mitzvah* (holy deed) is a prayer in the form of a deed. The *mitzvoth* are the Jewish sacraments, sacraments that may be performed in common acts of kindness."[9] If this is accepted, then the deed does in truth become the life center of religiosity.

At the risk of over-quoting Buber, we believe we must affirm with him that

> genuine religiosity has nothing in common with the fancies of romantic hearts, or with the self-pleasure of indulgent souls, or with the clever mental exercises of a practiced intellectuality. Genuine *religiosity is doing*. It seeks to carve the unconditioned out of the matter of this world. The face of God rests, invisible, in an earthen block; it must be wrought, carved, out of it. To engage in this work means to be religious—nothing else.[10]

8. Buber, *On Judaism*, 110–11. He adds, "I repeat: not truth as idea nor truth as shape or form but truth as deed is Judaism's task; its goal is not the creation of a philosophical theorem or a work of art but the establishment of true community."
9. Heschel, *Moral Grandeur*, 278.
10. Buber, *On Judaism*, 93 (emphasis ours).

Surely this is no different from the words of James, the brother of Jesus, "Religion that God our Father accepts as pure and faultless is this: to look after orphans and widows in their distress and to keep oneself from being polluted by the world" (James 1:27).[11]

Mission is a task! It defines us and gives God's people their distinctive and irreplaceable direction and purpose. To return to the imagery of the Menashe story, mission gives us our *name*. Any spirituality that attempts to avoid this must surely be a spurious one.[12] An inactive, purely reflective, personal faith is not typical of that modeled by Christ. This isn't to say that the reflective practices are not helpful. They surely are, but only when part of a broader actional, missional Christian life. In fact, we believe one worships more fully, prays more deeply, and studies more diligently when all are done in the context of a life of action and spiritual momentum.

A helpful illustration for this is that of sailing. In sailing, as in life, momentum is a valuable asset. President Woodrow Wilson once said,

> What is liberty? We say of a boat skimming the water with light foot, "How free she runs," when we mean, how perfectly she is adjusted to the force of the wind, how perfectly she obeys the great breath out of the heavens that fills her sails. Throw her head into the wind and see how she will halt and stagger, how every sheet will shiver and her whole frame will be shaken, how instantly she is "in irons," in the expressive phrase of the sea. She is free only when you have let her fall off again and have recovered once more her nice adjustments to the forces she must obey and cannot defy.[13]

Anyone who has ever been under sail will understand what Wilson is describing. When a sailing boat slams headfirst into the wind, she stops dead in her tracks. The expression, to be "in irons," says it all. The feeling of a boat at once in full flight then slapped in irons is a jarring one. Once the momentum is lost, its recovery can be slow and arduous. This betrays a clear and simple

11. So much of Scripture puts emphasis on action and nonaction. A classic example is Matthew 25, which is literally made up of a series of parables of judgment culminating in the profoundly unsettling parable of the sheep and the goats, which places the emphasis on action or nonaction as the gauge for judgment. Any Christian that is not unsettled by that parable, and many like it, must surely be in denial and is more than likely quoting Paul in favor of what Bonhoeffer called "cheap grace." This is precisely the way we must not use Paul. He would have been horrified. The Gospels are the primary texts of the missional church.

12. "From every deed an angel is born, a good angel or a bad one," wrote Buber in *The Life of the Hasidim*. "But from half-hearted and confused deeds which are without meaning or without power angels are born with twisted limbs or without a head or hands or feet." Maurice Friedman, *Religion and Psychology*, 6.

13. Quoted in Richard Bode, *First You Have to Row a Little Boat* (New York: Warner, 1995), 53.

principle governing movement and inertia. That is, a body in motion tends to stay in motion—and a body at rest tends to stay at rest. We think it no different for the life of a Christian. A life of action, movement, energy, and striving is the best place for the reflective practices of meditation, prayer, and reflection.

The Christian experience is richer when it has developed momentum under the steam of the Holy Spirit. In Luke's Gospel, Jesus sends out seventy-two disciples in pairs to do mission throughout the land. Luke reports, "The seventy-two returned with joy and said, 'Lord, even the demons submit to us in your name'" (Luke 10:17). Momentum has been established through action. It's in the doing of it that its meaning will become apparent. Just do it.

However, we are not advocating busyness for the sake of action. There's too much of that in the church as it is. Too many members of the clergy are run off their feet trying to keep the machinery of church oiled. A messianic spirituality gives rise to intentional, missional activity. Referring to the great biblical heroes of the faith, Martin Buber pointedly remarked,

> Once the great doer expected to alter the face of the world with his deed, and to inform all becoming with his own will. He did not feel that he was subject to the conditions of this world, for he was grounded in the unconditionality of God, whose Word he sensed in the decisions he made as clearly as he felt his blood in his veins. This confidence in the suprahuman has been undermined; man's consciousness of God and deed had already been stifled in his cradle; all one could hope for was to become the exponent of some small "progress." And whoever can no longer desire the impossible will be able to achieve nothing more than the all-too-probable. Thus the power of the spirit was replaced by busyness, and the might of sacrifice by bargaining skill.[14]

"Whoever can no longer desire the impossible will be able to achieve nothing more than the all-too-probable." That seems to describe the current malaise of the church.

How Then Shall We Live?

We want to suggest some possible missional implications of a shift from a more passive to a more active spirituality. Clearly the missional church that claims the deed as sacrament will be fully involved in life, evangelism, work among the poor, community groups and causes, and pubs and cafés. This is because the missional church realizes that it is finding God (or is God finding

14. Buber, *On Judaism*, 35.

us?) in those places previously perceived as "outside" of God because they were outside of the local faith community's mission program. Actually there is no such thing as seeking God, for there is nothing in which he cannot be found. It's all in the "seeing" and the perceiving. Having broadened our concept of God's involvement in the world and our part in it, Christians can then be free to engage missionally in any and every place. The whole world becomes an arena for the inbreaking of God's kingdom.

But an interesting spin-off of seeing action as sacrament is that it allows others to join in around a common activity. People have done this in all kinds of places. Any community that gathers around a cause, be it a justice issue or a common activity, is inviting action to be the center of its life together. Indeed many social movements begin when people gather to collectively voice concern or interest. Whether it is a sociopolitical cause (e.g., the campaign to free Nelson Mandela) or a social activity (e.g., a mural art project), the action itself can unite a wide variety of people around that activity. And these activities can become wonderful places for evangelism and mission. We witnessed some very interesting projects of this type in San Francisco recently when visiting with a missional group called *ReImagine* and in Los Angeles with a group of wild, radical believers called *Ichthus*, both of which we have referred to earlier in this book. They were doing what we will call *arts activism,* using art as a medium for missional change. Both these groups gather people around art projects and use these as their medium for church planting and incarnational mission. The missionaries in all these contexts are fundamental parts of the host community.

One of the most remarkable versions of arts activism we have seen is a project called *Cellspace* in downtown San Francisco. *Cellspace* is not a Christian organization; in fact, it is run by Marxist-Buddhist radicals. Cashed up by a $20,000 inheritance from the death of a grandparent, and inspired by a clear sense of vision, this group put down a deposit on a disused factory in San Francisco. A few guys moved in to live there, and they transformed the factory into one of the most vigorous incarnational cultural centers that we have witnessed. It is operated as a local cooperative, so anyone can join, and they use all forms of art to make social statements about the city and its policies. One night we visited, they were hosting an art exhibition in the front of the building and in the middle of the factory were running a short film festival about the plight of the homeless in the gentrification of downtown San Francisco. This is what Christian mission could look like. If God's people in this time are willing to be courageous enough to reconceive themselves as incarnational communities gathered for the purpose of changing the world (missional action), we believe they will have a significantly more profound impact than the current, passive, come-to-us and sit-in-the-pew mode of most churches. Besides being a better use of resources, multi-use buildings commit the church to a local work and invite many others to join together around that work. Action can become the organizational center of a community and so become a concrete expression of justice, mercy, and faithfulness (Matt. 23:23). For instance, many churches are now redesigning their buildings into sports or health centers, thus giving the church a less privatized and a more outward, missional thrust.

This is what *Elevation* (Alan's café project) aims at doing. The aim is to provide for what we earlier called "proximity spaces" for people to come from all walks of life and join in a host of activities. Most of these are not-yet-Christians, but in journeying together, and in doing things together, they will be invited into an ongoing conversation about God, meaning, and so on. Some of the activities include art classes, philosophy discussion groups, film reviews, mural projects, dance classes, cooking classes, cooperative purchasing, and anything in between. Activities become the focal center of the gatherings in all their forms. People vote with their feet and by their interests. In the case of *Cellspace* or *Ichthus*, the appeal is through art, but it can be anything. Art is a great medium to enter into organic discussion on meaning and purpose because true art is always dealing with these issues in some form or another. It does not have to be forced and inorganic.

In all the cases above, action has become a focal point of mission, and people are experiencing grace through the actions of Jesus' people. The church can begin to see itself as an agent of missional-action grace. The great strength of this approach to community development is that it allows for many people to join in, even if they might or might not be Christian in the classic definition of the term. It allows for the "centered set" of faith to draw people into an experience of Jesus in and through his community without the slightest loss of the evangelistic edge of the gospel. People experience God through what we do, and that is the secret.

Only a messianic spirituality offers us the resources to sacralize the ordinary and to make daily connections between heaven and earth. What postmodern people are crying out for is not better doctrine or clearer theology, but simply kindness in a chaotic and haphazard world. As Jesus himself said, "Let your light shine before others, that they may see your good deeds and praise your Father in heaven" (Matt. 5:16).

9

The Medium Really Is the Message

Everything is fine, but the ship is still heading in the wrong direction.

—Edward de Bono

The Great Escape

In the charming film *Chicken Run*, a group of hens are imprisoned in a chicken coop that is akin to a POW camp and made to work tirelessly producing eggs. Whenever a chicken fails to reach its quota, she is tagged for elimination—that is, the dinner table. In scenes reminiscent of the classic movie *The Great Escape*, Ginger, the heroine of *Chicken Run*, refuses to give up trying to organize a mass escape. She has a vision of what could be if they lived free. In a rather tragic scene, she is trying to share her vision and stir up another escape attempt when she realizes that most of her fellow hens have no concept of freedom. For them, this is the way it has always been. Why try and change it, when, as one hapless chicken claims, "This is a chikin's lot"—to lay eggs and then die.

Ginger is a real hero, because she refuses to give in to the prevailing consciousness of the prison camp. She's a prophet and a visionary and a darn good leader. At risk of her life and by enduring incarceration and suffering she eventually succeeds in organizing the most daring (and very unchickenlike, mind you) escape by building the most extraordinary flying machine. Through her vision and sacrifice, the entire flock are driven from their inertia, freed from their cowardice, saved, and finally delivered into a new life of security and freedom—all this not without significant risk to their lives. They all had to put themselves on the line.

Without being too dramatic, we believe this is precisely what is needed for missional leaders and radical disciples who know that the urgency of the day requires a significant shift from the predominant image of "church." It is not too harsh a judgment to say that most people in the Western church simply cannot see beyond the Christendom mode they know so well. Sadly, like Ginger's fellow prisoners, they simply cannot see things in another way at all. It's not uncommon in churches to hear leaders claiming that the way it is now is the way they've always done it. Those who call for radical change are often told to stop rocking the boat. The greatest silencing of the call for change often comes from leaders of large churches. They seem to be unaware of or untouched by any effects of significant social change. We have both been told more than once by large-church pastors that the church isn't doing so badly at all. This false sense of security is chicken-run thinking, where the shackles are primarily in the minds and consciousness of the inmates.

It is true that most concentration camp victims give up the hope of freedom and die a death of the spirit long before they die physically. This is because they've given up their inner freedom. Freedom is a condition of the soul whereas liberty is a condition of the body. One can have one's liberty removed, but no one can ever take away our sense of freedom. Inner freedom, therefore, as a function of our spirit, is our spirituality, as Søren Kierkegaard so profoundly perceived in his writings. And to break free from the shackles of a dying Christendom, we need to awaken a Christian spirituality that can nurture and envision an alternative reality of communal life together. If ever there were a time to act, it is now. This is the time for a new expression of authentic New Testament messianic spirituality to dream up an alternative vision of what the church and Christian life can be.

We believe that such a spirituality must be *missional and evangelistic* because it must be inspired by the gospel in all its dimensions, and it needs to adopt the same stance in relation to surrounding cultures that Jesus and the early church did—as the object of mission. To break out of the stultifying Christendom mode is going to require a courageous effort on the part of the few, already marginal Gingers in our midst. In this chapter we hope to awaken your desire to set out on a journey of discovery to search for a richer, more vigorous, relevant, and effective mode of Christian communal life. In order to do this, we will suggest what has been useful for us, and also propose different ways to interface with the basic elements of community, God, and world. We will also recommend a very powerful tool for critique, both of the messages that our lives communicate and also the message of our communities.

Who I Am Will Determine What I Do

Core to a messianic spirituality is the understanding that God changes us by changing our identity, our sense of self-definition. It really is that simple. In Christ, we are new creatures; we are inheritors of the kingdom; we are God's children; we are saints (holy ones). These are not just little tags used to describe the same reality we knew before we were saved. They are identities we take on when we are made alive with Christ (Rom. 6). Having undergone union with Christ in regeneration, we are then called to live out our basic identity shifts that took place in that event. If we are made into saints by our relation with Jesus, then we are exhorted to live consistently with that identity. What do "holy ones" do? They live holy lives. This is what scholars have called the *indicative* and the *imperative*. The *indicative* defines us, and the *imperative* calls us to live the definition out in daily life. Incidentally, this is how the New Testament, especially the Pauline Epistles, is structured. In almost every case the first half of Paul's letters are framed in the indicative (you are saved, justified, etc.). The second half is framed in the imperative (*therefore live as . . .*).

Who I am, or rather who I have become, in Jesus, *must* change the way I behave and determine to a great extent what I do. For example, if a person defines himself as a gourmet chef, you know what that person does. If someone defines herself as an athlete, then you can be sure she does a lot of athletic type activities. Our secondary identities determine our secondary purposes in life, and our *primary* identities determine our *primary* purposes in life.

We can both say that one of the greatest identity shifts that has taken place in our post-conversion life has been the embracing, and the subsequent living out, of a missionary identity. For Michael, it evolved as he began to embrace a role as an evangelist, preaching right across Australia in every denomination and every state. Simply preaching the gospel in churches where nary a nonbeliever could be found was a life-sapping experience for an evangelist. He became more and more aware of his need to train a new generation of missional leaders in order to free evangelism and mission from the pulpit and the local attractional church. This led to his appointment to the faculty of a seminary in Sydney. For Alan, it took place when he accepted a role with his denomination that placed him in charge of mission and revitalization for one of the southern states of Australia. He also remained in leadership at a local church to ensure that he remained a practitioner, not just a denominational bureaucrat. We both felt the imperative to be "in two places at once"—that is, as practitioners and theoreticians. As a result we were both involved in the inception of Forge, a missional training network in Australia, the US, and Canada. This ambidextrous approach has given us a unique strategic perspective of the church and Christianity in our land and highlighted the dilemma the church faces in the emerging global culture. It also highlighted that the church in the West had to adopt a missionary stance in relation to its cultural contexts or die. And so God birthed the missionary in us both.

This was no secondary identity shift, but rather something primal and *totally* reorienting. It changed everything, absolutely everything—the way we perceived the church, how we do ministry, why we even exist. It even included a thorough reconceptualization of the way we connected with God and perceived his working in the world, and how we could find him in the stranger places, places normal good ministers never ventured. Being missionaries to Australia has meant that we saw the whole function of ministry differently. In fact we no longer call ourselves ministers. For us both, being a *missionary* better defines us totally. This is so much the case that we have concluded that ministry itself must be redefined missionally. We would go so far as to say that ministry itself is a means to mission.[1]

We report this personal "conversion" because we believe that such a conversion is necessary for all who wish to become truly missional-apostolic. This is the genre of difference that made Ginger different from the other hens in the compound. She knew things could be, *had to be*, different if they were to survive and thrive as a community of chickens. The only way to see the real issues is to view them as a missionary would and to adopt exactly the same stance as a missionary would in any culture. It requires a conversion, no less. Anyone who dares to embrace a similar conversion will find themselves as a committed revolutionary, because you will know things are not what they seem in the matrix of the average Christendom church. It's time to fly the coop . . . literally!

We have chosen to address this issue in our section on messianic spirituality because it is an issue of the spirit and of the spirit's identity. Freedom always

---

1. We both believe that if we aim at ministry, we seldom get to do much mission. But if we aim at mission, we have to do ministry because ministry is the *means* by which mission is achieved. The established church has generally got this wrong. Most never get to do real mission with real outsiders because they aim primarily at the "saved." This we believe is a distortion of authentic New Testament faith and praxis. The church does not exist for itself but for its mission. Or as Emil Brunner said in his oft-quoted maxim, "The church exists by mission as fire exists by burning."

involves a certain danger because in every important choice one's whole personality is at stake. It also involves a willingness to see God differently and to fly from the confines of a previously binding paradigm. Another movie, *The Matrix*, struck a resonant chord with many Christians because it alerted them to that dangerous something that lies dormant at the heart of their identities as disciples of an untamable and wildly free Messiah. The name *disciple* should be synonymous with history maker. We are a people commissioned with a unique purpose that no other people group can, or will, do—namely, making disciples of Jesus. But to embrace such a commission one must, as in *The Matrix*, become committed to a certain *response*-ability, that of becoming a revolutionary, an activist committed to changing the way things are.

The Medium Is the Message

In the sixties, a significant thinker called Marshall McCluhan expounded a unique set of ideas on technology and media that brought the philosophy of existentialism and discipline of media studies together.[2] It was McCluhan who invented the phrase "the medium is the message."

To help us understand this as a powerful tool of assessment of the church and its missional impact, we will try to summarize what his seminal book, *On Media*, was about. When McCluhan uses the word "media," he is actually using it as a synonym for what we might call technology and technique, not media in the narrow sense of the word. He does this because he rightly maintains that all technologies, all tools, are essentially extensions of our selves and the human body. For instance, the wheel is essentially an extension of the foot. Weapons are basically extensions of the hand, the teeth, or the foot. A calculator is just an extension of our brain's ability to do addition, subtraction, and the like. Any technology is therefore a medium through which we outsource basic functions normally associated with human consciousness and bodily functions.

Now, having established that, McCluhan can say that the "message" of any medium or technology is the change of scale or pace or pattern that it introduces into human affairs. In other words, technologies create new social patterns and behaviors. For example, the railway did not introduce movement or transportation, nor did the wheel or roads, into human society. These were tools that had already been in use for a long time. What they did do was accelerate and enlarge the scale of previous human functions. And the result

2. Marshall McCluhan, *On Media* (London: Abacus, 1964), and Marshall McCluhan and Quentin Fiore, *The Medium Is the Message: An Inventory of Effects* (Watford: Penguin, 1967).

was to create totally new kinds of cities and new kinds of work and leisure. The invention and introduction of the steam engine, seen in this light, actually created what we now call the Industrial Revolution. Consider the impact of the printing press or the discovery of iron or of ships. The fact is that technologies have massive impacts on the way we perceive ourselves and our worlds, and how we pattern our societies—for good or ill (in most cases it is both).

Some of us have totally outsourced our brains to our smart phones. Even an ordinary tool like a diary can change our modes of awareness and our patterns of behavior.

Essentially the idea behind the phrase "the medium is the message" is this: *we shape our tools, and then they shape us.* What McCluhan wanted us to look at was the reciprocal effect that our tools and technologies have on us. They are not neutral things. They impact us deeply—much more than we are wont to believe—and we would do well to really think about what effects they have on us. Remember that this applies to all tools and techniques, including the ones the church has traditionally used.

One of the most significant and frightening aspects of this phenomenon is the electronic media, and here McCluhan sounded a particularly prophetic note. When one considers the electronic media like television, radio, and the internet, it's not difficult to see that they are extensions of the human capacity for thinking. McCluhan says that electronic media are extensions of human consciousness, and as a result we are in global embrace and have leased out our consciousness to corporate interests. The media moguls have in effect rented out our consciousness and are selling it back to us at a profit. In short, we are being shaped by the dollar and by corporate interests. Let us take McCluhan's theory and apply it to the tools that have been used by the Christendom-era church to do mission.

The Sermon

Let's face it! The entertainment industry—in particular, film—has changed traditional education and communication in profound ways, and the church had better take notice. If we think of Hollywood's making movies as just visual storytelling (and they are that), we miss seeing the reciprocal effect, i.e., movies make us! To apply a McCluhanite phrase, people have outsourced their imaginations to Hollywood. Movies have changed expectations about how we receive communication. With the average American seeing around one hundred movies a year, not to mention TV programs, music videos, and the net, preachers are forced to compete with multi-million-dollar film budgets in their efforts to get a message across. Sadly, in the communication of the gospel up until now, we have generally relied on one single tool—the mono-logue sermon. Will future generations be so overstimulated (is there any doubt that postmodern people today are extremely so?) that they will no longer be able to access a thirty-minute monologue in the same way their parents and grandparents did?

Now a preacher has to do amazing things to even catch folks' attention, let alone *really* communicate. The film-addicted generation thrives on hyperreality, in postmodern cultural theory language, and it's serious business. As a result of this appetite for hyperreality, the era of the monologue sermon that can have an impact is coming to an abrupt and sad end. It's worth asking whether Billy Graham will be the last of the great mass-communication preachers. We're not signaling the end of the spoken word to communicate, but preach-ers will need to have a long hard look at how they speak if they expect to be heard. Except for the preaching of outstanding communicators (and they have to be very good), sermons have little or no impact.[3] And let's not forget that preaching as we know it is only a tool and a somewhat overused one at that, one that comes more from Christendom's love of the philosophical art of rhetoric than it does from the Bible. Furthermore, it addicts the congrega-tion to the communicator. (Incidentally, that is another part of McCluhan's theory—technology is addictive! He uses the word "narcotic." Try doing without your computer.) Try envisaging church without a trained minister. We shape our tools and then they shape us. We invented the sermon (actually we borrowed the technique from the Greek and Roman philosophers), and then it reinvented us. We have become totally reliant on it! If you are a minister in the evangelical heart of the US, see what happens if you decide not to preach in church next Sunday.

The Building

Let us look at another area of church life to prove the profundity and usefulness of McCluhan's intellectual bequest to us; and then let's look at its

3. To test the validity of this statement, try to remember last week's sermon. Then, the previ-ous week's sermon. If you are not already struggling, try the one three weeks ago. Perhaps we've made our point. Research done in the US and in Australia asked recipients, "What are the main reasons you come to church?" Generally "community" scored number one, and preaching was consistently way down the list. We must take this seriously! If we do not, we are living in a fool's paradise. And in many cases it's not even paradise. Missionally speaking in Australia at least, nonbelievers are not coming to our churches at all precisely because of the perceived boredom factor. The Emperor of preaching has no clothes. We suggest you try dialogue instead—it cer-tainly goes better with the emerging global cultures and postmoderns when people are involved and add to the learning experience.

significance for a missional-apostolic spirituality. We discussed the impact of buildings on limiting our levels of incarnational ministry in the second section of this book. Our church buildings can create an us-versus-them mentality, but they can do more than that. They not only affect how we see *others*, they impact how we see *ourselves*. Let us return to an expression we used earlier. To paraphrase McCluhan: We *shape our buildings and then our buildings shape us.* We have been so profoundly shaped by buildings in Christendom that it is extremely hard to assess the real impact they, as tools, have had on our consciousness and our social patterns. For the vast majority, perhaps even all, of the congregations that Alan or Michael have ever done consultations with, it has been almost impossible for them to conceive of "church" without a building. Even the new church plants tend to think they are incomplete without them, kind of "churchless churches," as ridiculous as that sounds.

Most people know in their hearts that the Bible affirms that church is not a building but a community. When Jesus said, "I will build my church," we are sure he didn't have a construction program in mind. Buildings are merely tools, and it is always appropriate to remind ourselves of that fact. Christianity was at its most effective and most true to its nature as the people of God when it did not own any buildings. It was Christendom that gave us beautiful buildings and cathedrals and steeples and pews; all these have shaped us and imprisoned us and kept us from discovering real community for so long that it must be called a tragedy. Let us be clear here—buildings are useful. They are tools, sometimes vital tools, *but they are only tools nonetheless.* And when the use of a tool blunts our ability to fulfill our mission and purpose in the world, it must be questioned and dealt with appropriately.

A dear friend of ours and one of our heroes is a man named Ashley Barker who heads up a missionary order among the poorest of the poor in Melbourne and Bangkok. A few years ago Alan and Ashley attended a denominational conference together, one that was held in a brand-new megachurch building. Ash, in a totally nonjudgmental manner, asked the question, "I wonder what this medium says about the message?" It was an interesting question in that context, so we got to work on it. To begin, the walls were painted apricot and gray with no art or symbolism on them at all. The vast majority of the building was just row upon row of seating facing a large stage at the front featuring excellent lighting and sound equipment. So what indeed was the nonverbal message of that building? Our interpretation: the vast majority of the people were passive consumers. The few active people were the ones on the stage presented in a highly professional manner. They were the producers. The church looked like it was designed for the presentation of a show of some sort. The building exuded wealth, success, and professionalism. All the needs of the consumer were catered to. But what did that building (or even any traditional church building) say to the average not-yet-Christian about the gospel?

Our mission and our context must determine the selection and the nature of our tools, not the other way around. If we are not deliberate about this, the reciprocal effect of our tools will catch us out. Sell the building and free your congregation or rework it missionally so then its effect will be missional. Run a basketball camp in it during the week, operate a medical health center, operate a café, develop a cooperative supermarket, run a community vegetable garden. But move from the static, attractional, once-a-week, high cost building use to missional buildings—ones that create proximity spaces between God's people and the surrounding communities. We can design buildings that people flow organically toward. Churches could provide community health during the week. Make the building shape the congregation positively and missionally. We need to design our tools, not let our tools design us.

The Seminary

There is another tool used by the church that has significant strategic implications for the development of missional leaders and churches in our day. The issue is that of our ministry development systems. They have such a massive impact and are so central in renegotiating a future that we simply must have a look at them in light of McCluhan's dictums.

There seems to be something about the way we are training leaders that is making the church dysfunctional. Consider the "tools" of our training systems—the seminaries—and the techniques being employed in them and then ask, "How have these tools reinvented us?" Then to seek the answer, we have to observe the effects of the tool on the leadership and ministry of the churches that these tools helped produce. If the medium is the message, what is this medium saying about the message? What is the implicit "message" of the seminary? If the shape of the academy looks like a room full of chairs all facing the front with a platform and a lectern, it oughtn't to surprise us that church buildings look the same. Likewise, the model of having one expert passing on information isn't too different from a church service.

Of course, we acknowledge there's much more to church life than just this, but is this not the archetype which is produced in almost every dimension of church life? We've outsourced biblical knowledge and discipleship to the experts. And we all collaborate with this because it's the system and it's comfortable (remember *Chicken Run*?). For this reason Michael has pioneered one of Australia's leading internship-based models of leadership development. At

Morling Seminary in Sydney his students are not expected to simply sit in rows and absorb volumes of words presented in monologue form. He has sought to embrace an action-reflection style of learning. Many seminaries around the world are trying this shift, but the vast majority continue to perpetuate the classic lecture style. The medium *is* the message! You can say something verbally a thousand times, but the time when you truly communicate will be the time when your point is more deeply learned. People reproduce what they have experienced. There is much truth in the popular dictum, "Your actions are speaking so loudly, I can't hear your words."

Many might be content with the classic model and its implications for ministry and mission, but for us there are serious issues of vital strategic importance involved when it comes to trying to experiment with new forms of Jesus communities and in trying to develop forms of incarnational-contextualized mission. To birth a truly missional-incarnational church, we need a new tool. Remember, the seminary is just that—a tool. Is it time to rethink and reimagine what leadership and theological formation would be like in a new paradigm? It's worth asking about the ways Jesus developed disciples during his ministry and then considering to what degree the theological academy has mirrored this. Has the traditional model been effective? In other words, is the medium of the "academy" the right medium for the message of disciple making and mission?

We Are Our Messages

What we want to do now is bring McCluhan's probing questions to bear on the related issues of personal and corporate spirituality. If we take seriously that the medium is the message, then there's no way around the fact that our actions, as manifestations of our total being, do actually speak much louder than our words. There are clear nonverbal messages being emitted by our lives all the time. We are faced with the sobering fact that we actually *are* our messages.

Søren Kierkegaard, the Danish philosopher, called this "existence-communication" by which he meant that our lives—our very existence—is our communication. Your existence as an authentic human being communicates more than what you *say* or even what you think. Kierkegaard despised the philosopher Wilhelm Hegel who held that all truth could be grasped objectively. With stinging irony he points out that "Hegel builds a magnificent tower but lives in a hut." What he meant by that is that Hegel could not live in the real world in the ideological system he had produced. It was all ideas. And he was not a "player" in that world, so to speak, but a distant observer. In other words, he was not his own message. Living in ideas is the very contradiction to living in actuality, but to live in books is the philosopher's constant temptation. The only essential sermon one can listen to and appropriate comes not from the pulpit via the minister's words but from one's own existence.

This is essentially the message of biblical existentialism. Commenting on Kierkegaard's thinking, Frederick Sontag says,

> Existence corresponds to the individual, not the concept of the universal. To conceptualize is to dissolve existence into possibility and away from actuality. As far as contact with actuality is concerned, to increase our powers of conceptualization is a step backwards. The aim is to move from possibility toward actuality, that is, to determine a concrete action. For instance, to transform Christianity into "science and scholarship" is an error, since if it succeeds Christianity will be abolished. Its existence lies on another plane of individual decisiveness. Christianity is not a doctrine but an "existence communication."[4]

This has been the problem of Christendom—the reduction of Christianity into science and scholarship. We need to take seriously the fact that the medium—our lives—conveys very definite messages, ones that are being read all the time by the people around about us. This is a rather disturbing truth as it has already been noted that "your actions are so loud I can't hear your words." So what is the message of my life? Am I being read as a disciple? Do people see a clear picture of Jesus through my personhood?

Take our middle classness for instance: We seldom stop to question some of the very unbiblical assumptions that are built into the experience of being middle class. Assumptions about security, prestige, power, money, competition, family, education, and so forth, make up the sociological category of class. And so many of these assumptions remain quite untested in terms of the gospel. And yet we would have to confess that so often our middle classness undermines and attenuates the gospel message. To be perfectly honest, Alan confesses to an internal struggle that driving a company car and owning a house in inner-city Melbourne communicates a status that he does not wish to communicate. These things are not neutral. Our cars, houses, and education symbolize status in a profound way. And what do they say about the gospel? If we are going to effectively evangelize our relevant cultures, these things *have* to come under scrutiny. We can never just leave the issue of our class or our culture out of the equation of what it means to be disciples of Jesus. His life must interpret ours, especially at the level of class and culture. And if we wish to embody the message of Jesus, and we wish for people to

4. Frederick Sontag, *A Kierkegaard Handbook* (Atlanta: John Knox, 1979), 42–43.

see him through us, then these things must be tested—for the sake of the message and the mission.

Many philosophies and theologies attempt to understand existence by subtracting the human person/actor/individual from the equation, as if truth is something out there and irrelevant to being human. But in Kierkegaard's world, knowing the truth and being the truth is the same thing. The truth is not "out there"; it must be "in here." This complex piece of Kierkegaardia is worth tussling with. Though the following quote sounds confusing, read it over carefully to distill its power:

> The truth consists not in knowing the truth intellectually but in *being* the truth. . . . Knowing the truth is something which follows as a matter of course from being the truth, and not conversely. And it is precisely for this reason it becomes untruth when knowing the truth is separated from being the truth, or when knowing the truth is treated as one and the same thing as being the truth, since the true relation is the converse of this: to be the truth is one and the same thing as knowing the truth.[5]

J. V. Taylor, the British missiologist, once remarked, "How secondary, indeed how futile, are all the means of communication unless they are actually born out of the very truth they are meant to convey." With this statement we are back to that age-old question of *personal integrity* (living true to that which we hold as true).[6] Truth cannot be known divorced from life itself. If it is true, then it must be my truth. It must change me. I must be involved in it. Truth means subjective change and involvement.[7]

To turn to Martin Buber again, he says,

> A "zaddik" (a righteous person) said about the rabbis who "speak Torah" (i.e., who interpreted the Scriptures for others) "What is the sense of their speaking Torah? Man should act in such a way that all his behavior is a Torah, and he himself is a Torah." At another time it is said, "The aim of the wise man is to make himself into a perfect teaching, and make all his acts as bodies of instruction; and where it is not possible for him to attain to this, his aim is to be a transmission of the teaching and a commentary on it, and to spread the teaching by each of his movements." . . . The people in whom this Torah-nature fulfills

5. Søren Kierkegaard, "Training in Christianity," quoted in Abraham Heschel, *A Passion for Truth* (London: Seckler & Walbury, 1973), 163–64.

6. One of our friends, Mark Collier, says that if he could be the same person in three places, he would have achieved holiness. The challenge is to be the same person at church, at work, and at home.

7. Perhaps another way of saying this to theologians would be that *the imperative is implicit in the indicative.*

itself are called zaddiks, "the righteous," the law-*full*. They are the bearers of . . . teaching, not only as its apostles, but more as its effective reality. *They are the teaching.*[8]

Buber says in another place: "Every person, by living authentically, shall become a Torah, an instruction."[9] Isaiah, Jeremiah, Paul, James, Tertullian, Francis, Luther, Wesley, Bonhoeffer, Martin Luther King Jr., and Jesus—especially Jesus—belong to those central figures in the history of our faith who have done their work by *living* in a certain way; not from out of a teaching but toward a teaching, who have lived in such a way that their lives acted as a teaching not yet translated into words. Their lives communicated their message.

On another somewhat disquieting note, and this relates particularly to missional apostolic leadership, we need to recognize that an authentic community can only be founded on changed relations between people; and these changed relations can only follow the inner change and preparation of the people who lead, work, and sacrifice for the community. In other words, it must begin with leadership. We must embody our visions and our values in such a way that people can "see" the vision in and through our existence. It will take sacrifice on the part of the leader. It must, especially if he or she is asking for sacrifice! We simply don't believe that people in the "crap-detector" generation, savvy people who understand what it means to be constantly targeted by hundreds of thousands of clever sales messages, are going to follow other people who don't live out their messages. If leadership fails to embody the message, no one is going to follow. Leaders, you cannot lead where you will not go; you cannot teach what you do not know.

Beyond the Either/Or Church

In this section we want to suggest ways in which the church can structure its communal life in a way that embodies a missional-messianic spirituality. Behind this is the belief that the medium of the church itself must communicate a message that helps people find God in every sphere of life and not just within the confines of the church and in church activities.

To do this we need to go back briefly to the issue of dualism. We raise the issue of dualism again because it is so easy to embody this belief in the very structures and activities of the church in a way that counters any life-affirming message we might wish to portray verbally. Again, the actual medium of the

8. Italics ours. Buber, *Mamre*, 79–80.
9. Buber, *On Judaism*, 92.

church is the message. If we could diagrammatically demonstrate this dualistic structure of church it might look like this:

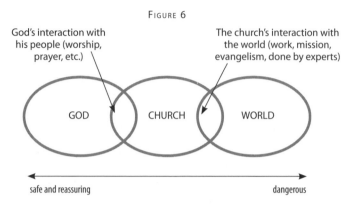

FIGURE 6

God's interaction with his people (worship, prayer, etc.)

The church's interaction with the world (work, mission, evangelism, done by experts)

GOD   CHURCH   WORLD

safe and reassuring   dangerous

Dualistic/Christendom Mode

In this diagram one can envisage the unconscious perception of the average churchgoer's church experience as something like this:

One enters the church (the middle circle). This is a neutral space of like-minded people. It is kind of safe and reassuring to be there. Then one goes into the chapel area (symbolized by the interface between the "God" and "Church" circles) and there hears the call to worship; the music kicks in, and the worship starts. Now one is beginning to experience God. After the communal singing and the intimacy with God that is experienced there, our typical churchgoer (let's call her Jane) is then exposed to the Word of God in the sermon. She then experiences God deeply as personal Savior in the sacraments. Some more songs and Jane is out again into the middle circle having a coffee or a soda with her Christian friends. She then has to face going out into the world (symbolized by the "World" circle). The world in Jane's (dualistic) perception is a dangerous place for Christians. God is not perceived as being "in the world." It's a harassing experience and she barely makes it to midweek cell group where she again encounters God in the same way as she did on Sunday. Also, she has her quiet times when God "turns up," but other than that she is on her own in a spiritually dangerous place.

If you'll forgive the over-simplification, we're sure that all of us raised in evangelical Christendom can relate in some way to the basic experience described here. This is pretty much the standard experience of "church." The tragedy is that *everything* in this medium of church sets Jane up to experience her life as fundamentally dualistic. Even the sermon is unrelated to life and overly conceptual. No one has necessarily intended it to be this way—it's just somehow in the medium and in the fundamental assumptions that underlie much Christendom theology and practice. No matter how seeker friendly one might wish to make the service, it still communicates dualism. In the end God is experienced as a church god and not the God of all of life, including church. There is no missional edge to a community structured in this way. Its institutional message always works against, and thus cancels out, its overt verbal messages. And its spirituality sets people up to fail in seeing their work, play, and study as ministry or mission. Ministry is a churchy thing and is done by the experts. It is almost ridiculous to say at this point that the New Testament church was nothing like this. It's that Christendom thing again.

Can we suggest that there is another way to configure these three elements of the diagram? There is another stance we can take in relation to God, World, and the Church. This stance in our phraseology is missional-incarnational-messianic-apostolic. It brings together the four elements of this book. We believe it is a powerful shift from the normative Christendom church. Consider the following diagram:

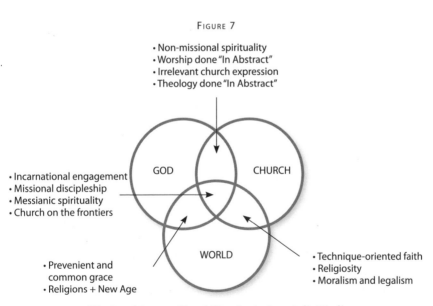

FIGURE 7

• Non-missional spirituality
• Worship done "In Abstract"
• Irrelevant church expression
• Theology done "In Abstract"

• Incarnational engagement
• Missional discipleship
• Messianic spirituality
• Church on the frontiers

GOD   CHURCH

WORLD

• Prevenient and
  common grace
• Religions + New Age

• Technique-oriented faith
• Religiosity
• Moralism and legalism

Missional-Incarnational-Messianic-Apostolic Mode

By reorienting the three circles we can visualize the Christian experience in an altogether different way. When we conceive of all three circles as coming together at the center, there we have a church that is truly missional, deeply incarnational, and acting in a way that extends the ministry of Jesus into the world. In this mode our worship of God is always done in the context of our mission, is culturally meaningful, and has definite missional edges, as it is open to all. Our evangelism and social action is communal, we join with God in redeeming the world (he's already there!), and our spirituality is of the all-of-life variety.

This is exactly what *Elevation* (the café project in St. Kilda, Melbourne) was all about—a convergence of God's people, mission, spirituality, and community in an organic incarnational way that has the potential to literally transform whole districts. And this is what we try to engender in the interns of Forge Mission Training Network; one of the most rewarding elements of working with the Forge interns is when we see the lights go on as the idea dawns on them that they really can bring all the disparate elements of their lives together and still call it "church." Church needn't be something excluded from the rest of life. In fact we believe it is only true to God's own purpose when it ties together all the loose ends under the one God. The fact is that God is everywhere. He is already deeply involved in human history and in all people's lives. The challenge for us in transitioning to this mode lies in the circle named "church." The church needs to adjust its position in relation to God and the world. And to do this we must break the bondage of dualism. We've got to "fly the coop" with Ginger.

Partners with God

There's a riddle in the Talmud that goes like this, "If God intended man to live on bread, why didn't he create a bread tree?" And the answer is that, in fact, God could have created a tree that produced crusty loaves of bread, but he prefers to offer us a grain and invite us to buy a field and plant the seed. He prefers that we till the soil while he sends the rain. He prefers that we harvest the crop while he sends sunshine. He prefers that we grind the grain and knead it and bake it while he gives us air in our lungs and strength in our arms. Why? Because he would rather we become partners with him in creation.

Of course, God could simply supply our every need and solve our every problem. But our God invites us into a creative partnership with him. He supplies the earth, the air, the water, the sun, and our strength and then asks us to work with him. So it is with mission. We suppose he could have converted the whole world by now, but he prefers partnership to mere accomplishment.

One of the truly great missional leaders in Australia is a man named John Smith. He heads up one of the most prolific incarnational mission movements in that country. He has done evangelism in many schools, pubs, motorcycle gangs, Parliament, and anything in between. John is a true Wesleyan and has taken this teaching and really run with it. John tells some stories that exemplify this teaching—here is just one of them:

One day, after an evangelistic campaign, a beautiful young woman approached John and begged him to come and meet her. She was deeply moved by what he said and needed to talk further. Sadly, John explained that he needed to go quickly to his next speaking engagement and couldn't spare the time right then. But she was so insistent in her need to find out more about Jesus that he agreed to come and meet with her later that night. She thrust a piece of paper in his hand, asking him to meet her at that address, and ran off. Later when he checked the note, he realized that she had arranged to meet him at one of the city's most notorious strip clubs. He was in a bit of a dilemma. It is John's normal practice that whenever he is entering edgy places, he always takes another member of his team. But John thought this could well be a setup by one of the sleaze newspapers to take a photo of one of Australia's leading evangelists going into a strip joint, so he decided to go, but to go alone. (Whatever one might think of the wisdom of that choice, we ask you to hold your judgment and so get to the core of the story.)

And so he arrived at the striptease club, found a table, and asked the waitress to get Linda (not her real name). When the waitress returned, she brought him a drink but not Linda. When he told her that he had been asked to meet Linda there that night, the waitress, still not believing the story, asked for his name. When he told her his name was John Smith, she replied, "Oh yeah sure, everyone is John Smith in this place." Eventually he persuaded her to get Linda.

When she arrived Linda thanked John profusely for coming and began to tell the story of her life. She had always loved dancing and always wanted to be a performer. At seventeen she met a young Christian guy and fell in love. He took her to hear John at his church (called Truth and Liberation Concern in Melbourne), and that day she became a Christian. However, her boyfriend came from an ultraconservative denomination that looked down on all types of worldliness, especially dancing in all its forms. And so the parents forced the young man to end their relationship. It was dancing or him. She chose dancing. This devastated Linda because she quite rightly associated Jesus with the actions of his people, in this case some exceedingly narrow people. Subsequently she gave up on the church, her faith, and devoted herself to a career in dancing. Life didn't go all that well for her—she could get no jobs, dancing or otherwise; and against her better judgment she ended up stripping for a living, claiming that at least she could dance and that the money was good. It's the story of so many in that sad industry.

As they talked about her family, her dreams, Jesus, and the meaning of things, she felt that it was time for her to come back to Jesus. John led her back to Christ right there in the club. This might have been the end of a simple story of a young woman's journey back to Jesus but for the strange twist at the end of the tale. When it came time for her to strip again, she turned to the man who had just prayed a prayer of recommitment with her and asked him to stay and watch her dance. Not many evangelists find themselves in this situation because most of them confine their "witnessing" to churches. Here was Australia's leading evangelist being begged by a recent convert to watch her routine. John thought this was taking it a bit far, but again Linda prevailed, and he stayed for the dance. (Again we ask you to withhold your moral judgment here; John has always kept a very rigorous accountability in these things and sees himself as an ambassador of Christ in the toughest of places.) Anyhow, she did her dance. The choice of the song was "Only Seventeen" by Janis Ian. The song is all about rejection and being an "ugly duckling." She had woven the story of her loss of faith into her strip act.

Now the question John asks, and we now ask of you, is this, "Was Jesus in that strip club that night?" You must attempt an answer here. Can God be found in that place of tragedy and brokenness? We believe that to be biblical you must answer in the affirmative. Well, the question that follows is the key missional one. If God was in that place, wooing Linda to himself through Jesus Christ, was it all right for John to join him in mission in that place? In the act of redeeming a broken life? Had God prepared the soil, caused the sun to shine and the rain to fall? Had God prevened the situation so that John might watch that striptease and lead that woman away from sin and into wholeness? And the answer we leave to you. We believe you can guess ours.

The point we want to make here is not that we should all go to the strip clubs and evangelize the strippers. Both of us (Michael and Alan) agree that we probably couldn't go there without stumbling. But that isn't the point. That's incidental to the real God story going on in the narrative. The question that must drive us is the question of whether we can join with God in his mission—in whatever place we find ourselves. The evangelicalism that grips the church in the West teaches us (implicitly and explicitly) that we take God with us where we go in mission. We "tell" people about God, assuming quite falsely that they have had no God experiences, or epiphanies as we called them earlier in the book, prior to that point. This is simply unbiblical! The fact is God was already there! He was always there wooing, forever courting, constantly wowing, and acting redemptively by drawing people to himself. It's like he's saying, "Look at my magnificent Son! Isn't he something! Go on, talk with him. . . ."

Let's go back for a moment to figure 7 above. It represents the three coinciding circles where missional faithfulness is rendered—where God *and* world *and* God's people meet. That is the space for prevenient grace to transform into saving grace. We have for so long done our church thing and our spirituality, even our evangelism, apart from the world that we have no real concept of real missional-incarnational engagement. This again was not the case in the book of Acts and in the early church. And it most certainly was not the case for Jesus, who couldn't seem to get enough of hanging out in the pubs with the Lindas of his world. It was precisely this that offended the sensibilities of the religious people of his day. Jesus did it anyway because he loved the lost and the broken, the "sinners" and the marginalized, and wanted them to come to know God through him. The kingdom of God came upon them in Jesus, and it can come upon others through us (we are agents of the kingdom, aren't we?) if only we can get out and mix it up with normal people on their turf. A small attempt at South Melbourne Restoration Community, a church committed to being a gateway for twenty- to thirty-somethings, has them holding their Alpha program in the local pub where people can come and join the discussions. This is only a small way in which a church can break out and the kingdom can break in.

Toughen up! Get out of the chicken coop, trust God, get accountable, go out in twos, and let it happen. If you don't know what you're doing, follow Jesus; he's the best model of mission we know. It's time to fly the coop!

PART FOUR

APOSTOLIC LEADERSHIP

10

The Genius of APEST

There is one thing stronger than all the armies in the world: and that is an idea whose time has come.

—Victor Hugo

A New Kind of Leadership

In this chapter we want to explore perhaps one of the most significant aspects needed for the transition from Christendom mode to a missional mode of church—a shift to apostolic leadership. In fact, without this the missional church is unlikely to rise at all, and if it does manage to survive birth, it will not last long because it will lack the leadership structure to sustain it over the long distance. If anything, a new *type* of leadership must precede any meaningful transition to missional church. And so, in this section, we want to properly introduce the final part of our four key characteristics of the new forms of church emerging in our day—namely, *missional, incarnational, messianic,* and now *apostolic.* When combined with the first three in various ways, *apostolic* leadership provides an essential element for the new expressions of church.

A renewed focus on leadership is absolutely essential to the renewal and growth of the church. But that begs the question, "What *kind* of leadership?" The church has got plenty of "leaders" now, but they're not effectively impacting our culture. So it follows that we must be speaking about a very different type of leadership. Alan's most recent book, *The Permanent Revolution,* is a book completely dedicated to exploring a missional leadership for a

P.F.S.G.

missional movement.[1] There, as well as here, we argue that the development of a new kind of leadership is possibly the single most important question of strategy in this decade, and whether the church responds correctly or not will determine to some extent its survival as a viable expression of the gospel in the years to come.[2]

To answer the question about what new kind of leadership is required, we turn again to the Apostle Paul and his directions in Ephesians 4:1–16:

> As a prisoner for the Lord, then, I urge you to live a life worthy of the calling you have received. Be completely humble and gentle; be patient, bearing with one another in love. Make every effort to keep the unity of the Spirit through the bond of peace. There is one body and one Spirit—just as you were called to one hope when you were called—one Lord, one faith, one baptism; one God and Father of all, who is over all and through all and in all.
>
> *But to each one of us grace has been given as Christ apportioned it. . . . It was he who gave some to be apostles, some to be prophets, some to be evangelists, and some to be pastors and teachers, to prepare God's people for works of service, so that the body of Christ may be built up until we all reach unity in the faith and in the knowledge of the Son of God and become mature, attaining to the whole measure of the fullness of Christ.*
>
> Then we will *no longer be infants*, tossed back and forth by the waves, and blown here and there by every wind of teaching and by the cunning and craftiness of men in their deceitful scheming. Instead, speaking the truth in love, we will *in all things grow up* into him who is the Head, that is, Christ. From him the whole body, joined and held together by every supporting ligament, grows and builds itself up in love, as each part does its work.

We will examine some of the implications of this text by seeing it from two perspectives: theological and sociological. Before we begin to explore the text theologically, it will be helpful if we introduce our use of various terms (we direct you to the glossary at the rear of this book for further clarification). We will refer at times to the "ministry matrix" and "leadership matrix" as two dimensions of what has traditionally been called the fivefold ministry pattern found in the Ephesians text. And in order to avoid the cumbersome term "fivefold ministry," we have substituted it with the term APEST. APEST simply describes the five functions in this text: Apostle, Prophet, Evangelist, Shepherd, and Teacher. As the above text progresses, we perceive a shift in focus

---

1. Alan Hirsch and Tim Catchim, *The Permanent Revolution: Apostolic Imagination and Practice for the 21st Century Church* (San Francisco: Wiley, 2012).

2. It was with this in mind that we developed Forge. The idea was to train and develop a distinctly new breed of leader in the *pioneering, missional* mode. Refer to chapter 12 on structure for a more comprehensive philosophy of missional-apostolic training and development.

from organic and theological unity to APEST ministry and leadership, or to what we call the mechanism of maturity. It is our intention to make a case for the rediscovery of an APEST type of ministry and leadership in our churches.

The Theology of APEST

When we turn our attention to Paul's words above, we begin with the assumption that the book of Ephesians is one of the *General* Epistles and that, like most of these general letters, it was circulated among the house churches in the region of Ephesus. This is important to note at this point because it means that this letter provides insights into Paul's general teaching and practice in all the churches, not just one. This has implications for all churches everywhere, and we would add, at all times.[3]

Furthermore, this teaching is found in Ephesians, which is Paul's primary tract on the nature of the church itself and the nature of the ministry of the church. Ephesians and its teaching forms part of Paul's fundamental ecclesiology, and as such, ought to be read as a fundamental description, even a prescription, of the church in all ages.

The flow of the passage seems clear enough as the diagram below illustrates:

FIGURE 8

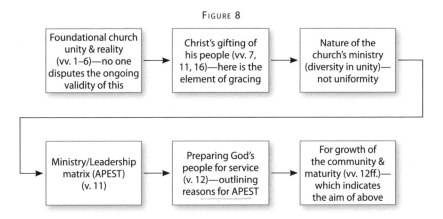

It begins with that timeless call to strive to maintain the essential unity of the church in spite of its complex diversities and contexts. This makes even more sense when you consider that Paul was about to commend an egalitarian community of leaders, all offering different types of leadership to the body of

3. There is no New Testament hermeneutic principle, other than the ones based on purely ideological assumptions, that would limit the scope of this text to just the early church period.

Christ.[4] With the acceptance of diversity comes a heightened call for unity, a unity based in one Spirit, one faith, one baptism, one Lord, one God and Father of all (4:1–6).

Paul then goes on to speak of Christ's act of gifting or gracing of his people for ministry.

> But to *each one of us* [read literally as "to *all* Christians"!] *grace has been given as Christ apportioned it. . . .* It was *he who gave* [i.e., he distributed them in this way] *some* to be apostles, *some* to be prophets, *some* to be evangelists, and *some* to be pastors [shepherds] and teachers. (vv. 7, 11)

These verses seem to underscore the fact that the church's ministry is fundamentally charismatic by nature.[5] This is important to recognize because it allows us to move away from the notion of APEST ministry as *office* to that of *function*. Jesus' gracing of his church cannot be institutionalized into office.[6]

What we are arguing for here is a rediscovery of the fullness of Pauline teaching about Christian ministry. In effect, this will mean for many traditional-Christendom churches a full inclusion (as opposed to the historic exclusion) of the invigorating roles of apostle and prophet and evangelist in the church today. The Pauline logic that asserts the church is gathered around *one Lord/faith/baptism* is the same logic that says God has specifically and deliberately (and with purpose) placed this pattern of ministry/gifting in his church. We therefore claim that this text is grammatically, theologically, and thematically indivisible. There simply can be no other conclusion. One cannot break the text into compartments without destroying its total meaning and force. It seems that the doctrine of the church's unity and faith is therefore inextricably linked with a comprehensive understanding of the function of APEST in the life of the church. The church and its fundamental ministry are one. In fact the mission is here *directly* related to its ministry structure.

4. We prefer not to use the term *egalitarian*, because it is such an Enlightenment idea that is so historically loaded. We don't believe the New Testament posits any leadership in a simply democratic sense. It seems much more subtle than that, being more about gifting, character, and especially, calling. However, we cannot come up with a better term.

5. Not necessarily charismatic in terms defined by the sociological phenomenon called the "charismatic movement," but mainly in terms of its theological implications; i.e., of God's enabling/empowering grace for ministry. At core, *charis* lies at the root of all charisma and therefore at the heart of ministry.

6. If this is recognized, then we can avoid the unhelpful historic controversy about the unique historical function of the original twelve apostles in relation to the ongoing validity of apostolic service and ministry. Clearly, any further apostolic ministry cannot replace the fundamental eyewitness role of the original twelve. In asserting an apostolic dimension to ministry, in no way do we suggest a reinstitution of the apostolic office of the original apostles.

More than this, if we read the passage as a unit, the church's inherent capacity to mature is inextricably interwoven with its capacity to foster a full-fledged APEST-style ministry and leadership system. The connection between this APEST and the church's maturity and mission is direct and undeniable. Listen again to Paul in verses 12–16:

> To *prepare* God's people for works of service, so that the body of Christ *may be built up* until we all *reach unity in the faith* and in the knowledge of the Son of God *and become mature, attaining* to the *whole measure* of the fullness of Christ.
> *Then* we will *no longer be infants,* tossed back and forth by the waves, and blown here and there by every wind of teaching and by the cunning and craftiness of men in their deceitful scheming. *Instead,* speaking the truth in love, we will in all things *grow up into him* who is the Head, that is, Christ. From him the whole body, joined and held together by every supporting ligament, grows and builds itself up in love, *as each part* [namely, APEST] *does its work.*

As we interpret this, Paul actually sees APEST ministry as *the* very mechanism for achieving mission and ministry effectiveness and Christian maturity. He seems to be saying that without a fivefold ministry pattern we *cannot* mature. If this is true, it is impossible to estimate what terrible damage the church has done through the loss, even active suppression, of this crucial dimension of New Testament ministry and leadership. But if we take these verses at face value, then it is our contention that the impact has been significant indeed. Perhaps the fact that APEST has not been intentionally nurtured and practiced might have something to do with the immaturity we find in the Western church that inhibits fulfillment of its mission. Verse 14 could well be a description of church history in the West—we have been tossed about, immature, infantile.

We think it is to the detriment of the mission of the church that the role of evangelist has been marginalized and made itinerant rather than localized. And we see it as even more concerning that the functions of prophet and apostle have been ignored by mainstream churches altogether. But we reiterate our belief that only when all five are operating in unity or harmony can we see effective missional engagement begin to occur. Shepherds and teachers have had more than their share of responsibility in church leadership. It's time for the recovery of some sense of balance.

For clarification, we offer the following definitions of the five foundational leadership functions as mentioned in Ephesians 4. In doing so, we are not ascribing them to *any* office.

- *Apostolic function,* usually conducted translocally, pioneers new missional works and oversees their development.

- *Prophetic function* discerns the spiritual realities in a given situation and communicates them in a timely and appropriate way to further the mission of God's people.
- *Evangelistic function* communicates the gospel in such a way that people respond in faith and discipleship.
- *Shepherding function* oversees the people of God by leading, nurturing, protecting, and caring for them.
- *Teaching function* communicates the revealed wisdom of God so that the people of God learn how to obey all that Christ has commanded them.

These functions are primary areas of ministry but are not mutually exclusive. For example, a person who teaches may lead a person to Christ; one who operates apostolically in establishing a new missional work may also function in pastoring and teaching; one who communicates the gospel may establish a new missional work or may teach the new disciple; and one who is used of God prophetically may also be used evangelistically. The point is that these are descriptions of the primary functions of people called to these spheres of mission.

All these working together result in the equipping of the saints to do the work of ministry and in the maturity of the body. The whole framework of the letter to the Ephesians expects mutual recognition of these callings and a mutual accountability for their operation.[7] The following table is a helpful summary. It looks at each of the five ministry and leadership functions and explores each one's focus, myopia, and impact.[8]

Role	Definition	Focus	Myopia	Impact
APOSTLE	One who is sent to establish	Urgency of tomorrow	Demands of today	EXTENSION
PROPHET	One who knows the direction	Demands of today in the light of tomorrow	Demands of today	UNDERSTANDING
EVANGELIST	One who champions the cause	Urgency of today	Demands of today	EXPANSION
SHEPHERD	One who cares for God's people	Demands of today	Urgency of tomorrow	NURTURE

7. We are thankful to our colleagues on the International Missional Team (IMT) of Churches of Christ in the following three nations: Australia, the United Kingdom, and New Zealand, for hammering out these working definitions. The IMT is an example of a strategic body that is taking APEST seriously enough to try and work it right through the denominational system.

8. Modified and adapted from a diagram by Dwight Smith.

Role	Definition	Focus	Myopia	Impact
TEACHER	One who clarifies the truth	Integration of the whole	Time	INTEGRATION

As you can see, we are defining some of these functions more broadly than some (particularly Pentecostal) leaders have drawn them. We would see an apostle as being someone who is moving the church into extension, church planting, crossing frontiers, and embracing significant movement beyond itself. We would see a prophet as one who knows the mind of God on issues affecting the church and who speaks into the community eliciting transformation and growth. And let us emphasize that for maximum, missional impact, APEST functions must not merely be limited to the leadership community within the church, but must be exercized by the whole church. In other words, we want to suggest a two-dimensional reading of APEST—one dimension that describes the *leadership system* (the leadership matrix) and the other that describes the *whole church's ministry* (the ministry matrix). Some will be called as apostles, but the whole community is to be apostol*ic*. Some will be called to be evangelists, but the whole community is to be evangelis*tic*. This can be diagrammatically represented as follows:[9]

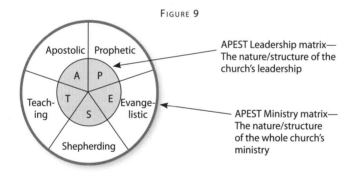

FIGURE 9

Paul wrote in Ephesians 4:7, "But to *each one of us* grace has been given as Christ apportioned it. . . ." And in verse 11, "It was *he who gave some* to be apostles, *some* to be prophets, *some* to be evangelists and *some* to be pastors [shepherds] and teachers." And here comes the revolutionary paradigm: What we have called the ministry matrix suggests that the fivefold ministry belongs to, and describes in some way, the whole church. If we take the phrase

9. For being introduced to this two-dimensional reading of the text we are very thankful to the leadership team of St. John's Church in Sheffield, England, who spent significant time with a group of Aussies looking around the UK for manifestations of the missional church.

"to each one of us" together with the repeated distribution formula *"he . . . gave some to be"* quite naturally, this implies that all Christians are included in some part of the fivefold APEST structure.

Paul was not primarily describing, as is so often quoted, the official leadership of the church in this text, but rather the church itself, which we agree with. Paul didn't labor under any misconceptions of ordained ministry that is so much a part of Christendom's assumptions of "the ministry." There are no clergy and no laity in the New Testament—all are ministers (we know we keep saying this, but it needs to continually be reinforced in the light of 1,700 years of Christendom). And so here Paul described everyone in the church in some way. In other words, if we had some way to analyze the gift-typing of the entire church, all would in some way fit somewhere into APEST, into the fivefold nature of the church's ministry. This signifies a fresh perspective on the gifting structure implicit in the whole church. This aspect alone, if accepted and practiced, would unleash significant renewal in church life as people connect with the primary giftings.

While this might seem like a fresh reading of the text, we don't think it's so difficult to see God working its implication out in local churches. The fact is you only have to look for it. Take any average person in your church and try to place him or her into one of the five segments of the pie chart above. We know many people who are classic pioneering types, and while they are not in "the ministry," their gifting can be seen as being clearly apostolic. Others we know are great teachers of the Bible. They seem to have an innate grasp of its ideas and the ability to communicate even though they might not have had any significant training. Some have two or more primary gifts in APEST ministry, but might not be part of the leadership structure of the church.

This is not to say that we are disregarding Paul's instructions for elders (or leaders) within the church. We see the leadership matrix as the community within the community, made up of certain people who are called to exemplify and embody these ministries in such a way as to be an APEST leader to the rest of the APEST body. In other words, some leaders are classic pastoral leaders. Some are prophetic types, some apostolic types, and so on. They already had the gifting by being part of Jesus' gracing act, but then they are called beyond that to actually lead in the mode they were already gifted in. This can be seen as a "calling within the calling."[10]

As we have mentioned several times already, all Christians are ministers, but we want to emphasize that there will be no significant mission or ministry until

10. Thanks to Mike Breen of St. John's Sheffield for this phrase.

we take that fact very seriously.[11] It is important for us to recognize the brute fact that not all existing ordained ministers are necessarily leaders. Leadership is a different thing altogether from APEST giftings. The equation that ministry capacity equals leadership capability does not compute in reality. Frankly, one can be a good minister and a terrible leader. Most people can identify someone in this category. Being a prophet might mean a person can speak from the heart of God, but put into a leadership role, such a person might well prove organizationally clumsy, even destructive. But there are some seriously prophetic leaders. Leadership is that added something that enables one to influence and get others to follow. In short, leadership must be viewed as conceptually distinct from gifting and ministry. In some people they do overlap, but not in all.[12]

Another comment about the implications of the text is that the APEST matrix (either leadership or ministry) does not function in isolation, but is always a functioning unity (a body) played out in multiplicity. Each role's legitimacy comes from the total system. We bemoan the current preference in churches for pastors (shepherds) and teachers at the exclusion of apostles, prophets, and evangelists. In fact, such a bias is a perversion of the Pauline idea—as would be true for a ministry comprised of only apostles or evangelists. This commits the missional-apostolic church to a corporate understanding of church, ministry, and leadership. The missional-apostolic church must operate as a body at all levels and perhaps especially at the *leadership* level because it is leaders who model ministry to others. There is no room for the loner or the one-man band in the New Testament model. We repudiate the classic hierarchical, triangular model with so-called senior pastors at the top. Biblically, it must be APEST.

At South Melbourne Restoration Community, under the leadership and direction of team leader Debra Hirsch, the church has adopted a most invigorating restructure of the church around the two-dimensional understanding of APEST. No longer is the church run by pastors alone but by a developing APEST

11. It is worth noting here that part of the revolution of missional church, like all revolutions, will have to bring down the dominant ideological system that imposes the old system. We simply have to break the power of clerical*ism* if we are going to see new movements start and flourish. Why? Because clericalism (the dominance of the ordained clergy class) serves to enshrine the old system and has too much to lose in the new—it will resist the change that disturbs the system that legitimizes it. Again we refer the reader to a study of movements in general. The dominant official leadership has always persecuted new movements. Witness the New Testament examples in Jesus and Paul. Witness the great missional movements and leaders in the church, the early monastics, Francis, Luther, Wesley, Booth, Martin Luther King Jr., the Pentecostals, etc. But as Jesus revolutionaries we do well to heed Jesus' old warning to his original disciples in not too different a situation than ours: "Be wise as serpents and innocent as doves."

12. Nouns and adjectives: Perhaps it would be more helpful to describe the APEST nature of church in adjectival form rather than noun form. Hence *apostolic* rather than apostle, *prophetic* rather than prophet, and so on.

leadership team whose aim is to help all the other ministers (everyone) to find their parts in the whole and to pursue them. Much further down this path is the amazing St. John's in Sheffield. Under the leadership of Mike Breen and Paddy Mallon, the church has actually developed a way to help people discover what their APEST gifting really is; and then they have developed a whole pathway of discipleship training and leadership development built around each gifting. The church is exploding in wonderful mission and ministry all over the place.

So much then for the clearly theological implications of Ephesians 4. We now turn to some of the sociological dimensions of the text, especially in terms of organizational theory and the implications for leadership.

The Sociology of APEST

If we look at the church as any set of human beings and explore the impact of differing leadership styles, we discover that Paul's radical plan for the Christian movement is affirmed by the current best practice in leadership and management theory and practice. In fact, given that the theological or biblical terms employed by Paul are so historically loaded, it might help to step out of the text for a minute and look at the issue from the viewpoint of contemporary sociology. We do this, bearing in mind that historically the church has been squeamish about the roles of apostle, prophet, and evangelist.[13]

Most human leadership systems acknowledge that there may be one or more of the following leadership styles:

- The *entrepreneur* is the groundbreaker and strategist who initiates an organization's mission.
- The *questioner* disturbs the status quo and challenges an organization to move in new directions.
- The *communicator/recruiter* takes the organization's message to those outside and sells it to them.
- The *humanizer* provides the organizational glue by caring for the individuals inside it.
- The *systematizer* organizes the various parts into a working unit and articulates that structure to the other members.

13. Again, it is rather interesting to us that the argument has waged around the terms and roles of apostle, prophet, and evangelist, and not at all with the functions of pastor (shepherd) and teacher. This is curious, isn't it? What does this say about the prevailing consciousness of the established leadership style and order? Why do they seem so frightened by these roles? Is it because such roles by nature challenge the status quo and the static institutional security of the Christendom mode?

Various social scientists use different terms for the above categories. In most leadership management theory it is assumed that the conflicting agendas and motivations of the above leaders pull them in different directions. However, imagine a leadership system in any setting (corporate, government, political, or other) where the entrepreneurial groundbreaker and strategist dynamically interacts with the disturber of the status quo (the questioner). Imagine that both these are in active dialogue and relation with the passionate communicator/recruiter, the person who carries the message beyond organizational borders and sells the idea(s) or product(s). These in turn are in constant engagement with the humanizer—the carer, the social cement—and with the systematizer and articulator of the whole. The synergy in this system would be significant in any context. Clearly the effective combination of these different leadership styles is greater than the mere sum of its parts.

This is the model proposed by Paul in Ephesians—a dynamic synergy of different giftings and motivations pulling *together* in harmony and unity for the building up of the whole. A possible sociodynamic view of the APEST matrix can be represented as follows:

FIGURE 10

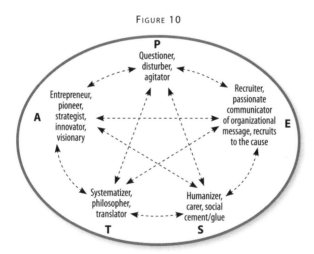

It is a useful exercise to take one leadership mode out of the equation (say the entrepreneur) and then ask the question, "What is lost by that removal?" Write down the possible answers. After you've done this for each type of leadership ask the question, "Is any style or leadership factor missing? Does any factor need to be added?" These exercises should highlight something of the apostolic genius and synergy of the whole APEST system. We would see the above sociological terms correlating with Paul's model in the following way:

- The entrepreneur = the apostle
- The questioner = the prophet
- The recruiter = the evangelist
- The humanizer = the shepherd
- The systematizer = the teacher

While the terminology is different, the concepts are the same. Current secular leadership theory yearns for the synergistic, creative, dynamic, interactive community proposed by Paul. Organizations are the poorer for majoring on only one or two styles of leadership. And so is the church.

The Ecology of Missional Growth

We wish to state briefly now and explore further later three primary principles for organic organizational development. They are to always create *organic,* *implicitly reproducible,* and *self-sustaining* systems in whatever we do. Organic, reproducible, self-sustaining: This constitutes something of the best practices in systems theory of organizational development. But here it is locked into this ancient text long before systems theory ever "discovered" it. When we look at the APEST system, we find that it fulfills the criteria of organic development in a remarkable way.

It is organic: In fact the Ephesians text itself is imbued with organic images (the body, ligaments, unity-diversity balance). There is a definite "ecology" at work here—an ecology and a balance we have messed with to our detriment by our excluding of the apostolic, prophetic, and evangelistic types of ministry and leadership. Another organic metaphor we can apply is DNA. A body has many different organs and systems (e.g., digestive, nervous, cardiovascular, etc.). These systems are held together by the unique distributions laid out in the DNA. We believe that APEST is part of the DNA of the church and ought not to be tampered with.

It is reproducible: An APEST-led church is reproducible both in the local and regional setting (vv. 7, 11–12). The ministry matrix is inherent in the nature of the church itself and a healthy church will always be able to find people with these ministries.

It is self-sustaining and self-invigorating/regenerative: When the church operates in APEST mode, it will grow itself. In fact the text directly states that the

APEST matrix is the very cause for growth and the built-in mechanism for maturity (vv. 14–16).

But there are even more factors that make for organizational health that are built into the model. The APEST system allows for great diversity within a context of an even deeper, underlying unity. This is the "secret formula" of all profound and creative organizational development. The deeper the theological-existential unity based "in Christ," the greater the opportunity for a wide diversity in terms of personality, spirituality, leadership style, *and* gifting. Any missional church that embraces the APEST model will find itself more equipped to embrace the classic ecclesiological dilemma of maintaining unity in diversity.

This Pauline model allows for what is termed in organizational structuring as "fit and split" and "contend and transcend."[14] The term "fit" refers to that which binds an organization together (unity). It is the group's common ethos and purpose. "Split" is the inclination of the organizational culture to intentionally develop great diversity of expression (plurality) in relation to the fit. "Contend" is the permission, even encouragement, given by leadership to disagree, debate, and dialogue around core tasks (duality). "Transcend" is the corporate agreement everyone makes to overcome disagreement and find new answers (vitality). APEST, well directed, can operate in a similarly invigorating way. It should rightly foster a church culture that fits and splits, that contends and transcends. This is a healthy organizational structure. Unfortunately the Christendom-era church, with its preference for hierarchical structures, favors a chain-of-command approach. Such a culture doesn't fit and split. Decisions are made at the top end of the structure and filter down to the grass roots. There's no interaction, no broad participation. As can be seen in many denominational structures as well as many local churches, the membership at the so-called bottom of the system often feel silenced and resentful. An APEST model allows for the church to contend and transcend by welcoming a variety of giftings and equally recognizing all segments of the church.

It creates a learning system: The dynamic nature of the whole matrix built as it is with APEST leadership structures will ensure that an open learning system results. The more outward-looking members (in this case A, P, & E) will ensure incoming information from outside the system and guarantee a dynamic engagement and growth with the organization's environment.

There is a wonderful ecology at work in the APEST system. It is a remarkably organic understanding of leadership and organization, especially for ones that wish to be missional. In fact it would be hard not to be missional if one were

---

14. Richard Tannee Pascale, *Managing on the Edge: How Successful Companies Use Conflict to Stay Ahead* (London: Viking, 1990).

to intentionally develop this into the life of God's people. It is worth noting here that Alan was involved in a similar organizational reconstruction around the APEST idea for his denomination both at state and international levels in the form of a nonformal, very talented, trinational body called the International Missional Team (IMT). The IMT has been responsible for significant stimulation of the missional cause in his denomination in the UK, Australia, and New Zealand, as these ideas have been employed at a strategic level. We say this to assure the reader that these ideas have been tested in practice at local, regional, and international levels; and while the full impact has not yet had time to be assessed, they are working.

APEST and the Movements of God

Believing that the missional church will likely see itself as a movement rather than as an institution, we want to make reference to the direct connection between movements, organizational life cycles, and APEST ministry and leadership systems.[15]

All organizations go through what theorists call a life cycle from birth to death. And insofar as the Christian community is an organization in its strictly human dimension, it, too, goes through life cycles. This should not be surprising as it is part of the organic nature of God's people. The life cycle of a local church or denomination can be viewed as follows:

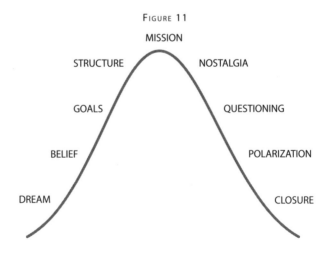

FIGURE 11

15. We wish to acknowledge the thinking of Steve Addison, the Australian director of Christian Resource Ministries (CRM), for this material on organizational life cycles.

A classic life cycle starts with a dream and ends with closure. Along the way a group has embraced certain beliefs and developed compatible goals and structures. At the peak of the cycle the organization is involved in fulfilling its mission as first conceived by the initial dream. It isn't difficult to think of examples of churches or other organizations you've been part of in which this bell curve is or has been reality. Think of a group that had a dream to plant a church in a new suburban area of a large growing city. At the peak of the curve, they will be a dynamic, growing suburban church, full of young families and children, and offering a variety of ministries and activities. But as the demographic of the suburb shifts and teenagers move out and young families cannot afford to buy in, the curve begins to fall. Before long, churches become nostalgic about "the good old days." This is followed by questioning about "what we're doing wrong," which often leads to polarization and eventual closure. It is not an unusual scenario.

However, looking at this life cycle in terms of leadership dynamics can be quite revealing. In short, different types of leaders play different roles at the various stages of the life cycle. For example, starting an organization from scratch requires the vision of an entrepreneurial, risk-taking type of leader such as the apostle. As an organization grows, on the other hand, it needs to change; and the apostolic type, if this person exercises too great an influence, can actually hinder the organization's growth. At this stage in the organization's life, a prophet or perhaps a teacher might be better equipped to redirect the original vision or restructure the organization for maximum effectiveness. The details will differ from organization to organization, but we must recognize that certain styles of leadership tend to predominate in certain critical periods of an organization's life cycle.

Of course, a properly conceived APEST approach is always taken as something of a fivefold *whole*. That is, such a system does not have one leadership type at a time in a kind of sequence but has all types operating all the time, both in leadership and in ministry. Keeping this in mind, it is possible to place the APEST model on the life-cycle curve as a way of identifying which types of leaders exercise the greatest influence during various stages of an organization's life. What we see is that during the early phases of the church plant or movement, the apostolic, prophetic, and evangelistic modes of leadership will tend to predominate over the pastoral and teacher types. That is, before the church reaches the top of the bell curve and moves into a maintenance phase, the apostolic, prophetic, and evangelistic leadership types need to come to the fore. This does not mean that pastors and teachers should be absent, but they will take less of a lead than the other three. On the other hand, later in the life cycle the situation might well be reversed, as pastors and teachers take the lead in order to help the church deal with its declining numbers. The symbiotic relationship between these two groups can be diagrammatically represented as seen in figure 12.

During the initial stages of an organization's life, the culture or feel of the group might be a bit feisty and somewhat hard edged. The group's belief systems are likely to be more narrowly defined, seen in black-and-white terms, and passionately held. The softer, more humanizing edge is underplayed while the triumphalist aspect is highlighted because of the typology of leadership and ministry. While this does not make for the softest landing in terms of organizational culture, it does create growth. The group is highly motivated by the organization's vision, mission, and directive purpose.

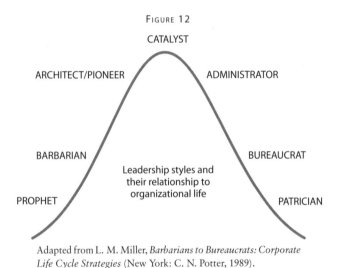

FIGURE 12

CATALYST

ARCHITECT/PIONEER   ADMINISTRATOR

BARBARIAN   BUREAUCRAT

Leadership styles and
their relationship to
organizational life

PROPHET   PATRICIAN

Adapted from L. M. Miller, *Barbarians to Bureaucrats: Corporate Life Cycle Strategies* (New York: C. N. Potter, 1989).

On the other hand, during the latter stages of an organization's life, the group will become more stable, though at the expense of a dynamic commitment to mission. In fact, using our APEST model to interpret much of our current malaise, we would have to say that this is the case in the vast majority of Christian churches and agencies and in fact much of Christendom in the West.

In APEST terms, the pastoral and teaching types of leaders have predominated over the apostolic, prophetic, and evangelistic types. We can say this with some assurance because history allows us to test this. Even the theological debate that has always raged around the issue of apostles and prophets directly indicates that the pastoral and teaching types have ejected the other types from the system. These are forced to express their innate gifting in contexts

other than the established local church or denomination. They have ended
up in parachurch agencies, government, business, overseas mission, and the
like. We know numerous highly talented (APE type) people who felt a call
to ministry and were told that they had no future in ordained, local church
ministry. This again highlights the sheer tragedy for the church in the loss of
an APEST system. We need to reiterate our belief that our current decline
and malaise is directly linked to this loss of missional-apostolic leadership.

The fact is that we need the whole system. Whenever a nation's early pioneers set out to conquer and subdue the wilderness, they faced significant
odds. The establishment of rural societies across the American Midwest is
a case in point. It took a strong pioneering spirit to do it. But once the land
had been opened up, it needed settlers to come along and build towns and
establish the infrastructure. Pioneers find new ground, and settlers build on
it. Without the pioneers there would be no place to settle, and without the
settlers the pioneers would never see their work bear fruit.

The APEST system can also be likened to a motor vehicle. There are at least
two pedals on the floor of the vehicle—an accelerator and brakes. You need
both to drive effectively. Just so, healthy leadership needs both accelerator-
and brake-type people. Not to put too fine a point on it, APE-leadership
types tend to be accelerators or pioneers and ST types are brakes or settlers.
We need all operating effectively for a more missional and holistic model of
leadership to emerge.

Just Like the Geese

We began this chapter by indicating that a missional-apostolic church will only
flourish under APEST leadership. And again we have to emphasize that we
believe it will take the emergence of the pioneering-missional type of leader
to accomplish this. Sadly, the Western church simply does not have enough
of the apostolic, prophetic, and evangelistic leadership types at present to get
the job of mission done.

As we keep saying, what the church needs is a deep-seated restructuring
in order to make a place for the genuinely missional types of leaders in our
churches. There are of course exceptions, but by far the majority of seminaries
that we know basically produce pastoral and teacher types of people who are
then sent to maintain established churches. This is not a time for more maintenance! In the West at least, maintenance is tantamount to decline, and we
have effectively been in long-term decline since the Enlightenment. It *is* within
our power to make a difference in this area if we will exercise strategic focus

and discipline in recruiting, training, and mobilizing a full-fledged leadership and ministry matrix for our times. But such a focus will require significant will to realign our resources strategically. It will also mean a major paradigm shift in terms of organizational/denominational culture. Giving space for those disturbers of the status quo will require massive permission-giving from all levels of the established denominations, who currently give little indication that they are really willing to let that happen.

We do wholeheartedly believe that the future hope of Christianity in our respective countries is directly linked to our ability or inability to become a dynamic mission movement in our day. The church, however, cannot become a movement without the rediscovery and implementation of the ministry and leadership matrix precisely because we will lack the mechanism to grow and mature. Stated simply: The renewal of the church and its mission has a direct relation to our ability to strategically develop and nurture a full-fledged ministry and leadership matrix. We have come to the conclusion that if we fail to make significant place for APE-type leadership in our time, it is unlikely that the missional church will get footholds into the various Western contexts in which we are called to be faithful. We finish this section with a retelling of one of Søren Kierkegaard's famous geese parables and allow it to speak for itself.

> Imagine what it would be like if geese could talk—then they surely would have ordered their affairs so that they too had their divine service, their worship of God. They would gather every Sunday and listen to the gander's sermon. The gander would dwell on the high destiny of geese, the high goal for which the Creator had destined them—and each time His name was mentioned the lady-geese would curtsey and the ganders would bow their heads. Their wings would carry them away to distant regions, blissful regions, where they truly belonged, for on earth they were like strangers in a foreign land.
>
> Thus every Sunday. When the service was over the congregation would rise and the geese waddle home. And again next Sunday they would attend divine service—and go home—and that would be that. They would thrive and grow fat, become plump and tasty, and eventually they would be eaten on St. Martin's Eve—and that would be that. Yes, that would be that. For while listening to resounding sermons on Sundays, on Mondays the geese would have a lot to tell each other, among other things what happened to a goose who tried in earnest to use the wings the Creator had given it, destined for the high goal set before it; yes, what happened to it, the horrors it had to endure. The geese, among themselves, knew all about it. But of course it did not behoove them to speak of it on Sundays, for, as they said, then it would become obvious that our worship actually is a mockery of God and of ourselves.

There were also among the geese a few who began to look peaked and were losing weight. Of those the other geese said, "Well, now we certainly see where it leads, this wanting to fly in earnest. For because they constantly have this idea of flying on their minds they lose weight, don't thrive, don't enjoy God's grace like ourselves, which is why we grow plump, fat, and tasty—for God's grace makes one plump, fat, and tasty."

And again next Sunday they would go to church, and the older gander would preach about the high goal for which the Creator (here the lady-geese curtsied and the ganders bowed their heads) had destined them, the goal for which they had been given their wings.

Thus it is with the worship of God in Christianity. Man too has wings; he has imagination. It is meant to help him really to soar—but all we do is play, we let imagination entertain us in a quiet hour, in a Sunday reverie, and for the rest we stay as we were; and then on Monday we regard it as God's grace that we grow plump, fat, tasty and put on an extra layer of yellow fat, save money, acquire prestige in the world, beget many children and are successful—all this we regard as proof of God's grace. But all those who really get involved with God and who therefore—it cannot be otherwise and according to the New Testament it isn't—suffer and look worried, have trouble, toil and affliction—of those we say, "There, it is quite obvious that they don't enjoy the grace of God."

Then when someone reads this he will say, "How fine, how very fine." And that is that—then he waddles home and strives with all his might to become plump, tasty, and fat—but on Sunday the parson delivers a sermon and he listens to it—just like the geese.[16]

---

16. See Søren Kierkegaard, "The Tame Geese: A Revivalistic Meditation," ed. Robert Bretall, *A Kierkegaard Anthology* (Princeton, NJ: Princeton University Press, 1946; paperback, 1973), 433.

11

Imagination and the Leadership Task

We are the people of the parenthesis—at the end of one era but not quite at the beginning of the next one. Maps no longer fit the new territories. In order to make sense of it all, we must cultivate a vision.

—Jean Houston

The Death of the Art of Ministry

As part of the research for this book both Alan and Michael (separately and together) traveled around the world in order to dig out some of the more innovative missional expressions of the church. The itinerary included the US, the UK, Italy, France, Israel, New Zealand, and South Africa. One of our lasting impressions of the churches in all those contexts is that, by and large, in spite of language differences, they tended to be invariably dull and rather predictable. They had a disturbing propensity to look, feel, and act in basically the same way. They sang the same basic songs and followed the same basic order of service in their corporate worship. The sheer predictability of it all was quite shocking and deeply disturbing. It sometimes seems as if there is some form of "template" at work in evangelical churches all over the world, regardless of language and culture.[1] These historical cultural forms seem to dictate to us how we should behave, and they keep us captive to a distinct mode of thinking.[2] Where the church has embraced an alternative approach, it has been marginalized and is often so underground it's hard to find. All this, we believe, amounts to nothing less than the triumph of technique over substance—the death of the art of ministry and mission.[3]

We would love to know who, or what, exactly is responsible for this malaise of the spirit, this absence of creativity. Who can tell us where this stifling "template" came from in the first place? And why do we seem to follow it so unquestioningly in almost every setting in the Western church? Primary responsibility must be placed at the feet of church leadership, since it is the task of leaders to set direction and shape organizational culture. To be more precise, we locate the problem in the standardized mode of pastoral leadership so predominant in the Western church[4] and with the ministry training systems, past and present, whose defining vocation should be the formation of leaders and through them the shaping of all future ministry. Furthermore, there seems to be painfully little permission, either from denominational, local, or personal leadership, to "go for it" and try new things. This failure to make space for active creativity is a problem of organizational *culture* long before it is a problem of fact. Therefore it is a failure of leadership when imagination as a vital resource for mission and ministry is not truly valued.

1. It is actually a useful exercise to assess evangelicalism, not so much by its distinctive theological formulation, but by its cultural formulations. We so often confuse the culture and the theology that sustains it. This has led to much debate, particularly in the UK, about evangelicalism and so-called postevangelicalism. The issue at the heart of the debate is, in our view, not so much a dismissal of evangelical theological perspectives, as a rejection of the culture that pervades the evangelical world. Evangelical culture is seen as a somewhat stifling, middle class, and at times schmaltzy, unvarying cultural typology that has little or no place for the marginal or other atypical expressions of culture.

2. One is reminded of Paul's warnings about the "elemental spirits" (RSV) or "elemental principles" (NIV) in Galatians 4:3, 9 and Colossians 2:8. These *stoixeia* control human behavior through human institutions, traditions, ideas, and religious philosophies, and serve to limit the freedom gained for us through Christ in the gospel. See James F. Cobble Jr., *The Church and the Powers: A Theology of Church Structure* (Peabody, Mass.: Hendrickson, 1988).

3. Art, it has often been noted, is the tense struggle between form and substance, outer expression and inner meaning. The act of mission, let alone of ministry and worship, should in this sense be no less an art form. We must always struggle to express the gospel in new forms. This loss of the art of mission has contributed directly to the dullness of most churches.

4. The leadership styles of the Western church, molded as it is by the Christendom paradigm, have tended to be predominantly pastor-teacher (or priestly) types. While necessary to the total health of the church, taken out of a more multidimensional style of leadership, these *types* of leaders have tended to be maintainers of the status quo rather than initiators or pioneers of new mission and producers of innovative forms of the church. Refer to chapter 10 on the ministry and leadership matrix.

Imagination and the New Millennial Culture

It was Winston Churchill who once prophesied that "the empires of the future will be the empires of the imagination." This not merely anticipated the demise of the British Empire as it was then, but also gives us a direct clue as to the vital role of imagination in the social, religious, and political (re)construction of the future. Imagination for our purposes is:

The ability to visualize: that is, the ability to form images and ideas in the mind, especially of things never seen or never experienced directly.

The creative part of the mind: the part of the mind where ideas, thoughts, and images are formed.

Resourcefulness: the ability to think of ways of dealing with difficulties or problems.

A creative act: an act of creating a semblance of reality, especially in art and literature. This refers not merely to fantasy but, more importantly from a missional perspective, to creative or poetic genius. Imagination and creativity are closely associated ideas. John Kao defines creativity as follows:

> Creativity [is] the entire process by which ideas are generated, developed, and transformed into value. It encompasses what people commonly mean by innovation and entrepreneurship. . . . it connotes both the art of giving birth to new ideas and the discipline of shaping and developing those ideas to the stage of realized value.[5]

This need for creativity and imagination is particularly true as we shift from the modern era to the emerging new millennial culture. As it relates to the declining Christendom "empire" and the rise of the missional church in the West, imagination must be embraced as a priceless resource for mission; if it is not, the Christian cause, like that of the British Empire, will be lost. Much work has been done to contrast the cultures of modernism and postmodernism. One of the major shifts in this massive cultural transition we are experiencing has been the move from being a predominantly left-brain culture to being a right-brain culture. We have moved from being a rational-linear culture to being much more an experiential and nonlinear one. It can be said

5. John Kao, *Jamming: The Art and Discipline of Business Creativity* (Glasgow: Harper-Business, 1997), xvii.

that we live in a "designer" culture. Even a cursory glance at the internet gives one a direct experience into this creative, visually rich aspect of the new cultural epoch. In other words, we live in an age where creativity and diversity are at a premium, and the church has yet to adjust itself missionally to this shift. We believe that this is a time for Christianity to activate its dormant right brain—we need to cultivate imagination and creativity afresh in order to communicate meaningfully into the emergent cultural paradigm in the West.[6]

In order to try stimulating active creativity we are going to use three statements by Einstein to frame a discussion on imagination and its importance for the life of the missional church.[7]

Imagination Is More Important than Knowledge

Einstein once said, "I am enough of an artist to draw freely upon my imagination. Imagination is more important than knowledge. Knowledge is limited. Imagination encircles the world." This is a remarkable statement, particularly from the mouth of Einstein, one of the world's all-time great thinkers and history makers. Imagination is more important than knowledge! If this is true, we need to explore why it is so. And can this be something of an indication of one of the strategic priorities for the missional church?

Creativity is certainly being taken seriously as *the* corporate resource for twenty-first-century companies. Innovation is recognized as the most significant training need by corporations as they engage the new global economy in the fluid cultural environment of emerging millennial cultures. Witness the proliferation of courses in innovation and entrepreneurship in business schools all around the globe. Most governments now give significant tax incentives for all forms of research and development, particularly in aspects that relate to the new economy. It is *the* arena for strategic positioning of both national and corporate interests.

Similarly, aesthetics and design have become central aspects in product development. Pure functionality is no longer enough to guarantee marketability.

6. Two books that Alan has coauthored delve deeply into the nature of missionally motivated innovation and entrepreneurship. They are *On the Verge* (section 3) and *The Permanent Revolution* (part 3). The reader is encouraged to explore these issues there.

7. Certainly the line between imagination and fantasy is not neat—there are no guarantees in the life of the imagination; it is a risky business. However, if we avoid the nurture of missional imagination, we will likely fall backward into mere fantasy. The more we attempt to avoid the uncertainties of imagination, the more likely we are to lapse into the fantastic. Whitehead wrote, "Imagination is a dangerous gift which has started many a conflagration." Imagination is creative while fantasy is not and whatever the risks, without it there can be no new missional-incarnational church. Urban Holmes, *Ministry and Imagination* (New York: Seabury, 1981), 103.

Design is now considered to be a major factor, if not *the* major factor in the success of a given product.[8] At the risk of sounding crass, and without surrendering either the inner meaning or the countercultural implications of the gospel, the church needs to seriously consider this element of design and style if it is going to meaningfully communicate its message to a sophisticated, design-savvy, postmodern audience. But it's more than just sharpening up our communication techniques to be more cool and relevant. It's about the church's very identity as a missional agency. It's about progress.

This idea of *church-by-design* incorporates the need for a very active creative process as part of the leadership mix. It also means that we need to be quite deliberate about how we appear, what total impression we make in the eyes of the outsiders, and in making sure that we are communicating very precisely with all aspects of our being. The church must be very intentional about this. Edward de Bono highlights this implicit relationship between design and progress when he notes that "if there is a known and successful cure for an illness, the patient would much prefer the doctor to use this cure rather than seek to design a better one. Yet there may be much better cures. How are they ever to be developed if at each moment the traditional treatment [is] preferred? It is little wonder that the judgment mode of the last millennium restricts us to past successes. . . . *Design is at best a risky process but without design there is no progress.*"[9]

Returning for a moment to the axiom that art is the struggle between inner meaning and outer expression, creativity and imagination add the element of art to church life, which in so many settings can be artless, predictable, controlling, and functional. Who would deny our near desperate need to recover the distinctly artistic element—that ingredient of surprise—in our worship, discipleship, mission, and community life together?

Furthermore, creativity gives an organization an edge. As corporations work to constantly adapt themselves to an always-changing, ever-evolving market, businesses that expect to survive, let alone thrive, are finding that they must actively value creativity and pay highly for it as *the* corporate resource that gives them the much-vaunted competitive edge. Mission requires a similar edge for very different reasons, and imagination opens the door to accessing that edge.

Also, as the life cycle of organizations gets shorter and shorter because of constantly changing market conditions and an unforgiving competitive environment, corporations are finding that they regularly need to reinvent themselves.

8. "The Redesigning of America," *Time Magazine*, 20 March 2000.
9. Edward de Bono, *New Thinking for the New Millennium* (St Ives: Viking, 1999), ix (emphasis ours).

This process requires significant imagination and vision as a company grapples with its very identity and mission. Adaptability, by its very nature, demands imagination and creativity. And as profoundly true as this is for the corporate world with its innate sensitivity to markets and the constant motivation of the "bottom line," it is even more significantly true for the church in the West.

This is especially so in light of the massive missiological gap that exists between the average church and its "market" so to speak. It is our belief that one of the core tasks of missional leadership is to assist the church to find new forms and expressions of church or bear the responsibility of the church's effective extinction in our day. One calls to mind the age when the British motorbike industry led the market. The names BSA, Norton, and Triumph were synonymous with quality and desirability in motorcycles. Who remembers them now? Except for Triumph, which has brilliantly reinvented the name and the company, these vehicles are merely collectors' pieces, relics valued for their historical interest alone. The companies refused to adapt, and so they died. Instead of adapting, they refused to proactively value the critical tasks of creativity and developmental change. They had no R&D departments.

Ours is an era that prizes knowledge. In many ways the new economy is built entirely on information and knowledge. But information in itself is not useful, particularly when there's so much of it around. Imagination, creativity, and design are needed to process information from being mere data to being something useful and desirable. Creativity as such adds value to knowledge by providing a meaningful interface, a medium of accessibility, for the user of knowledge. In this function, creativity adds new meanings to old activities and rituals; it reinterprets and restores old and outworn symbols and gives them currency and meaning.

In light of the above, we can understand what Einstein meant when he said that imagination is more important than knowledge. Allow us to consider now another Einsteinian comment on imagination.

If You Can't Imagine It, You Can't Do It

David Bosch, in his magisterial book on mission, remarked, "The mission of the church needs constantly to be renewed and reconceived."[10] Without directly referring to Einstein's axiom "If you can't imagine it, you can't do it," Bosch nonetheless refers to the same dynamic process by which the people of God are to relentlessly reimagine their fundamental tasks in the world. This

10. Bosch, *Transforming Mission*, 519.

is a reimagining that must regularly take place in the light of new missional contexts and of the changing natures of the existing ones.

It seems so obvious, doesn't it? Without first being able to imagine something, be it a task, object, or whatever, one would not be able to create it or do it. But alas this fundamental task of conceptualizing or reconceptualizing the basic elements of mission, ministry, or even church is so lacking in our ecclesiastical and missional practice in the West that it is alarming.

Just reflect on this in relation to the building you are now in as you read this book. You might question aspects of the design and its functionality, but you can be sure of this—it could not have been built unless there were a blueprint of sorts. Even the crudest of buildings requires some forethought and conceptual preparation. The building must have "existed" in the mind of the designer or builder before it existed in concrete reality. The same is the case for all artistic expression, but is also as true for the social structure of human communities as it is for the mission of God's people in the world.

In terms of mission, Stephen Covey, in *The Seven Habits of Highly Effective People*,[11] calls this "first and second creations." The first creation must take place at the level of imagination before it can take place at the level of actual realization. The second creation must follow the first or it cannot be done. Covey incorporates this aspect under the overall habit of *beginning with the end in mind*. This phrase states so self-evidentially why imagination is so fundamental to mission, ministry, leadership, and church life—begin with the end in mind. The end, insofar as it is in the future, can only be accessed by an exercise of the imagination—by that God-given ability to dream up the world we want to live in. It is one of the fundamental jobs of the imagination in life—to produce out of the society we *have* to live in a vision of the society we *want* to live in.

One of the best working definitions of poverty is not just the lack of money but the lack of a dream, a vision, hope. Darryl Gardiner, the director of Youth for Christ in New Zealand, believes that one of the core missional tasks when working with the poor is to help them to begin to dream again. The poor, in Darryl's view, are people without a dream. It is the missionary's task to rouse the imaginative abilities that lie at the base of the human soul in order to awaken the possibilities for a new gospel future and to access the deepest sources of human motivation—faith, love, pleasure, and hope. It is to awaken a sense of purpose, of mission, in life. No less is needed to help birth and nurture the missional church in the West. We need to dream again, and to do this we must cultivate a love for imagination. Before we can do it, we need to dream it.

11. New York: Simon & Schuster, 1989; Melbourne; The Business Library, 1989.

And it's one of the core tasks of leadership to help the community to dream again. It is a disturbing trait of the more gung-ho Christian leader today to believe that he (usually male) is the sole visionary and the people are mere receivers of the vision and must adhere to it because of the position of the leader in the organization. While many of us reject this approach to leadership, a watered-down version of this kind of thinking exists in many so-called leadership development programs. They teach that all is well when graduates of these programs simply (super)impose their vision on a community without first listening very deeply to the longings and dreams of the local people in that community.

A much more wholesome view of vision and visionary leadership is contained in the idea of the *management of meaning*. Considered philosophically, all that a great visionary leader does is awaken and harness the dreams and visions of the members of a given community and give them deeper coherence by means of a grand vision that ties together all the "little visions" of the members of the group. The fact remains that no one will be prepared to die for *my* sense of purpose in life. She or he will die only for her or his own sense of purpose. My task as a leader is to so articulate the vision that others are willing to embed their sense of purpose within the common vision of the community. Only if they think that the common vision legitimizes their vision will they be motivated by the leader's vision. In this sense, willingness to partake in corporate vision is the greatest compliment that a person can pay to leadership. It is holy ground and should be treated with reverence.

When Martin Luther King Jr. so compellingly articulated the vision of a better America in his legendary "I Have a Dream" speech, he was not articulating ideas that were particularly new to the people, or for that matter to history itself. The Old Testament prophets gave us the basis of that moral vision in the first place. Something much more primal was going on in his hushed audience—he was acting like something of a midwife to the great primal dream of God lying at the heart of every human cry for justice. Rather than just espousing a new vision, he was awakening their innate sense of purpose and their longing for justice and peace by giving that dream a vocabulary, legitimacy, and direction.

And so it is for all authentically visionary leadership. It is this capacity to articulate a preferred future based on a common moral vision that allows people to dream again. This is true of all genuine apostolic leadership. And in a profound sense the leader is the key person in the release of spiritual creativity and innovation in any setting—the catalyst for reconceptualizing the mission of the church.

But imagination takes courage, as it involves risk. In fact if there were no courage, there could be no imagination. And if there were no risk, there could be no apostolic leadership, only priestly maintenance and more of the same boring stuff that is keeping people from getting in touch with that most radical and dangerous person. The person is one who required his hearers to risk all to gain the kingdom of God and even more to advance it. This person? None other than Jesus.

And faith, when we think about it, is not merely intellectual assent to a set of propositions but the supreme gamble in which we stake our lives upon a conviction: It is far closer to raw courage than it is to mere belief.[12] A missional church is as imaginative as it is bold. And missional leadership is courageous and willing to try new things and risk all if necessary to see the kingdom come. Every church should have a Research and Development department—that is, a forum for dreaming, where nothing is impossible and no thought too outrageous. And every authentic missional church will experiment like mad in order to find new and accessible ways of doing and being the people of God.

Imagination of a Different Order

On to our final Einsteinian structure for imaginative thinking:

> The Kind of Thinking That Will Solve the World's Problems
> Will Be of a Different Order
> to the Kind of Thinking That Created Them in the First Place.

What Einstein is simply saying here is that problems cannot be solved at the same level of awareness that created them; that square-shaped thinking creates square-shaped paradigms, which in turn create square-shaped solutions. But the square paradigm also creates distinctly square-shaped problems. What Einstein is saying is that it is impossible for square-shaped thinkers to solve the square-shaped problems using the same mode of thinking that created the square-shaped problems in the first place. In order to solve the problems of the square, we need to access a different sphere of thinking from square-shaped thinking.

Or as Bill Easum says in his book on post-Christendom-style leadership, "Churches wanting to break free from the quagmire of their dysfunctional systems and climb out of their downward death spiral must learn to feel, think,

12. This is the fundamental insight of Blaise Pascal. That faith is not supine acceptance of dogma but rather something in the nature of a gamble has been accepted by almost all subsequent thinkers. Faith, in biblical perspective, is not the acceptance of conventional standards of behavior, and it is not primarily an effort to save our own puny souls: it is the exciting venture of faith in which we bet that God really is, that this is his world, and that he is like Jesus Christ. It is the essence of a gamble that the gambler either wins or loses; he is either right or wrong. So it is with the supreme gamble presented to us in the call to trust the person and work of Jesus Christ. Our faith is either true to reality or it is a horrible delusion. If it is not true, it is an evil.

234   Apostolic Leadership

and act differently than they do now. The times in which we live require us to change our Life Metaphors, something akin to rewiring the human brain."[13] This is no easy feat as it often amounts to the "king" of our beloved institutions being exposed as naked by the "child" of the innovator. But whatever the difficulties, it is absolutely necessary if we are to genuinely move from being a Christendom church to being a truly missional one. How do we do it?

Before we look at practical ways to engender new (out-of-the-box) thinking, we think it is vital to comment on the dynamics of paradigms and paradigm shifting. Thomas Kuhn gave us the foundational text on this subject in his seminal book *The Structure of Scientific Revolutions* in which he describes the transitions between various scientific worldviews and how they were effected.[14]

A paradigm in Kuhn's sense is a self-contained and self-referential mode of thinking in relation to scientific and cosmological problems. It is a way of trying to both understand our world and also to solve the problems of understanding by relying on a set of assumptions that give rise to the solutions in relation to the problems. And because science is always searching, its method drives it. It is so committed to the search for answers based on verifiable truth that there have been a number of significant, clearly discernable paradigm shifts in its history. Most notable have been the shifts from the pre-Copernican to the Copernican, from the Newtonian to the Einsteinian, from relativity to quantum physics, and so on. Or as Lewis Mumford says it, "Every (transition) . . . has rested on a new metaphysical and ideological base, or rather, upon deeper stirrings and intuitions whose rationalized expressions take the form of a new picture of the cosmos and of (humanity)."[15]

In that the church is also meant to be a community embracing the search for truth, Kuhn's book is a tremendous resource in our attempts to reframe the mission of the church in the new millennial context. It also serves as a warning to us as to how easily vital new perspectives can be stifled by a predominant paradigm, something that has sadly been so much a part of the historical Christendom project. It is important for the church to know something about how the shift from one paradigm to another takes place.

A paradigmatic shift involves the following stages:

1. We begin with a well-established paradigm that dominates the thinking or consciousness, scientific philosophy, and cosmology of a period.

13. Bill Easum, *Leadership on the Other Side: No Rules, Just Clues* (Nashville: Abingdon, 2000), 39.
14. Thomas Kuhn, *The Structure of Scientific Revolutions* (Chicago: University of Chicago Press, 1962).
15. Quoted in Easum, *Leadership on the Other Side*, 31.

Though dominant, the preexistent paradigm should encourage a sense of expectation and searching, and so the quest for answers goes on. This is also a vital clue to us as it legitimizes an ongoing search for truth.

2. An increasing sense of anomaly develops from within the paradigm, that is, a feeling that something is wrong with the paradigm. That something might be as yet indiscernible, but there is a sense that something is awry. Oddly enough, this occurs precisely because the current methodology within the given paradigm enables the real experts to master all aspects of the paradigm. This means that they (the experts) are the ones most able and likely to perceive when things are wrong. Consequently, it is those who understand the paradigm the best who are often the first ones to break from the consensus and begin what Kuhn calls "a roaming of the mind," a new sense of freedom to perceive anomalies without recourse to preconceived assumptions, without reference to the paradigm itself. This is an interesting intimation of the inner workings of the prophetic spirit in the social sense of the word. Those who *really* understand the problems of the paradigm most acutely are the first to sound the alarm that something is wrong. The Apostle Paul and Martin Luther come to mind.

3. A slow-growing (but inexorable) recognition of the above occurs. The trickle becomes a flood. A group of dissenters emerges followed by a flurry of new theories in search of an alternative understanding of things. The beginnings of the process of transition is now taking place.

4. A new paradigm (answer) begins to emerge, most often with opposition by those who still hold strongly to the established paradigm. Copernicus saved his neck only by recanting from the "heresy" implied in his theory but was imprisoned for life. It is interesting that people are willing to persecute dissenters based on their assumptions about the world. This is probably because they have invested much of their sense of selfhood in the current paradigm and so receive their legitimacy from it. This is also why denominations seldom permit a questioning of their core organizational beliefs—commonly called sacred cows.

When we established the Forge Mission Training Network in Melbourne, we knew we were confronting the existing paradigm of theological education. Forge is a network of agencies set up to develop missionaries to the Western world, itself an innovation. Its *action-learning* (discipleship-coaching) paradigm of leadership development is difficult for established seminaries to affirm. The academy is generally staffed by academics, people who get their vocational legitimacy from, and have vested interests in, the system that promotes knowledge, as opposed to action as the key means of ministry formation.

This highlights how innovation, and therefore real progress, can so easily be marginalized and locked down in the Christendom paradigm of church. It is rare that an established institution can tolerate a serious questioning of its legitimacy implicit in a new, alternative model. It was Machiavelli who noted that innovators are always persecuted and their innovations resisted. In fact, the more compelling the innovation, the more powerful the resistance to it.

Some Keys to Paradigm Shifting

One of the most important things we have learned in working particularly with established churches is that people must be convinced that there is a problem before they are interested in a solution. People will not change unless they believe they really have to. So many leaders come in with a great sense of what the solution might be, but they encounter resistance because they have failed to communicate the problem. What can a leader do to promote paradigm shift? We offer the following ideas.

Encourage Holy Dissatisfaction

One of the great weapons in the revolutionary leader's arsenal is to cultivate a sense of *holy* dissatisfaction—to provoke a basic discontent with *what is* and so awaken a desire to move toward *what could be*. It must be holy because it is very easy to awaken the unholy variety of discontent.[16] The old Marxist slogan "Rub raw the sores of discontent" is brilliant. The early Marxists knew how to create the environment of insurrection, of revolution, of *movement*. This ought to be no less true for the revolutionary missional leader. We must not be afraid to be unpopular, to be seen as revolutionaries, if we want to really effect the missional-incarnational paradigm in our time. The real revolutionary, perhaps the only one, is the person who has nothing left to lose. Rub the discontent raw and then throw salt on it—our times are urgent; Christendom must be brought down and apostolic faith and practice established if we are to be true to our call as followers of the revolutionary Jesus in our day.

Embrace Subversive Questioning

Another invaluable tool for the reconceptualizing of the ministry and mission of the church is the art of subversive questioning. It has been said that

16. In fact, this is one of the subversive practices in the advertising industry. They generate dissatisfaction (most often with an unholy appeal to our covetous natures) so they can sell you something you don't really need.

behind every question lies a quest and that every quest, when rightly pursued, ultimately leads the searcher to God. This is exactly the kind of radical questioning we are suggesting. Questions are subversive because they force the hearer to self-awareness and a personal search for answers. Socrates was the master of the question. Far more revolutionary than the provision of answers is the radical use of questioning. Ministers are often expected to be answer people rather than the more effective (and Christlike) question people.

One of the great advances in organizational theory and development in the 1990s was the movement that took seriously the role of questions in the ongoing development of healthy organizations. In its essence the theory taught that learning takes place when questioning is added to programming (i.e., how we are inclined or "programmed" to think). If the theory is correct, and it seems obvious that it is, then one must ask: What are the right questions? In Kuhnian terms, what questions will cause us to step out of our paradigm and take us to the heart of learning? Here are some examples that we have found helpful.

- Is a can opener a can opener if it can't open cans?—All of us have experienced using a can opener that can't open cans anymore. It sure looks like one, but it doesn't do what a can opener should do. So, Q here is "Is it still a can opener?" This is a very, very subversive question because it forces those questioned to tackle the distinction between form (it looks like one) and function (it doesn't operate like one). And it's not long before some bright button in the group will apply the formula to the church. "Is the church still a church if it doesn't function like a church anymore?" This is actually quite a sophisticated theological question. By now you can guess our answer, but we'd prefer you think about it yourself.
- If you could start all over again, would you do it the same way?—We answered this question ourselves earlier in the book. Alan has asked this question many times in groups and churches who are struggling to revitalize the ministry of the church. In every setting, he has yet to hear someone say they would do it the same way. Well the Q here is "Why are you doing it the same way now?" If all human progress is predicated on the assumption that everything can be done better, why have you stopped progressing? We have not arrived at a state of perfection, have we? Then when and why did we stop trying to do church better? And what are we going to do about it now that we cannot plead ignorance anymore?
- What would your experience of church be like: (a) if you no longer had a building? (b) if you could no longer meet on Sundays? (c) if you had no pastor or clearly identifiable leadership team?

All of these questions are designed to force us to reflect *biblically* and *radically* on our experience of church. They expose just how deeply the Christendom-mode of church has framed us and set us up for failure. Christendom is always associated with buildings, Sundays, and clergy! Always and everywhere. Yet the New Testament church had none of these.

In terms of questioning, we would encourage missional leaders to develop a whole list of questions like these, and to use questioning far more extensively than is currently common practice. Use parables and storytelling like Jesus did, for they, too, "wound from behind" (to quote Søren Kierkegaard) and invite the hearer to fill in the gaps and find themselves in the story (e.g., Matt. 21:45).

Become a Beginner

Another great way to evoke the creative juices is to learn to think like a beginner, not like an expert. This is particularly the case when we think we are sure about the way forward. Actually expert-type thinking is often only thinking that has been set in an already hardened paradigm. Try to think how you would do something if you were doing it for the first time. This takes us back to the Emperor's New Clothes story. The adults were trained to think in set ways, but the child had yet to be set in the same way. So much of what we think we know needs to be *un*learned. Exercise unlearning as much as you apply learning techniques.

Social psychologists have long sung the praises of playfulness as an essential part of general health. Christianity, especially in the Western tradition with its historic antipathy and active suppression of pleasure and frivolity, can easily make us into very uptight and often unpleasant people. We need to learn how to play again. This is so important for the recovery of a gospel ministry that we cannot emphasize it too much. But there is more in play than meets the eye.

Have you ever noticed how many uses children can make of, say, a chair? For us it is just a chair that exists only to be sat on. For a child it can become literally *anything*. A child can use a chair as a house, an antiaircraft gun, a building block of sorts, anything. Researchers into human behavior have called this distinction "associative" and "dissociative" thinking. The adult *has learned* to see the chair in a one-dimensional manner. The adult has *associated* it with only one basic function. The child exercises a far more dissociative approach to objects in his or her world, and this renders the world of the child multitalented and full of possibilities closed to the adult. It is precisely this aspect of childlikeness that we need to recover in our approach to reimagining community, mission, and ministry. Be playful with things, ideas, activities, people. It opens up new possibilities all the time.

One of the most important lessons from history is that the renewal of church always comes from fringes, and we mean *always*. And it is the movements of mission that in turn create movements of renewal. This can be tested in every context of the church. The lesson is that the church ought to remain in mission for God's sake, but also for its own sake. It is this radical openness to, and engagement with, the margins that so often brings that needed inrush of new thinking, acting, and feeling to Jesus' people.

There is an important and somewhat subversive subtext involved with the above statement, one that critiques the predominant bourgeois, middle-class, cultural blandness so prevalent in the Western church.[17] It is so often the culture of church brought about through various social forces that suppresses and marginalizes people who are different. "Fringy" people feel very alienated from the predominant expression of the church in the West. But it is so often these people who will bring a renewal of perspective, even spiritual rebirth, to God's people.

And if you are inclined to doubt this observation, we call you to consider that our real tradition as a missionary people, a gospel people, stems directly from the life and work of Jesus who was himself a marginalized person who hung out with people profoundly marginalized by the religious system and religious people of his time.

It is common for us to imagine the impact that Jesus must have had on those people, but it is also very interesting to think about the impact these people had on Jesus in his own culturally conditioned humanity. We would venture to suggest that much of the radicality of Jesus' message stemmed from his deep love and commitment to, but also from his profound relationship with, the rejected "sinners" of his time. We feel that we have been deeply enriched and irrevocably changed by hanging out with those on the edge of society and not only "normal" people. It was John Stuart Mill who once noted that "eccentricity has always abounded when and where strength of character has abounded; and the amount of eccentricity in society has always been proportional to the amount of genius, mental vigor and moral courage which it contained. That so few [people] now dare to be eccentric marks the chief danger of our times."[18]

17. One of the most jarring insights into middle classness was written recently by Douglas Coupland in his groundbreaking book *Generation X* where he noted, "You see, when you're middle class, you have to live with the fact that history will ignore you. You have to live with the fact history can never champion your causes and that history will never feel sorry for you. It is the price that is paid for day-to-day comfort and silence. And because of this price, all happinesses are sterile; all sadnesses go unpitied." Douglas Coupland, *Generation X* (London: Abacus, 1991), 171.

18. John Stuart Mill, *On Liberty* (Mineola, NY: Dover Publications, 2002), 56.

But we must not only be radically open to those at the margins; we need to make space for mavericks of all sorts. These renegade types have a vital part to play in proposing a consciousness alternative to the dominant consciousness of the "average." In a real sense, a true biblical maverick acts in a prophetic manner by exposing the lies that the dominant group tells itself in order to sustain its shared illusions—and all groups, including the church, have them. The Old Testament prophets clearly embodied this "gift" to the people of God. But you need look no further than Jesus for a perfect example of a biblical maverick. He never accepted the norms and definitions of spirituality and religion. He didn't fit into the box. He hung out with the sinners and was routinely accused of being a drunkard and a glutton (Matt. 11:19), and yet he embodied *perfectly* God's message to the world. He was the Word. In him the medium is the message.

The point is that the holy, nonconforming "rebel" is very useful to us in exposing our illusions—some the very illusions that keep us from experiencing God afresh and doing things differently and better. While often hard to take, they nevertheless play a vital social role, and we should be at pains to listen to their irritating whining and complaining for hints of God's voice and will for us. There have been stranger ways in which God's Word has come to us—just look through the Old Testament.

Take More Risks

Moving on from eccentrics and holy rebels to something less strange but no less important, we would like to commend risk taking as a stimulus for creative reimagining. It has already been noted that imagination and creativity are dangerous, but we believe that without risk there can be no growth and no progress. If you want to help birth and nurture a truly missional-apostolic church, then put both yourself and your organization *at risk* because without it you will be neither missional nor apostolic.

Simply stated, when you are out of your depth, at risk, the creative juices start really flowing. The fact is that when we are doing things we have learnt well and are part of the safe and the habitual, we really don't learn all that much. We don't have to. However, when we are out of our depth and out of our comfort zone, we have to learn. Mission involves risk, but risk involves wonderful new learning for you or your organization.

In his constant teaching on the ideas associated with what he calls *lateral thinking*, Edward de Bono makes the seemingly self-evident observation that you cannot dig a hole in a different place by digging more in the same place.[19]

19. See for instance his books: *Conflicts: A Better Way to Resolve Them* (New York: Viking Penguin, 1986); *Eureka!* (New York: Holt, Rinehart & Winston, 1974); *The Greatest Thinkers* (New York: Putnam, 1976); *Thinking Course* (New York: Facts on File, 1985).

This is similar to Einstein's remark about the impossibility of problem solving by using the same type of consciousness that created the problems in the first instance. It is also sometimes called organizational insanity—the belief that you can get significantly different results by doing the same things "better." And yet this is precisely what we do all the time. Surely Christendom has been worked and reworked and tweaked every which way possible, and yet we still persist in doing it the same way, only "better."

Lateral thinking emphasizes the search for alternatives, but it looks laterally (sideways) for different approaches and different ways of looking at things. If you want to dig a hole in another place, then cease digging where you are and move to another place and start digging there. Move sideways as opposed to up or down in the same place. Vertical thinking builds on the same way of doing or thinking. Lateral thinking means to shift ground. The term covers a variety of methods including provocations to get us out of the usual line of thought. Lateral thinking is cutting across patterns in a self-organizing system and has very much to do with perception. And like all true creativity it can sometimes be provocative. The church hasn't generally shown much inclination to move sideways (just look at history). It has commonly preferred its own brand of organizational insanity to the rigors of change.

Create a Climate of Change

Less dangerous perhaps, but no less important for the imaginative process, is the need to establish a climate for creativity. In other words, develop a certain ecology where creativity can thrive. In a real sense, the church is just like all natural ecological systems that allow for plant and animal life. In the church's case it is a function of the leadership to passionately value imagination and creativity and rate them as essential resources for mission, ministry, and leadership. The leadership of a given community will need to give organizational permission for rethinking and allow for lots of experimentation, recognizing that this process is dangerous, tricky, and inevitably chaotic. It can do this by encouraging a questioning of the culture and praxis of the organization and by getting a whole lot of people together in hothouse events like "think tanks" around key topics. Be prepared for some failures, but also be prepared for massive exponential learning and missional openings you never dreamed possible.

Try to ensure you have a balance of left-brained and right-brained people on your leadership teams. Seminary-trained (ordained) leadership in the West has tended to be left-brained and rationalistic. To counteract this overreliance on rationalism, the church must intentionally create space and opportunities for creative types and rational types to work side by side as together they reshape the church into what it was intended to be. Like all organic systems, the mix is vital not only to fully understand the congregation and to minister effectively to them but especially if you want to give space for creative activity.

A climate of change can be promoted by a preparedness to act outside of the box. At Forge we throw some of the following challenges at the interns. They're like curve balls that cause you to duck and weave.

Ask a fool: That's what the Renaissance kings did to break out of the dead-end environment of their yes-men. The fool's job was to parody any proposal, to make it appear in a fresh light.

Break out: The more you do something the same way, the more difficult it is to think about doing it in another way. Eat some ice cream for your breakfast. Go see a film you wouldn't normally see. Take a different way to work for a change. Drive down your street in reverse.

Learn from mistakes: Before Thomas Edison invented the light bulb, he discovered 1,800 ways not to make it. Columbus was looking for India. Errors are natural—one of life's primary vehicles of learning.

Try a different approach: Most of our advances have occurred because someone challenged the rules and tried a different approach. What rules should you challenge here and now?

Get out of your box: Anyone can look for fashion in a boutique. Anyone can look for history in a museum. Explore. Look for fashion in a hardware store or an airport.

Combine different ideas: Guttenberg combined the wine press and the coin punch to create moveable type and the printing press. Combining unusual ideas is at the heart of creative thinking.

Dig deeper: Nothing is more dangerous than an idea when it is the only one you have. The best way to get a great idea is to have lots of ideas.

In *Built To Last,* James C. Collins and Jerry I. Porras offer some more ways to stimulate creativity and movement:

Good enough never is: Encourage a continual process of relentless self-improvement with the aim of doing better and better, forever into the future.

Try a lot of stuff and keep what works: Try to develop high levels of action and experimentation—often unplanned and undirected—that produce new and unexpected paths of progress and enable visionary companies to mimic the biological evolution of species.

Accept that mistakes will be made: Since you can't tell ahead of time which variations will prove favorable, you have to accept mistakes and failures as an integral part of the evolutionary process.[20]

Be challenged: Take a new challenge each week. Work on a new problem each week, explore something new with the purpose of solving it, or generating ideas.

Adopt a genius: You can benefit by learning from the lives, ideas, and actions of the great geniuses of history. Adopt a role model. You can probably tell by now that our heroes include Einstein, Kierkegaard, and Buber. But we also love Van Gogh, Heschel, Simone Weil, Robert Frost, and David Bosch. Your resident genius might be Dorothy Sayers, Picasso, T. S. Eliot, Thomas Edison, or Hannibal (not Lecter!).

Brainstorm: If properly carried out, brainstorming can help you not only come up with sacks full of new ideas, but can help you decide which is best.

Take notes: Always a notebook (or a note-taking app) around with you. That way, if you are struck by an idea, you can quickly note it down. Upon rereading your notes, you may discover about 90 percent of your ideas are daft. Don't worry, that's normal. What is important is the 10 percent that are brilliant.

Exercise creativity: If you're stuck for an idea, open a dictionary, randomly select a word and then try to formulate ideas incorporating this word. You'd be surprised how well this works. The concept is based on a simple but little known truth: Freedom sometimes inhibits creativity. There are nothing like restrictions to get you thinking.

Define your problem: Grab a sheet of paper, electronic notebook, computer, or whatever you use to make notes, and define your problem in detail. You'll probably find ideas positively spewing out once you've done this.

20. James C. Collins and Jerry I. Porras, *Built to Last* (London: Century, 1996). While their thoughts on stimulating creativity are helpful, they maintain the scientifically naïve view that all evolution means progress. While evolution can be progressive, it can also be regressive. It's a statement of value to say that progress results from evolutionary processes.

The Six Thinking Hats

We close this section on imagination by introducing Edward de Bono's game involving the six thinking hats. This is a social game in which participants agree to help solve problems. The six hats represent six modes of thinking. In fact, they are directions to think rather than labels for thinking.[21] Participants agree to switch hats for a period of time in order to take a certain approach that they would not normally take to the problem. While wearing a particular hat, each participant is committed to thinking only as that hat allows. The method promotes fuller input from more people. In de Bono's words it "separates ego from performance."

Everyone is able to contribute to the exploration without denting egos. The hat releases them to think of and speak out a solution they might not agree with, or might not have come to without wearing the hat. The six-hats system encourages performance rather than ego defense. People can contribute under any hat even though they initially support the opposite view. The key point is that a hat is a direction to think rather than a label for thinking. You can use this great tool for anything, even as a way to do group Bible study. You don't need actual hats, just the imagination to think and speak in different modes.

The six hats are as follows:

White hat: Think of white paper. It's neutral and carries information. The white hat has to do with data and information. The white hat asks, "What information do we have here?" "What information is missing?" "What information would we like to have?" "How are we going to get that information?"

Red hat: Think of red as fire and warmth. This has to do with feelings, intuition, hunches, and emotions. "Putting on my red hat, this is what I feel about the proposal." "My gut feeling is that this will not work." "I don't like the way this is done." "My intuition tells me prices will soon fall."

Black hat: Think of the stern judge wearing black robes who comes down heavily on wrongdoers. This is the caution hat. It prevents us from making mistakes, doing silly things, and doing illegal things. It points out why something cannot be done or why something will not be profitable. "The regulations do not permit that." "We cannot raise the money for that." "He has no experience in that."

21. From Edward de Bono, *Serious Creativity* (London: Fontana, 1993), 71–85.

Yellow hat: Think of sunshine. The yellow hat is for optimism and the positive view of things. This looks for feasibility and how something can be done. It looks for benefits—but they must be logically based. "That might work if we moved the production plant nearer the customers." "The benefit might come from trying that out several times before we adopt or reject it."

Green hat: Think of vegetation and rich growth. The green hat is for creative thinking, for new ideas, additional alternatives, putting forward possibilities and hypotheses. This requires creative effort. "We need some new ideas here." "Are there any alternatives? Don't worry how bizarre they might sound at first." "Could we do this differently?" "Could there be another explanation?"

Blue hat: Think of the sky and an overview. This is for process control. The blue hat thinks about the thinking being used. It sets the agenda for thinking. It suggests the next step in the thinking. The blue hat can ask for the input of other hats. It asks for summaries, conclusions, and decisions. It can make comments: "We have spent far too much time looking for someone to blame." "Could we summarize how far we have got?" "I think we should look at the priorities." "I suggest we try some more green hat thinking now." This is usually for the chairperson or organizer of the meeting.

Try using the six hats when next brainstorming new direction or ideas for your organization or church. We offer them as one possible tool, along with all the other ideas we've outlined, for fostering creativity and reimagining. To use Gerard Kelly's expression, it is time for some "reimagineering" to happen in our churches. And it will be up to an emerging apostolic leadership to bring it about. As Gary Hamel says in *Leading the Revolution*, "Whatever I can imagine, I can accomplish. I am no longer a vassal in a faceless bureaucracy. I am an activist, not a drone . . . I am a revolutionary."[22]

---

22. Gary Hamel, *Leading the Revolution* (New York: Plume, 2002), 29.

12

Organizing the Revolution

Strategy is all about commitment. If what you're doing isn't irrevocable, then you don't have a strategy—because anyone can do it. . . . I've always wanted to treat life like I was an invading army and there was no turning back.

—Troy Tyler

The Church as a Missional Movement

What we have said about an apostolic mode of leadership will be easier to ground if done in the context of a number of other missional priorities. We want to conclude our discussion of the emerging missional church by simply introducing these other priorities. It might sound strange to be introducing concepts in our final chapter, but we do so because each of the areas suggested will require much more rigorous work than the scope of this book allows. We believe apostolic leadership works more effectively when the church rediscovers itself as a missionary movement; when it organizes itself as a centered set; when it builds organic structures, gears for metabolic growth, and develops a missional leadership training system. We suggest them here because of the absolute strategic value that each of these areas presents to the long-term effectiveness of new expressions of missional church. Also we present them here in the hope that many of the readers will pursue these critical areas of study and so develop ways forward for the missional church in the twenty-first century.

The first of the areas of critical mission focus that we will explore is that of the nature of movements. We have already looked at the nature of organizational life cycles and their relationship to styles of leadership. Here we wish to explore a little more deeply the nature of a movement itself.[1]

It is perfectly true to say that all social groupings that have impact on either a local, national, or international level always begin with a form that sociologists call a *movement*. That is, there are some common characteristics that mark off the early phase of dynamic social movements that are distinct from the social structures of the later institutions that arise from them. This is as true of the church and other Christian agencies as it is of corporations, community projects, political parties, and other social movements. Whether it be a denomination, parachurch agency, or local church plant—all are launched with a certain ethos and energy that starts with a seminal vision or idea and swells like a wave to impact society 'round about it. Take early Methodism, the beginnings of the Salvation Army, and closer to our time, the Vineyard movement for examples of dynamic movements that have changed the world.

We believe it is therefore important to study the nature of movements, because it is in the movement's form, with all its fluidity, vision, chaos, and dynamism, that we find one of the most significant clues to transforming our world for Jesus. For our purposes, a working definition of a movement is as follows: a group of people organized for, ideologically motivated by, and committed to a purpose that implements some form of personal or social change; who are actively engaged in the recruitment of others; and whose influence is spreading in opposition to the established order within which it originated. We believe that this definition, however technical it may sound, describes the New Testament people of God accurately.

Consider again the organizational life cycle below; this one is more complex than the one presented in chapter 10. When looking at movements, it is helpful to observe the dynamics that make for the early growth phases of the organization (the foundation and growth periods). What's going on here? What kind of leadership is required? What is the focus of the organization? What makes for its growth? These are questions of fundamental importance for the missionary and church planter who is all about trying to pioneer some form of movement in varying contexts. Ask yourself these questions. Try asking the same questions of the historical movements you admire, of your heroes, and learn from them what makes for dynamic missional impact.

Looking at the bell curve below it can be seen that similar questions should relate to the decline phase: Here decline is directly related to the institutionalization and the eventual demise of the movement. What's going on in these stages? What mode of leadership is involved? What is the organization focusing on? What is it missing? These are absolutely pivotal questions especially as they relate to the revitalization of churches and denominations.

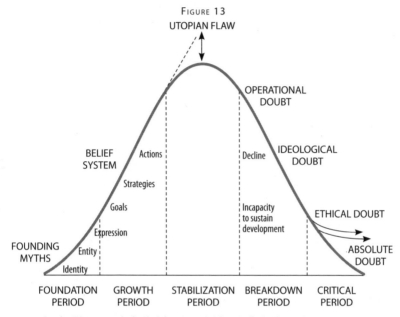

FIGURE 13
UTOPIAN FLAW

Based on "Management Studies" by Robert Hoover, David Rumkorff, John Sherwood, Bruce Roger, et al.

The goal of churches should be to achieve what strategists call "sigmoid growth," which is the capacity to constantly remain in a state of movement-like growth. This can be represented as follows:

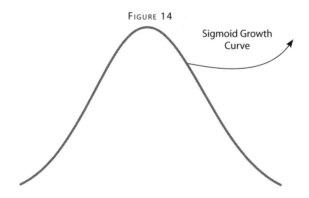

FIGURE 14

Sigmoid Growth Curve

Some movements in church history tend to focus on spiritual renewal (e.g., the charismatic movement and the monastic movement), and some tend to focus primarily on mission (e.g., the Wesleyan revival and the Society of Jesus). We would argue that the two forms are directly related, but we believe a close examination of all great movements will show that they really began with a sense of mission that has then been translated into a movement for renewal of the established church. Take the 1906–1909 Azusa Street Revival in Los Angeles, California. It began as an evangelistic outreach to the poor and developed into the Pentecostal movement, which in turn stimulated the charismatic movement. To make this clearer, it will be important to identify some of the characteristics of movements. For this we turn to Howard Snyder and his important book, *Signs of the Spirit*, which identifies the following as distinctives of renewal movements:

A thirst for renewal: A holy discontent with what exists precipitates a recovery of the vitality and patterns of the early church.

A new stress on the work of the Spirit: The work of the Spirit is seen not only as important in the past but also as an experience in the present.

An institutional-charismatic tension: In almost every case of renewal tensions within existing structures will arise.

A concern for being a counter-cultural community: Movements call the church to a more radical commitment and a more active tension with the world.

Nontraditional or nonordained leadership: Renewal movements are often led by people with no recognized formal leadership status in the church. Charismatic capacity is the key. Furthermore, women are more noticeably active in movements.

Ministry to the poor: Movements almost always involve people at the grassroots level. They actively involve the masses (the uneducated or socially outcast) and often start as mission among the poor (St. Francis, the Wesleys, Salvation Army).[2]

2. Renewal movements show us that deep renewal often begins at the periphery, or the margins, of the church. Howard Snyder, *Decoding the Church: Mapping the DNA of Christ's Body* (Grand Rapids: Baker, 2002).

Energy and dynamism: New movements have the ability to excite and enlist others as leaders and participants.[3]

It will be interesting to compare Snyder's distinctly Wesleyan perspective with that of sociologists. Gerlach and Hine, two sociologists who research movements, claim that movements are characterized by the following elements:[4]

A segmented, cellular organization composed of units held together by various personal, structural, and ideological ties. In other words a group of small faith communities (house churches or cell-groups) gathered around Jesus and his mission.

Face-to-face recruitment by committed individuals using their own preexisting, significant social relationships. Friendships and organic relationships are the primary means of recruiting people to the cause.

Personal commitment generated by an act or experience that separates a convert in some way from the established order, identifies him or her with a new set of values, and commits him or her to changed patterns of behavior. This is what believers have always called conversion—a radical reorientation of life and lifestyle.

An ideology of articulated values and goals, which provide a conceptual framework for life, motivate and provide a rationale for change, define the opposition, and form the basis for the unity among the segmented networks of groups in the movement. In other words, a clearly articulated and accessible philosophy of life and ministry that all can connect with in some real way is needed.

Real or perceived opposition from the society at large or from that segment of the established order within which the movement has arisen. This has occurred in almost every instance of the emergence of movements that we are aware of. Wesley was shunned by the Anglican Church, as was Booth. Martin Luther King Jr. was also rejected by the hegemonic Christianity of his day.

3. Howard A. Snyder, *New Wineskins: Changing the Man-Made Structures of the Church* (London: Marshall, Morgan and Scott, 1978).
4. Luther P. Gerlach and Virginia H. Hine, *People, Power, Change: Movements of Social Transformation* (Indianapolis: Bobbs-Merrill, 1970).

Movements generally have a nontraditional or nonordained leadership. Renewal movements are often led by people with no recognized leadership status in preexisting structures. Charismatic and not institutional power is the key (à la Max Weber). New missional movements almost always begin on the edges of society or culture and among the common people. They are nonelitist. And they have the ability to excite and enlist others as leaders and participants.

The similarities between Snyder's theological approach and Gerlach and Hine's sociological one are evident. While they use different language, they describe a similar phenomenon that is common to all human movements and social forces. For example, Snyder's observation that renewal movements typically live in tension with the dominant church institutions finds confirmation in Gerlach and Hine's recognition that movements generally experience some sort of opposition from the established order. In addition, both recognize the importance of nontraditional leadership for initiating and promoting change. Likewise, both observe that a renewal movement seeks to change people's behavior and work in a nonelitist fashion with the masses who live on the fringe of society. The only significant difference between the two analyses is Snyder's recognition of the work of the Spirit as a driving force behind renewal.

It is important to note these similarities in order to understand fully what we need to do to create a truly missional church and what can potentially keep us from doing so. It is clear that what these two studies describe is somewhat different from the feel of almost any denomination or established traditional church because they are on the decline side of the life cycle. Most established institutions will resist the movement ethos. It's just too chaotic and uncontrollable for most institutions to handle. That is why most movements are ejected from the host organization. This needn't be the case, but it requires a definite commitment to permission-giving at high levels of organizational leadership to ensure that they are not. The institutionalization of the church has robbed us of that dynamic that is needed to push beyond established boundaries to claim new missional ground in the name of the kingdom of God. In order to remain truly missional, we need to be very aware of the dangers of institutionalization.

On the other hand, we would venture to suggest that those readers currently involved in a new movement would recognize many of the above characteristics in their group. We point all this out because we believe that in order to recover the missional vitality of the early church, we have to reawaken a *movement ethos* in so many of the organizations we inhabit. As leaders we encourage our readers to take these elements seriously when establishing pioneering missional activities.

Jesus at the Center

We have already mentioned bounded and centered sets in chapter 3, "The Incarnational Approach," so we will not look at the issue exhaustively. But we do feel it not only has relevance for incarnational mission but also for the way we structure our life together and for leadership in the emerging global cultures.

In chapter 3 we outlined the difference between centered sets ("wells") and bounded sets ("fences"). We want to advance this idea one step further. In social-set theory, there are actually three kinds of sets that represent types of ways people gather together. First there is the bounded or closed set—a social system that has clearly delineated boundaries but has no strong ideological center. In the bounded set it is clear who is "in" and who is "out" based on a well-defined ideological-cultural boundary—usually moral and cultural codes as well as creedal definitions—but it doesn't have much of a core definition besides these boundaries. It is like a fenced farm. It is *hard at the edges, soft at the center.* Most established institutions, including denominations, are, for a host of reasons, bounded sets. It can be represented visually as in figure 15.

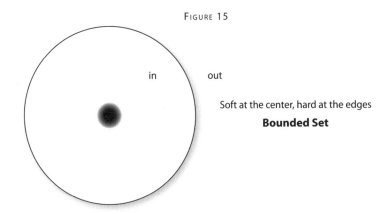

FIGURE 15

in   out

Soft at the center, hard at the edges
Bounded Set

Second, there is the fuzzy set, which has no real ideological center or boundary but is just made up of people hanging out together. They are not sure what has brought them together or why they meet. Usually these do not last very long. The fuzzy set is *soft at the center, soft at the edges.* In terms of the implications for mission, fuzzy sets can be either the early beginnings of what might become a movement, or what happens at the end of a movement. These can be illustrated by the following diagram:

Figure 16

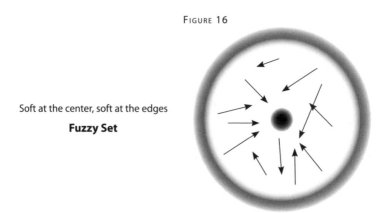

Soft at the center, soft at the edges

Fuzzy Set

The final set in the theory is the centered set. This is different from the bounded one. It is like the Outback ranch with the wellspring at its center. It has a very strong ideology or culture at the center but no boundaries. This set is *hard at the center, soft at the edges*. We suggest that in the centered set lies a real clue to the structuring of missional communities in the emerging global culture and the corresponding missional church. The centered set looks like this:

Figure 17

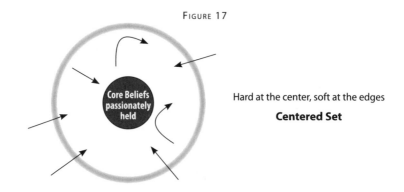

Hard at the center, soft at the edges

Centered Set

In our metaphor of the wells and fences, the notion of building fences to keep the livestock in fits with the normative idea of organizing churches. The traditional church makes it quite difficult for people to negotiate its maze of cultural, theological, and social barriers in order to get "in." In fact, "getting in" for some people takes a great deal of commitment and effort. And by the time newcomers have scaled the fences built around the church, they are so socialized as churchgoers that they are not likely to be able to maintain their connection with the social groupings they came from. They are fundamentally changed by the experience of wanting to be on the inside of the church. They become insiders and now have a clear notion of who the "outsider" is and why.

We propose that a far better and more biblical way is to organize like the Outback ranch. Sink wells. If you sustain your connection with the water source and ensure others can get to it, you will find a whole host of people relating to Jesus from different walks of life. We allow people to come to Jesus from any distance and from any direction. Our aim in mission is to fully present Jesus and to facilitate that vital connection. This is the essence of our priestly function—it is evangelistic (Rom. 15:15–16). The person of Jesus stands at the epicenter of what we do. He must shape everything. And the church must allow its connection with Jesus and the responsibility that this brings to determine how it will *be* and *do* church. The following flow chart illustrates this nonnegotiable movement from Christ as the source (in the center) to our peripheral decisions about the specific forms and functions of doing church (the edge):

FIGURE 18

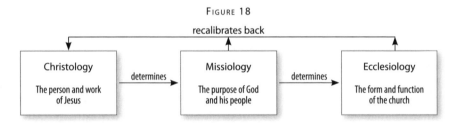

Our Christology informs our missiology, which in turn determines our ecclesiology. If we get this the wrong way around and allow our notions of the church to qualify our sense of purpose and mission, we can never be disciples of Jesus, and we will never be an authentic missional church. Churches that have got this basic formula wrong never really engage in mission and so lose touch with Jesus. These churches spend all their time discussing (or arguing) about the forms of worship, the church furniture, and the timing of services or programs, and fail to recognize that our ecclesiology flows more naturally out of our sense of mission. These churches become closed sets as a result, and their experience of Jesus at the center fades into a memory of the time when they were really doing something. It becomes a matter of history rather than an experience of mission now. It is important to recover the idea that the church connects with Jesus through mission, not through getting church meetings right!

But another advantage of the centered set is that it allows for massive diversity and for a deeper underlying unity based on Jesus and filtered through our distinctive organizational values. The hard at the center, soft at the edges paradigm allows for a wide variety of people to gather around Jesus through the church.

So what might this look like? And what constitutes the "hard center"? At South Melbourne Restoration Community (now called Red), Alan's original base community, the theological priorities at the core can be visualized as follows:

FIGURE 19

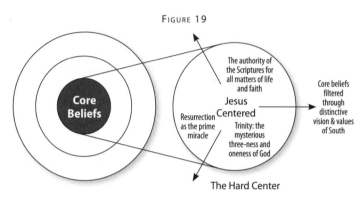

The theological structure of South Melbourne Restoration Community

In terms of theology, South was passionately committed to the central core of biblical faith (the authority of Scripture, resurrection, and Trinity) but it doesn't prescribe how these beliefs might be expressed. The leadership particularly is required to affirm these core tenets of the faith. But others are invited to explore these aspects of New Testament faith in order to make them their own. Furthermore, other more peripheral (e.g., mode of baptism) teachings of Scripture are taken seriously but are not made determinative for fellowship, and a wide variety of interpretations are allowed and encouraged. These core beliefs are filtered through the distinctive vision and values, the particular sense of destiny and mission that the church feels before God. What all this allows for is a wonderful quest by everyone. The faith is not predigested for each believer and made into easy formulas. It facilitates that vital journey that is so important for mission in the emerging global cultures.

We wish to mix two metaphors in order to put forth a way of leading so-called millennials, especially eighteen- to thirty-five-year-olds—that of herding cats and leading horses to water. Ever tried to herd cats? They simply will not go in lines and will climb over everything and scatter all over the place. Cats are rugged individualists. We suggest cats can be herded provided you are clever about it. Put down a dish of food when the cats are hungry and they will come. It is said that you can lead a horse to water but you can't make him drink. Wanna bet? Just give him salt, and he'll soon be gulping down that water. By extension, leadership in emerging global cultures will need to focus on (1) providing the right kind of food and (2) cultivating hunger. Again the issue of Christology comes to the fore. Jesus is always highly rated in public opinion polls. He is the church's primal mission "asset." It's time to place him at the heart of the church again.

Eco-Leadership

In chapter 10 we briefly mentioned that pioneered organizations should always be designed as (1) organic, (2) reproducible, and (3) sustainable learning systems. We raised these characteristics with reference to APEST ministry as set out in Ephesians 4. What we hope to do here is to enlarge on these themes and suggest them as fundamental starting points for all who are developing new missional initiatives and church plants. We refer to this as eco-leadership, because they are principles derived from the ecosystem in which we live.

Organic

What we mean by organic here is simply that the church in all its expressions remains true to its essential nature as a dynamic, living organism as opposed to a mechanistic-style structure. It also refers to the way a community is structured with a view to the interconnectivity and interrelationship between all aspects of its life, function, and purpose. And it implies an innate responsiveness to its environment. We believe that leadership must intentionally build an organic human system *before* actually triggering the activities of that system.

Without wishing to be unnecessarily provocative, both of us feel that post-Christendom missional leadership needs to be very wary about the related issues of size and programming. In the emerging global cultures in the West there is also a fragmenting and tribalizing as the age of the smaller, more organic, missional unit is dawning. The similarities to the early church are not coincidental. They, too, were on missional ground and could not claim a right to be at the center of culture as the later Christendom church did. This is related to size precisely because smaller missional units are more organically responsive to host communities in different subcultures. They are not automated organizations. They are not slick and polished but instead are rich and textured. They have an authentic human feel—a level of community and interconnectedness that can only be hinted at in the larger churches. We wish to be clear here that we are not denying the validity of the larger church. On the contrary, we firmly believe that we need a diversity of models of church in the emerging global cultures, and the large church surely must be one of the models. But that's the point—it should be only *one* of the ways of doing and being church. We need eco-diversity to create long-term organic, spiritual health.

Also, we are questioning the common assumption that church planting should always aim at founding the new church on a large church model. There is increasing diversity in the way that church is being conceived and done in the emerging missional churches, and there is a definite trend toward smaller, more rhythmic, organic communities. We are now seeing the emergence of churches that are meeting in houses, cafés, workplaces, dance clubs, nature parks, online, and other venues. Most of the more organic, missional churches we have been able to uncover are quite intentional about developing *smaller* communities and are attempting to fulfill the Great Commission by doing church planting rather than church growth. Not only is this more missionally responsive in the new context but, we believe, it is also much closer to New Testament ecclesiology and missions practice. The household church unit was the primary unit of missional community in the New Testament. Today whether they meet in homes like the contemporary house-church movement or not is irrelevant. What is important is that they tend to be smaller, more diverse, less organized, life-oriented, missional, relational, faith communities, not requiring their own specialized churchy buildings.

Related directly to size is the issue of programming. We have seen so many churches grow numerically through excellent programming but at the tragic cost of the loss of genuine community and long-term, organic health. It is very easy for key leaders to program the church out of a natural community experience. Says Mennonite missiologist James R. Krabill:

> Being more missional might actually mean doing fewer things. There is a Latin American proverb that says, "If you don't know where you're coming from, and if you don't know where you're going, then any bus will do." Some congregations are clearly riding too many buses! What they need is not more *flurry*, but more *focus*. Becoming disciplined about being a missional church can provide such a focus.[5]

We seem to have gotten so hooked on numerical church growth that we missed the idea of growth by multiplication of churches, which we know from nature and biology is the more organic/natural way to grow! The result is that

---

5. James R. Krabill, "Does Your Church 'Smell' Like Mission?: Reflections on Becoming a Missional Church," *Mission Insight* 17 (Elkhart: Mennonite Board of Mission, 2001).

we have large churches that have to manage the people, in part by building large, expensive, one-dimensional buildings, with an increasing emphasis on administrating programs. The cell group in this system can easily become a form of pseudocommunity filling in for the loss of the sense of broader community as the church grows beyond its optimum organic size.

It is so tempting (and so easy!) to try to institutionalize church life and in so doing develop an automated, production-line experience of church. In doing this we lose something of the much healthier, chaotic aspect of life that is the feature of healthy organic groupings. There is no doubting that the larger the church grows in terms of membership, the more machinelike and inorganic its systems, structures, and social patterns will tend to become. Church growth theory itself acknowledges the change in leadership styles as the church moves through the growth phases. The minister moves increasingly away from grassroots activity to being something of an ecclesiastical CEO. This is not dissimilar to corporate organizational growth patterns, and while it might work, it will also exact an immense cost in terms of the spiritual and missional health of the community. It is interesting that the Institute for Natural Church Development, in its massive international research on biotic (equivalent to our "organic") churches, actually found smaller churches having equivalent health indexing to that of larger churches. But they tended to be more effective in terms of missional growth and evangelism.

We have become very suspicious of programming as a means of filling in the gaps of ministry. Programs are important, but we need to remember that every medium has its own innate message—we invent our tools, and they in turn reinvent us. For genuine Christian community to develop and be maintained, it requires a gentle rhythm and a certain social ecology, an element of serendipity that simply cannot be planned or programmed. Our advice to leaders is to really justify another program before instituting it. Take all the clues from nature itself. In growing a healthy plant, one must have a view to its innate nature and its environment. If you give it too much or too little water or too much or too little fertilizer, it will die. It needs the cyclic rhythm of light and darkness to grow and produce.

Another very important factor in developing an organic church is the need for the church-planting missionary to acknowledge that he or she cannot know beforehand how a church might form and organize itself. As different garden plants have different natures, and the environment will in many ways determine how they will look, so, too, the emerging missional churches will have their own natures and senses of destiny (DNA) as well as their own particular contexts that will determine to a large degree what form and structure they take. We encourage church-planting missionaries not to assume they know what church is or what it should look like without first listening to its context very, very carefully. This is what we coach our interns to do:

- Observe the organic social rhythms of the host or target community.
- Watch for the social patterning.
- Ask where the social centers in your community are. Or as Brian Ollman at the Millennia Co-op in Los Angeles used to say, "Where are the ant trails? And where are they leading?"
- Ask "What is church for this group of people?" and "What will a Jesus-centered faith community look like among this people with their particular culture?"
- Do not import an alien or artificial model of church. Try to help develop one that is truly indigenous to that culture or subculture.
- Keep asking "What is good news for this community?"

Reproducible

It was Christian Schwarz and the Institute for Natural Church Development (NCD) that introduced the concept of "multiplication not addition" into the language of church growth. What NCD meant by this was that for too long we have been committed to the growth of the church through addition of new church members to a local church, rather than through multiplication by church planting and other means. We wish to use the term *metabolic growth* for this idea of multiplication as it describes exactly how organic growth actually takes place in nature and history.

The movie *Pay It Forward* illustrates metabolic growth in a profound way. In the film a teacher sets a project for each member of a class of twelve-year-old kids: The project? To change history. One child, played by Haley Joel Osment, decides to do a good deed to two people with the only condition being that they were not to pay him back but rather they were to do a good deed to two other people. In other words, they were to "pay it forward" instead of paying him back. The movie explores the world-changing impact of this simple idea. It begins with one person's good deed, which multiplies to two, then four, then eight, sixteen, and so on.

You may be familiar with the story of the inventor of the chess game. As a reward for his invention, he was offered one free wish by the king of India. As a most "modest" reward, he wished just for a kernel of rice on the first square of the chess board, two kernels on the second square, four on the third, eight on the forth, and so on. The king, who had initially smiled, thinking he would get off lightly, ended up unable to grant the wish. He would have had to produce 2^{63} kernels of rice, which is 9,223,372,036,854,780,000 kernels, or 153 billion tons of rice—more than the world can harvest for the next thousand years. This is what we mean by metabolic growth, illustrated like this:

FIGURE 20

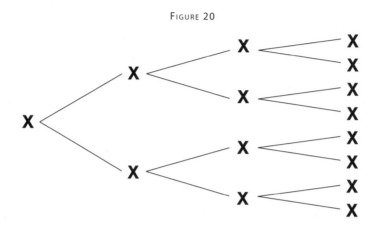

Seth Godin, a marketing guru, coined the phrase *ideaviruses* to articulate metabolic growth in relation to marketing and ideas in general. In Godin's conception an ideavirus is a big idea that runs amok across the target audience. It's a fashionable idea that captures the thinking and imagination of a section of the population, teaching and changing and influencing everyone it touches. And he claims that in our rapidly, instantly changing world, the art and science of building, launching, and profiting from ideaviruses is the next frontier. Have you ever heard of Facebook? Ever used it? If so, it's not because Facebook ran a lot of TV ads (they didn't). It's because the manifesto of Facebook, the basic commercial proposal at the heart of the company, somehow got to you through the medium of the promise of free email accessible anywhere and anyplace. It turned into an ideavirus. Someone you know and trust probably infected you with it. Knowing how such an idea spreads—and how to make it spread faster—underlies the genius behind unleashing an ideavirus. And it can, and indeed must, be part of strategic thinking in relation to missions in the West.

So an ideavirus is simply an idea that becomes contagious in precisely the same way that a virus does. Take for instance how a flu virus usually spreads—through the air or through contact with infected objects or people. Or ever watched how a computer virus can spread through the internet and jam the world's computers in one week? This is metabolic growth in action, and missional leaders cannot afford to ignore it. In fact we would argue that to miss it is to miss the possibility of truly evangelizing our world, because through mere addition the task is simply impossible.

We need to find the appropriate mechanism of organic multiplication. The question that this raises for us in our diverse contexts is, "What are the media through which we can develop the ideavirus of the gospel in this group or culture?" We need to locate the strategic medium into which we "sneeze" our message so that it can do what all great ideaviruses are made to do—*spread like mad*. Says Godin,

> If you don't have time to read the whole book, here's what it says: Marketing by interrupting people isn't cost-effective anymore. You can't afford to seek out people and send them unwanted marketing messages, in large groups, and hope that some will send you money. Instead, the future belongs to marketers who establish a foundation and process where interested people can market to each other. Ignite consumer networks and then get out of the way and let them talk.[6]

He goes on to give advice that, if taken seriously by strategic missional leaders, could help us transform the world.

> How does an ideavirus manifest itself? Where does it live? What does it look like? It's useful to think of ideas of every sort as being similar. They can be called manifestos. An idea manifesto is a powerful, logical "essay" that assembles a bunch of existing ideas and creates a new one. Sometimes a manifesto is a written essay. But it can be an image, a song, a cool product or process. The medium doesn't matter. The message does. By lumping all sorts of ideas—regardless of format—into the same category (manifestos) it's much easier to think of them as versions of the same thing. As long as you can use your manifesto to change the way people think, talk or act you can create value. In order to move an idea has to be encapsulated in a medium. It could be a picture, a phrase, a written article, a movie, even a mathematical formula ($e=mc^2$). The medium used for transmitting the ideavirus determines how smooth it is as well as the velocity of its growth. A medium is not a manifesto—every idea is a manifesto, trying to make its point, and the medium is the substance that the idea lives in.[7]

The medium could be word-of-mouth, the internet, organic church planting, pay-it-forward-type activities, or whatever means by which the idea of the gospel might travel to the host community. The trick is to find it, produce it if you need to, and use it to pass on your idea. It is not surprising then that Godin has marketed his ideas as a free download through the internet, the most powerful means of spreading an ideavirus to date.

6. Seth Godin, *Unleashing the Ideavirus* (www.ideavirus.com), 6.
7. Ibid., 13.

In a real sense the element of reproducibility (and ideaviruses) is actually an extension of the idea of organic church. Reproducibility is innate to all biological systems. One need look no further than to our own bodies or the nearest tree. Part of the fundamental aim of all living systems is to ensure a progeny in some form or another. The apple tree produces fruit, and at the heart of the fruit is a cluster of seeds. In the seed there is everything present to produce future apple trees. We wish to suggest that leadership should be profoundly attentive to learning from organic systems in their attempt to build healthy communities of faith. We should *always* aim at reproducibility.

The missional leader needs to genuinely commit to the idea of reproducibility prior to actually starting any new venture. The reason is that if the leader or missional team starts with reproducibility as a prior, nonnegotiable commitment, he or she will design the life of the church around that commitment and not try to add it as a subsequent, and somewhat inorganic, attachment. Over the last decade or two we have seen this happen all over the US, Australia, and the UK, as churches took on church planting as a strategy for growth and mission but lacked the DNA to legitimize, energize, and sustain it. The commitment to a truly missional form of growth such as church planting was commendable, but because it was somewhat artificial to the host church, many new church projects failed to take root. Seeds produce trees, which produce seeds—it's all in the DNA.

One final element that relates to reproducibility is that of fruitfulness, or what NCD calls functionality. Fertility and fruitfulness are built into all biosystems including the human body. Fruitfulness actually constitutes the very means of survival and growth for all of God's creatures. If fruitfulness is missing, the survival of the species is under real threat. In other words, if the animal or the tree is not reproducible, then something has gone wrong. We believe that we should apply the same test to churches and church life. We believe that churches that fail to reproduce organically actually fail the intention of the gospel implicit in the very gospel itself. The gospel is essentially a message (a seed, an ideavirus?) to be passed on; failure to pass it on results in infertility for the church in any given context. The Bible is full of images that relate to fruitfulness (and resultant blessing) or fruitlessness (and appropriate judgment). For instance John 15 and many of Jesus' parables raise the issue directly and unavoidably. We must be willing to ask hard questions in relation to our current systems if we are being unfruitful.

Sustainable

Sustainability is the final component of the ecology of healthy missional leadership and structuring. If *organic growth* ensures the right inner life and appropriate structure for the missional church, and *reproducibility* ensures that the church remains true to the gospel and missionally honest, *sustainability* ensures that the church keeps itself on task over the long haul.

Thinking in terms of sustainability as a fundamental assumption of pioneering leadership means that the leaders must pay serious attention to how the organization can take root, grow, and flourish over the long term in any given context. Furthermore, it means that leadership must look at ways in which to sustain the organization through all phases of its life cycle. The organization's ongoing *response*-ability is always kept in mind. The business world is good at this because it simply has to be. If a company fails in this area, it ceases to exist. Pain and difficulty faced by healthy business systems actually become wonderful teachers, forcing the leadership and the organization to respond and therefore adapt to new situations and challenges. Having to engage daily in active business decisions, secular leaders are aware that sustainability relates directly to what business has called the "bottom line." Having some form of bottom line means that management and leadership must always be responsive to the market and attentive to business infrastructure. One always has to improve, adapt, and respond, or face going out of business. While profitability is the bottom line for businesses, the church obviously does not measure its success by such a fiscal standard, but by whether or not it is fulfilling its mission—that's its bottom line. Harder to measure, for sure, but the church that commits to improving, adapting, and responding to the surrounding culture will be more sustainable than one that pays little attention.

Even though churches don't equate sustainability with making a profit, implementing a sound plan for supporting a growing and healthy church, agency, or ministry team is an important aspect of a church's sustainability. Normally churches assume one basic and unquestioned form of ministry support in Western contexts—that of centralized funding. A minister or leader is paid from the collected funds of the local church or agency. But allow us to question it for a moment. In this support structure, a church ministry team can only grow in direct relation to the size of the congregation—the ratio being perhaps one paid minister to seventy members depending on the relative wealth of the church community. In difficult missional contexts this is a formula for failure. Furthermore, centralized funding makes the minister or leader economically subservient to the dominant interests of the group. It's very hard to have a prophetic ministry to the group that provides your salary. And this incapacity to cultivate an authentic prophetic ministry contributes directly to the institutionalization of ministry and the church. Leadership is thus always hostage to the reactionary groups in the congregation. Change becomes inordinately hard.

It's much better if the leaders think organically about support systems. We suggest that pioneering leaders consider different ways of supporting themselves and the people they lead. We suggest here three tried-and-true methods of personal support:

Bivocational support or tentmaking: In this model, the leader, minister, or missionary works two places at once. He or she might work in non-church-based settings in order to support himself or herself for ministry in the direct missional setting. This has great advantages:

- It allows for a certain freedom to act as a leader in the church or mission agency.
- The group has less chance of manipulating leadership. It remains a labor of love.
- It keeps the Christian worker missionally honest as he or she has to interact meaningfully with non-Christians all the time.

Missional support: The church easily thinks of this in relation to overseas missions but seldom for missions in Western contexts, and yet this is one of the best ways to sustain oneself in mission over the long haul. The benefits of developing mission support systems are:

- The missionary has a direct, and often long-term, relationship to those who support him or her. Many of these are family and friends who are more likely to support the missionary because of the preexisting relationship.
- The missionary takes responsibility for his or her own support, and it becomes part of the ministry to maintain the support base. This ensures more prayer on behalf of the worker and the support group.
- The mission team can grow as big as needed depending on vision and capacity to recruit new members to the team. As such, this system is not only sustainable, but reproducible and organic as well.

Centralized funding: We have already mentioned this as the traditional form of ministry support, and while it has some problems associated with it, it is still a viable form of support. We suggest that centralized funding can be used to support administration-type staff while missional staffing can be bivocational or have a support team. This form of funding can come from a denominational resource or from a "mother church."

A mix of the above: Some situations could be handled by a combination of the above-mentioned options. We have seen a number of very effective missional agencies develop and grow in a sustainable way by adopting one or another of these ways to fund their key workers. Urban Neighbours of Hope, the mission order among the poor in Melbourne and Bangkok, has effectively planted many churches and has done wonderful work among the poor without a shred of centralized funding for its workers. The same is true for a group called Frontier Servants in Australia and India, and InnerCHANGE in America, Cambodia, and Vietnam. Some of our artist-missionary comrades in San Francisco and Los Angeles work similarly on mission support and tentmaking. It is the support system of the future. We suggest it is time for church planters and established churches to consider doing the same. Sustainability and organic growth are at stake.

Reproduce after Your Own Kind

The task of church planting and mission to the First World requires specialized training quite distinct from that of standard ministry formation pathways. The task-orientation for church planters and missionaries is different from that of normal church-based ministry and therefore requires a different approach. We believe that the gifting-clusters and therefore the training emphases required by missionaries and church planters in Western contexts is distinctive. If we accept that the description of ministry types and skills in Ephesians 4:11–12 (apostles, prophets, evangelists, pastors, and teachers) is normative for the church, it therefore provides an analytical framework to assess the provision of current training for all types. It is evident that the skills required for missional leadership development fit within the cluster of ministry skills associated with the apostolic, prophetic, and evangelistic giftings mentioned in this passage. Generalized ministry training, which is predominant in all denominational structures, focuses primarily on the gifting-clusters related to the pastor-teacher. Hence the predominance of biblical, theological, ethical, and counseling subjects. This does not disparage such training, because this type of ministry formation is vital to the ongoing health of established churches. However, there is a lack of emphasis on that particular ministry mix needed for the complex task of twenty-first-century church planting—a mix emphasizing the apostolic, prophetic, and evangelistic gifting-clusters.

We believe that in addition to theological and ministry skills, the church planter or missionary in Western, postmodern, cultural environments requires the following skills:

- A more actional approach that directly develops distinct entrepreneurial skills;
- A sharpened ability to interpret and engage popular culture, as opposed to church culture;[8]
- Capacities to implement marketing-type strategies;
- Skills in basic sociological research and in the interpretation of general social trends;
- Innovative evangelistic communication skills, including a "media awareness" and leadership and team development skills.[9]

The Dawn Project has stimulated successful pioneering leadership development programs, and it was with this in mind that Alan, Michael, and other missional leaders set about developing Forge Mission Training Network in Australia. We offer here some of the basic philosophy as examples of how the strategic task of developing missional leadership is being successfully done in one context. Our mission statement at Forge is simply *"To help birth and nurture the missional church in Australia, New Zealand, and beyond."* We have set our core values as follows:

- A holistic approach to mission;
- An action-learning approach to missional leadership development;
- A cross-cultural mission methodology in all settings;
- A grassroots movement ethos;
- A diversity of approaches and models;
- Networked, cross-denominational structures;
- A passionate action-based spirituality;
- Creativity, innovation, and experimentation in all we do;
- The priority of modeling for leadership and mission.

We set out to achieve the following outcomes:

- To stimulate mission as a strategic priority;
- To see growth in number of new churches and mission projects;
- To inculcate a missional leadership development;
- To provide service to, and leadership in, the Australian church;

8. The church mindset is different from the mindset of an unchurched culture. Ministry training for revitalization work focuses on changing the church and Christian people. The church planter works with a different "clientele."

9. The church planter does not begin with a church, a team, and a building. He or she must start from scratch. This requires different abilities, which must be cultivated.

- To nurture the development of the missionary identity of the church;
- To foster a networked and empowered body of missionaries and church planters in Australia.

And we set about doing it as follows:

- By raising up, and shaping, a future generation of missional leaders;
- By focusing on developing the distinctly pioneering type of leader;
- By helping birth and stimulate a distinctive missionary identity in all our interns and students;
- By contributing to the development of a missiology appropriate to each and every distinctive context;
- By actively stimulating innovation and creativity in any and every way;
- By coordinating an energetic community/network of leaders and activists focused on the task of mission.

And we believe that the following educational philosophy is of great significance to the development of effective missional leaders. Again we offer it as the guiding philosophy of Forge and not as normative for all systems, but we suggest that all these have important implications for training leaders in general.

Actional context is primary: We believe that one cannot learn mission divorced from the context of mission. The same applies to leadership and ministry. Therefore, the vast majority of the learning and training must take place in the organic context of the student or intern's workplace or mission setting. Furthermore different leadership styles will emerge from different mission contexts.

Context is everything: Interns are placed in edgy learning environments. We try to place interns in positions where they are "at risk" or out of their comfort zones and therefore most inclined to learn. We then bring the learning to them when they need it.

Action-reflection learning model: We believe that action is the starting point for reflection and therefore fundamental to the learning and discipling process. Real learning cannot therefore occur without a primary actional element.

Relational empowerment: We hold that relationships are the primary means of transferring leadership and influence and are, as such, indispensable in the training of missional leaders. Therefore, weekly and monthly coaching sessions form the backbone of the Forge internship process.

Practitioner-teachers: We believe that teachers cannot teach what they do not personally *know* and cannot lead where they themselves will not go. In light of this we expose our interns only to leaders and practitioners who have a *direct and current* experience at a cutting edge mission, church plant, or ministry project.

Inspiration, then information: We believe that people are not motivated by information alone; real motivation arises when they connect with their basic passion and calling . . . they must be *moved* and *inspired* to act with passion for the kingdom of God. Our intensives, therefore, aim primarily at inspiration, not just on giving new information.

Life-oriented experiential learning: We believe that the best educational theory confirms the fact that people learn best when learning matches the life experience of the learner. The idea that students are blank slates that come to be filled with knowledge is bad theology and even worse educational philosophy. Therefore we try to bring the experience and the learning moment together.

Imagination as a resource for leadership: Imagination is the basis of vision and innovation and creativity. Interns and students are stimulated to think in pioneering and innovative ways of doing and being church.

Leadership development, not just skill development: As we believe that leadership is the key leverage area for change and mission, our primary focus is on developing and nurturing distinctive *leadership* qualities and characteristics and then on providing skills.

Multi-dimensional leadership systems: We believe that the church needs to recover the apostolic, prophetic, and evangelistic functions to be an authentic missional church. Our training focuses primarily on developing these functions in relation to mission and leadership.

What is somewhat unique about Forge is the cross-denominational, inter-collegial, multiproject nature of the network. We were able to thus secure significant legitimization and accreditation for our interns while keeping them primarily in their local projects and coaching them in missional leadership formation. We don't think Forge is the cavalry sent to rescue the church from danger. Rather, we see it as our humble attempt to generate a creative, daring, innovative new generation of leadership for the Australian church. We commend you to find the methods and forums for doing the same in your context.

The Last Say

To conclude this section on leadership, indeed to conclude this book, we refer to a parable credited to that radical nineteenth-century disciple Søren Kierkegaard. Again the parable involves geese. Many of us, and especially those who have lived in the country, will have witnessed the migration of geese as they undertake a massive journey to follow spring and summer around the world. Characteristically, geese make a screeching sound as they fly. If one were able to observe the effect of this wild call on tame barnyard geese, the ones who have given up on the dangerous journey in favor of barnyard food and security, one would see that as the wild cousins fly overhead, the tame geese run along the ground and flap their wings wildly, somehow trying to imitate the mad flight of the migrating geese. The squawking seems to awaken something innate in them, a memory of wildness.

We want to suggest that this story has implications for us on many levels. On one level we suggest that it is the task of leadership to do exactly the same as the wild geese: to fly over the heads of those we lead in order to call them to the dangerous journey of mission and engagement in the name of God. To do this, we ourselves have to take flight and risk the long journey across the continents. The task of leadership and, by extension, the task of developing missional leaders, requires us to call people to do wild things—to remind them what they are made for. On another level, the story reminds us that at bottom, we are disciples of Jesus Christ. The disciple, too, has to take the journey of risk. In flying over the heads of the people in our culture, our task is to call them to the dangerous but marvelously instinctive journey to God through Jesus Christ.

The twist in the tale is this: that while it has been observed that wild geese have become tame . . . it has seldom been observed that tame geese can become wild again. We need to beware of the anesthetizing and stultifying effects that Christendom, the tame, nonmissional church, and our safe middle classness have had on us.

We began this book with the question "Evolution or Revolution?" We think it's that desperate. Either the church will seek to continue to evolve (or devolve?) into increasing irrelevancy and impotency in the West or it will answer the revolutionary clarion call. We have written this text with the hope that it might give some legitimacy to the missional church as it tries to break out of its chrysalis in the Western world. As it stands now, we believe the whole missional church project is no longer a marginal thing or as precarious. But it is not exactly fully mainstream either. Much will depend on how the now well-established forms of church and Christianity respond to the whole project. Will they give permission for experimentation and space to emerge or will they seek to further marginalize the fragile new expressions of churches popping up in the strangest places? The established church is simply going to have to put up with more chaos and lack of clarity for a while. Chaos usually goes hand in hand with creativity—uniformity will stifle any new effort in an attempt to control the situation. Whatever, the jury is out at present. But there are positive signs of a growing consensus among strategic and denominational leadership that things are not well on the good ship Christendom—enough consensus perhaps to let the new emerge even if they contain an implied critique of the existing systems of thought and activity.

Perhaps even more importantly, the birth of the missional church will depend on whether enough people will be found willing to respond to the critical issues of our time and have a go at dreaming up new forms of church and creating new ways of doing ministry and mission. We believe that the actual experimentation, the *revolution* if you will, will be actively led and executed by younger people—most revolutions are. The "people-power" revolution in the Philippines, the downfall of Suharto in Indonesia, the flower revolution of the 60s—these were all initiated and advanced by young people. Much of our future lies in the precarious hands and hearts of a generation that finds it difficult to decide and commit. Our heartfelt prayer is that our youth will find the necessary courage to break with the enslaving power of the habitual and familiar. There are signs that this is indeed happening all over the world, and in this we rejoice.

May we remember the words of Paulo Coelho, "The ship is safest when it's in port. But that's not what ships were made for."[10]

---

10. Paulo Coelho, *The Pilgrimage* (New York: HarperCollins, 1999), 22.

Glossary

APEST

The term we use to describe the fivefold ministry formula found in Ephesians 4. APEST is an acrostic for Apostle, Prophet, Evangelist, Shepherd (pastor), Teacher. Only when all five roles are operating within the leadership of a local congregation, and the congregation as a whole has embraced the five functions within its corporate life, can one say that an APEST version of leadership is occurring. We believe such a matrix is the antidote to the triangular or hierarchical model that empowers certain leaders and disempowers the majority of Christians.

Apostolic

We use the term very specifically to describe not so much the theology of the church but the mode of the New Testament church—to describe something of its energy, impulse, and genius as well as its leadership structures. An apostolic church is one gripped by the imperatives of the New Testament church. By apostolic leadership we are not suggesting the large-church leadership model or the supra-denominational leadership model favored by many Pentecostal leaders and writers today.

Attractional

An approach to Christian mission in which the church develops programs, meetings, services, or other "products" in order to attract unbelievers into the influence of the Christian community. While there is an element to which the New Testament church was attractive and enjoyed the favor of the broader community (in some contexts), we believe that the contemporary church now almost totally relies on an attractional approach to its community. We employ the term to describe the current mission stance of the church, a stance that is increasingly ineffective. Sometimes we use the term *extractional* to mean the same thing.

Biblical-Hebraic

Describes the worldview that basically formed, framed, and sustains the biblical revelation. When we use the term *biblical-Hebraic* we refer to the Hebraic worldview specifically found in the Scriptures. The term *Hebraic* on its own can encompass the insights of later Judaism as well.

Bounded Set

A bounded set is a group of objects defined by a boundary separating those in the set from those outside the set. When we use this term with reference to the traditional church, we are referring to the church's propensity to develop laws or prescriptions for determining who is in the church and who is out. While we hold strongly to holiness as a key feature of the missional church, such holiness should be judged by the degree of Christlikeness, not by some artificial human rule.

Centered Set

A centered set is a group of objects defined by its proximity to a central object. When we refer to the missional church as a centered set, we are saying that the church's membership should not be defined by some artificial (and often socially prescribed) set of criteria, but by proximity to Jesus. We claim that mission should therefore be Christocentric.

Christendom

As we use the term, it describes the standardized form and expression of the church and mission formed in the post-Constantine period. Essentially we see the Christendom church as fundamentally different from the New Testament church and from what we see as an authentic missional community. Christendom is marked by the following characteristics:

1. Its mode of engagement is attractional as opposed to missional/sending. It assumes a certain centrality of the church in relation to its surrounding culture. (The missional church is a "going/sending one" and operates in the incarnational mode.)
2. A shift of focus to dedicated, sacred buildings or places of worship. The association of buildings with "church" fundamentally alters the way the church perceives itself. It becomes more static and as a consequence, almost exclusively attractional. The early church had no recognized dedicated buildings other than houses and public spaces.

3. The emergence of an institutionally recognized, professional clergy class acting primarily in a pastor-teacher type mode. In the New Testament church people were commissioned into leadership by local churches or by an apostolic leader. But this was basically different from the denominational or institutional sanction or licensing we know in Christendom. This had the effect of creating two classes of Christians: the clergy and the laity. The idea of a separated clergy, we maintain, is as alien to a New Testament church as it is to a missional one.

4. The paradigm is also characterized by the institutionalization of grace in the form of sacraments administered by an institutionally licensed priesthood. The New Testament church's form of communion was the daily meal dedicated to Jesus in the context of everyday life.

Christocentric

This simply means that Christ is center. If something is Christocentric, then its organizing principle is the person and work of Christ. This is in effect a synonym for our use of the term messianic. This has implications also for our belief that the missional church will be a centered set, with Christ at the center.

Christology/Christological

Essentially Christology comprises the biblical teaching of and about Jesus the Messiah. When we say Christology must inform all aspects of the church's life and work, we mean that Jesus must be first and foremost in our lives and self-definition as church and disciple. When the word is used as an adjective, it simply means that the element being described must be referenced primarily by our understanding and experience of Jesus the Messiah.

Church Planting

The initiation and development of new, organic, missional-incarnational communities of faith in multiple contexts. We would affirm that all true mission aims at the development of communities of faith. Thus church planting is an essential part of any authentic missional strategy. Since we are not constrained by the belief in the parish model of church territorialism, we believe local neighborhoods can sustain several churches, each seeking to reach different strata of society. Church planting should not just be limited to new, middle-class housing communities.

Dualism

The Greco-Roman assumption that the world is divided into two competing realms: the sacred (spiritual) and the profane (material). Such a worldview tends to assume that the spiritual is the higher plane and the material world is devoid of meaning and is simply to be escaped by those seeking spiritual maturity. Dualism leads to other such divisions in thinking: the division between the clergy (spiritual) and the laity (profane); the church (spiritual) and the world (profane); between spirituality and sexuality; between so-called religious practices (prayer, worship) and so-called profane ones (work, art, eating). We believe such dualism undergirds virtually every tenet of the Christendom church (and therefore undermines the tenets of the missional church).

Ecclesiology

Classically this refers to the biblical teaching about the nature, life, and practices of the church. We believe that our ecclesiology should emerge from our missiology, which should in turn derive from our Christology.

Extractional

The practice of the Christendom-era church of converting unbelievers, then extracting them from their cultural setting to join the church, thereby making them ineffective as missionaries to their own people groups. It is a missiological term. An extractional mode of mission exacerbates the church's disconnection from its host culture. See also *attractional*.

Hebraic

Refer to *Biblical-Hebraic* above. Essentially, the worldview nurtured primarily by the Bible. Hebraic in the broader sense can also mean the worldview of the Jewish people as a racial group deeply influenced as it is by Judaism.

Incarnational

The Incarnation refers to the act of God entering into the created universe and realm of human affairs as the man Jesus of Nazareth. In relation to mission it means the followers of Jesus similarly embodying the culture and life of a host culture in order to reach that group of people with Jesus' love. We also use the term to describe the missionary act of *going* to a target people group as opposed to merely making the invitation for unbelievers to come to our cultural group (the church) in order to hear the gospel. We see it as a term that describes a missional stance taken by the church. If the church is incarnational, its stance is always inclined to go forth and enter into the lives of a host community. In this sense incarnational is different from attractional or extractional.

Kavanah

A term derived from Jewish mysticism. It describes the level of intentionality built into an action. As a deliberate spiritual exercise, *kavanah* involves the concentration of development of intentionality prior to acting and so filling one's actions with meaning and purpose.

Leadership Matrix

Our term for apostolic, prophetic, evangelistic, pastoral (shepherding), and didactic (teaching) leadership as it is drawn from the ministry matrix (see below). Viewed as such, leadership is a *calling within a calling*.

Messianic

Similar to our use of the term *Christocentric*. We use it to describe the church's spirituality and activity. It is messianic in that (1) it acts in the same way Jesus acts, (2) it is essentially structured around the person of Jesus, and (3) our actions in some way extend the messianic kingdom. Our actions are directly redemptive and related to God's activity in the world.

Ministry Matrix

This covers the entire church's being described in terms of being apostolic, prophetic, evangelistic, pastoral (shepherding), and didactic (teaching). See Ephesians 4:7 ("to *each one* . . . has been given") and 4:11 ("It was he who gave *some* to be apostles, *some* to be prophets, *some* to be evangelists, and *some* to be pastors and teachers"). This distribution formula describes the whole church and not just leadership as it is commonly interpreted. Leaders are drawn from the APEST (see above) nature of the church.

Missiology/Missiological

Missiology is the study of missions. As a discipline, it seeks to identify the primal impulses in the Scriptures that compel God's people into engagement with the world. Such impulses involve, among others, the *missio Dei* (the mission of God), the Incarnation, and the kingdom of God. It also describes the authentic church's commitment to social justice, relational righteousness, and evangelism. As such, missiology seeks to define the church's purposes in light of God's will for the world. It also seeks to study the methods of achieving these ends both from Scripture and history. The term *missiological* simply draws from these meanings.

Missional

A favorite term of ours—we use it to describe the church, leadership, Christianity, and more. A missional church is one whose primary commitment is to the missionary calling of the people of God. As such, it is one that aligns itself with God's missionary purposes in the world. A missional leader is one who takes mission seriously and sees it as the driving energy behind all the church does. The missional church is a sent church with one of its defining values being the development of a church life and practice that is contextualized to that culture to which it believes it is sent.

Mitzvah

A Jewish term meaning "good deed." It does not merely describe goodness in moral terms; rather its primary element is that of holiness or sacredness. It's a sacred deed because it is done toward God as an act of worship and obedience to his commands. When a *mitzvah* is done with *kavanah* (see above), the deed not only benefits the recipient but also the doer of the deed. Holy action is the primary focus of Jewish spirituality. The *mitzvah* is the sacrament of Judaism.

Mode

Another favorite word of ours—it simply describes the method, style, or manner of that which it refers to. For example, the mode of the early church describes its methodology, stance, and approach to the world.

Movement

In this book we use the term sociologically to describe the organizational structures and ethos of the missional church. We believe that the New Testament church was itself a movement. We believe that the missional church must always strive to maintain the style and ethos of a movement.

Additional Resources

Missional Church: Foundational Texts

Allen, Roland. *Missionary Methods: St. Paul's or Ours?* Grand Rapids: Eerdmans, 1962; London: Lutterworth, 1968.

Barrett, Lois Y., and Walter C. Hobbs. *Treasure in Jars of Clay: Patterns in Missional Faithfulness.* Grand Rapids: Eerdmans, 2004.

Bosch, David J. *Believing in the Future: Toward a Missiology of Western Culture.* Harrisburg, PA: Trinity, 1995.

Brownson, James V., Inagrace T. Dietterich, Barry A. Harvey, and Charles C. West. *Stormfront: The Good News of God.* Grand Rapids: Eerdmans, 2003.

Conder, Tim, and Dan B. Allender. *The Church in Transition: The Journey of Existing Churches into the Emerging Culture.* Grand Rapids: Zondervan, 2006.

Frost, Michael. *Exiles: Living Missionally in a Post-Christian Culture.* Peabody, MA: Hendrickson, 2006.

———. *The Road to Missional: Journey to the Center of the Church.* Grand Rapids: Baker, 2011.

Guder, Darrell L. *The Continuing Conversion of the Church.* Gospel and Our Culture Series. Grand Rapids: Eerdmans, 2000.

Guder, Darrell L., and Lois Barrett et al. *Missional Church: A Vision for the Sending of the Church in North America.* Grand Rapids: Eerdmans, 1998.

Hall, Douglas John. *The End of Christendom and the Future of Christianity.* Harrisburg, PA: Trinity Press International, 1997.

Hiebert, Paul. *The Missiological Implications of Epistemological Shifts: Affirming Truth in a Modern/Postmodern World.* Harrisburg, PA: Trinity Press International, 1999.

Hirsch, Alan. *The Forgotten Ways: Reactivating the Missional Church.* Grand Rapids: Brazos, 2006.

Hunsberger, George R., ed. *Bearing the Witness of the Spirit: Lesslie Newbigin's Theology of Cultural Plurality*. Grand Rapids: Eerdmans, 1998.

———. *The Church between Gospel and Culture: The Emerging Mission in North America*. Grand Rapids: Eerdmans, 1996.

Kenneson, Philip D. *Beyond Sectarianism: Re-Imagining the Church and World*. Christian Mission and Modern Culture Series. Harrisburg, PA: Trinity Press International, 1999.

Murray, Stuart. *Church After Christendom*. Bletchley: Paternoster Press, 2005.

Newbigin, Lesslie. *The Gospel in a Pluralist Society*. Grand Rapids: Eerdmans, 1989.

———. *The Open Secret: An Introduction to the Theology of Mission*. Grand Rapids: Eerdmans: 1978.

Rouse, Rick, and Craig Van Gelder, eds. *A Field Guide for the Missional Congregation: Embarking on a Journey of Transformation*. Philadelphia: Augsburg Fortress, 2008.

Roxburgh, Alan. *Missional: Joining God in the Neighbourhood*. Grand Rapids: Baker, 2011.

Taber, Charles R. *To Understand the World, to Save the World: The Interface Between Missiology and the Social Sciences*. Christian Mission and Modern Culture Series. Harrisburg, PA: Trinity Press International, 2000.

Tyra, Gary. *The Holy Spirit in Mission*. Downers Grove, IL: IVP, 2011.

Van Gelder, Craig, and Dwight Zscheile. *The Missional Church in Perspective*. Grand Rapids: Baker, 2011.

Wright, Christopher J. H. *The Mission of God: Unlocking the Bible's Grand Narrative*. Downers Grove, IL: IVP, 2006.

Church Planting

Benesh, Sean. *The Multi-Nucleated Church: Toward a Theoretical Framework for Church Planting in High-Density Cities*. Portland: Urban Loft Publishers, 2011.

Hjalmarson, Leonard, and Brent Toderash, eds. *Fresh and Re:Fresh: Church Planting and Urban Mission in Canada Post-Christendom*. Eagle, ID: Allelon, 2009.

Stetzer, Ed. *Planting Missional Churches*. New York: Broadman and Holman, 2009.

Missional Leadership

Benner, David. *The Gift of Being Yourself*. Downers Grove, IL: IVP, 2004.

Breen, Mike, and Steve Cockram. *Building a Discipling Culture*. Pawleys Island, SC: 3DM, 2011.

Breen, Mike, and Jon Tyson. *Multiplying Missional Leaders*. Pawleys Island, SC: 3DM, 2012.

Clinton, J. Robert. *The Making of a Leader: Recognizing the Lessons and Stages of Leadership Development*. Colorado Springs: NavPress, 1990.

Creps, Earl. *Off-Road Disciplines: Spiritual Adventures of Missional Leaders*. San Francisco: Jossey-Bass Wiley, 2006.

Easum, Bill. Leadership *on the Other Side: No Rules, Just Clues*. Nashville: Abingdon, 2000.

Ford, Lance. *UnLeader: Reimagining Leadership . . . and Why We Must*. Boston, MA: Beacon Hill: 2012.

Gibbs, Eddie. *LeadershipNext: Changing Leaders in a Changing Culture*. Downers Grove, IL: IVP, 2005.

Guder, Darrell L. "Leadership in New Congregations: New-Church Development from the Perspective of Missional Theology." In *Extraordinary Leaders in Extraordinary Times: Unadorned Clay Pot Messengers*. Vol. 1. Ed. H. Stanley Wood. Grand Rapids: Eerdmans, 2006.

———. "Walking Worthily: Missional Leadership after Christendom." *The Princeton Seminary Bulletin*, 28, no. 3 (2007): 251ff.

Halter, H., and M. Smay. *AND: The Gathered and Scattered Church*. Grand Rapids: Zondervan, 2010.

Heifetz, R. *Leadership Without Easy Answers*. Cambridge, MA: Harvard University Press, 1994.

Jacobsen, Eric O., ed. *The Three Tasks of Leadership: Worldly Wisdom for Pastoral Leaders*. Grand Rapids: Eerdmans, 2009.

Mancini, Will. *Church Unique: How Missional Leaders Cast Vision, Capture Culture, and Create Movement*. San Francisco: Jossey-Bass, 2008 (also available as full-text to Tyndale students via NetLibrary).

McNeal, Reggie. *Missional Renaissance: Changing the Scorecard for the Church*. San Francisco: Jossey-Bass, 2009.

———. *Practicing Greatness: 7 Disciplines of Extraordinary Spiritual Leaders*. San Francisco: Jossey-Bass, 2006.

Morse, Marykate. *Making Room for Leadership: Power, Space, and Influence*. Downers Grove, IL: IVP, 2006.

Nouwen, Henri. *In the Name of Jesus: Reflections on Christian Leadership*. New York: Crossroad Publishing, 1992.

Reese, R., and K. Anderson. *Spiritual Mentoring: A Guide to Giving and Seeking Direction*. Downers Grove, IL: IVP, 1999.

Senge, Peter M. *The Fifth Discipline: The Art and Practice of the Learning Organization*. New York: Doubleday/Currency, 1990; Sydney: Random, 1992.

Sheffield, Dan. "The Multicultural Leader: Developing a Catholic Personality. Clements, 2005"; and "Leadership Requirements for the Multi-Cultural Congregation." *McMaster Journal of Theology and Ministry*, vol. 5 (2002).

Sweet, Leonard. *AquaChurch 2.0: Piloting Your Church in Today's Fluid Culture*. Colorado Springs: David C. Cook, 2008.

Wheatley, Margaret. *Finding Our Way: Leadership for an Uncertain Time*. San Francisco: Berrett-Koehler, 2007.

Church in Emerging Culture

Bass, Dianne Butler. *Christianity for the Rest of Us: How the Neighborhood Church Is Transforming the Faith*. San Francisco: HarperSanFrancisco, 2006.

Clapp, Rodney. *A Peculiar People: The Church as Culture in a Post-Christian Society*. Downers Grove, IL: IVP, 1996.

Drane, John. *The McDonaldization of the Church: Consumer Culture and the Church's Future*. London: Darton, Longman & Todd, 2000; Macon, GA: Smyth & Helwys, 2001.

Gibbs, Eddie, and Ryan Bolger. *Emerging Churches: Creating Christian Community in Postmodern Cultures*. Grand Rapids: Baker, 2005.

Greig, Peter, and Andy Freeman. *Punk Monk: New Monasticism and the Ancient Art of Breathing*. London: Gospel Light and Regal Books, 2007.

Grenz, Stanley J. *A Primer on Postmodernism*. Grand Rapids: Eerdmans, 1996.

McNeal, Reggie. *Missional Communities: The Rise of the Post-Congregational Church*. San Francisco: Jossey Bass, 2011.

Middleton, J. Richard, and Brian J. Walsh. *Truth Is Stranger Than It Used to Be: Biblical Faith in a Postmodern Age*. Downers Grove, IL: IVP, 1995.

Murphy, Nancey. *Beyond Liberalism and Fundamentalism: How Modern and Postmodern Philosophy Set the Agenda*. Valley Forge, PA: Trinity Press International, 1996.

Sine, Tom. *The New Conspirators: Creating the Future One Mustard Seed at a Time*. Downers Grove, IL: IVP, 2008.

Sloane, Karen. *Flirting with Monasticism: Finding God on Ancient Paths*. Downers Grove, IL: IVP, 2006.

Smith, James K. A. *Who's Afraid of Postmodernism: Taking Derrida, Lyotard, and Foucault to Church*. Grand Rapids: Baker Academic, 2006.

Wilson-Hartgrove, Jonathan. *New Monasticism: What It Has to Say to Today's Church*. Grand Rapids: Brazos, 2008.

Spirituality and Missional Disciplines

Ausburger, David. *Dissident Discipleship: A Spirituality of Self-Surrender, Love of God and Love of Neighbour*. Grand Rapids: Brazos, 2006.

Bass, Dorothy C., ed. *Practicing Our Faith: A Way of Life for a Searching People*. San Francisco: Jossey-Bass, 1997.

Brueggemann, Walter. *Cadences of Home*. Louisville: Westminster John Knox, 1997.

———. *The Prophetic Imagination*. Philadelphia: Fortress, 1978.

Chittister, Joan. *Wisdom Distilled from the Daily: Living the Rule of St. Benedict Today*. Toronto: HarperCollins, 1991.

Foster, Richard J. *Sanctuary of the Soul: Journey into Meditative Prayer*. Downers Grove, IL: IVP, 2011.

Helland, Roger, and Leonard Hjalmarson. *Missional Spirituality: Embodying God's Love from the Inside Out*. Downers Grove, IL: IVP, 2011.

McLaren, Brian. *Naked Spirituality: Life with God in 12 Simple Words*. San Francisco: HarperOne, 2011.

Nouwen, Henri. *Reaching Out: The Three Movements of the Spiritual Life*. New York: Doubleday & Co., 1975.

Ogden, Greg. *The Great Commandment: A Disciple's Guide to Loving God and Others*. Downers Grove, IL: IVP, 2011.

Peterson, Eugene H. *Working the Angles: The Work of Pastoral Integrity*. Grand Rapids: Eerdmans, 1987.

Stock, Jon R., and Tim Otto. *Inhabiting the Church: Biblical Wisdom for a New Monasticism*. Eugene, OR: Cascade Books, 2006.

Taylor, John V. *The Go-Between God: The Holy Spirit and the Christian Mission*. London: SCM, 1972; New York: Oxford University Press, 1979.

Vanier, Jean. *Community and Growth*. Trans. Ann Shearer. London: Darton, Longman & Todd, 1979; Homebush, NSW: St. Paul, 1979.

Willard, Dallas. *The Spirit of the Disciplines*. New York: HarperCollins, 1998.

Wilson, Jonathan R. *Living Faithfully in a Fragmented World: Lessons for the Church from MacIntyre's After Virtue*. Harrisburg, PA: Trinity Press International, 1998.

Transforming Churches, Urban Environments, Parish

Benesh, Sean. *Metrospiritual: The Geography of Church Planting*. Eugene: Resource Publications, 2011.

Carlson, Kent, and Mike Lueken. *Renovation of the Church: What Happens When a Seeker Church Discovers Spiritual Formation*. Downers Grove, IL: IVP, 2011.

Holt, Simon Carey. *God Next Door: Spirituality and Mission in the Neighborhood*. Melbourne: Acorn Press, 2007.

Inge, John. *A Christian Theology of Place*. Farnham: Ashgate Publishing, 2003.

Jacobsen, Eric O. *Sidewalks in the Kingdom: New Urbanism and the Christian Faith*. Grand Rapids: Brazos, 2003.

———. *The Space Between: A Christian Engagement with the Built Environment*. Grand Rapids: Baker, 2012.

Roxburgh, Alan. *Missional: Joining God in the Neighbourhood*. Eagle, ID: Allelon, 2010.

Roxburgh, Alan, and Fred Romanuk. *The Missional Leader: Equipping Your Church to Reach a Changing World*. San Francisco: Jossey-Bass Wiley, 2006.

Scazzero, Peter. *Emotionally Healthy Spirituality*. Nashville: Thomas Nelson, 2006.

Swanson, Eric, and Sam Williams. *To Transform a City*. Grand Rapids: Zondervan, 2010.

Van Gelder, Craig. *The Missional Church and Denominations: Helping Congregations Develop a Missional Identity*. Grand Rapids: Eerdmans, 2008.

———. *The Missional Church in Context: Helping Congregations Develop Contextual Ministry*. Grand Rapids: Eerdmans, 2007.

Primers and Workbooks

Dickau, Tim. *Plunging into the Kingdom Way: Practicing the Shared Strokes of Community, Hospitality, Justice, and Confession.* Eugene, OR: Wipf and Stock, 2010.

Halter, Hugh, and Matt Smay. *The Tangible Kingdom Primer.* Missio, 2009.

Hjalmarson, Leonard. *The Missional Church Fieldbook: A Resource for Transition.* Raleigh, NC: Lulu, 2010.

Ogden, Greg. *Discipleship Essentials: A Guide to Building Your Life in Christ.* Downers Grove, IL: IVP, 2007.

Smith, J. B. *Spiritual Formation Workbook.* San Francisco: HarperOne, 1999.

Missional Texts by the Authors

Frost, Michael. *Exiles: Living Missionally in a Post-Christian Culture.* Peabody, MA: Hendrickson, 2006.

———. *Jesus the Fool: The Mission of the Unconventional Christ.* Grand Rapids: Baker, 2010.

———. *The Road to Missional: Journey to the Center of the Church.* Grand Rapids: Baker, 2011.

Frost, Michael, and Alan Hirsch. *The Faith of Leap: Embracing a Theology of Risk, Adventure, and Courage.* Grand Rapids: Baker, 2011.

Hirsch, Alan. *The Forgotten Ways: Reactivating the Missional Church.* Grand Rapids: Brazos, 2006.

Hirsch, Alan, and Tim Catchim. *The Permanent Revolution: Apostolic Imagination and Practice for the 21st Century Church.* Jossey-Bass Leadership Network Series. San Francisco: Jossey-Bass, 2012.

Hirsch, Alan, and Dave Ferguson. *On the Verge: A Journey into the Apostolic Future of the Church.* Grand Rapids: Zondervan, 2011.

Hirsch, Alan, and Lance Ford. *Right Here, Right Now: Everyday Mission for Everyday People.* Grand Rapids: Baker, 2011.

Hirsch, Alan, and Debra Hirsch. *Untamed: Reactivating a Missional Form of Discipleship.* Grand Rapids: Baker, 2010.

Michael Frost is an internationally recognized Australian missiologist and one of the leading voices in the missional church movement. His books are required reading in colleges and seminaries around the world, and he is much sought after as an international conference speaker.

Michael is the vice principal of Morling College and the founding director of the Tinsley Institute, a mission study center located at Morling College in Sydney, Australia. He is the author or editor of ten theological books, including *Jesus the Fool*, *Seeing God in the Ordinary*, and *Exiles*. These books explore a missional framework for the church in a postmodern era. Their popularity has seen him regularly speaking at conferences in the US, the UK, and across Europe, and as far afield as Nairobi, Rio de Janeiro, and Moscow.

He is the founder of the missional Christian community *smallboatbigsea*, based in Manly in Sydney's north, and the weekly religion columnist for *The Manly Daily*. He helped establish Action Against Poverty, a localized micro-financing agency, linking the cities of Manly and Manado, an impoverished Indonesian community. Michael was also instrumental in launching Street Pastors in Sydney, an incarnational ministry aimed at reducing the effects of alcohol-related violence in entertainment precincts.

Alan Hirsch is the founding director of Forge Mission Training Network. He is the cofounder of shapevine.com, and currently he leads an innovative learning program called Future Travelers, helping numerous megachurches become missional movements. Known for his innovative approach to mission, Alan is a teacher and key mission strategist for churches across the Western world. His popular book *The Shaping of Things to Come* (with Michael Frost) is widely considered to be a seminal text on mission. Alan's book *The Forgotten Ways* has quickly become a key reference for missional thinking, particularly as it relates to missional movements. His book *ReJesus* (again with Frost) is a radical restatement about the role Jesus plays in defining Christian movements. *Untamed* (with his wife Debra) is about missional discipleship for a missional church. His most recent book, *Right Here, Right Now* (with Lance Ford), is about everyday mission for anyone.

Alan's experience in leadership includes leading a local church movement among the marginalized, developing training systems for innovative missional leadership, and heading up the Mission and Revitalization work of his denomination. He is series editor for the Shapevine Missional book series as well as an associate editor for *Leadership Journal*. Alan is an adjunct professor at Fuller Seminary, George Fox Seminary, and Wheaton, and lectures frequently throughout Australia, Europe, and the US.

From Missional Experts

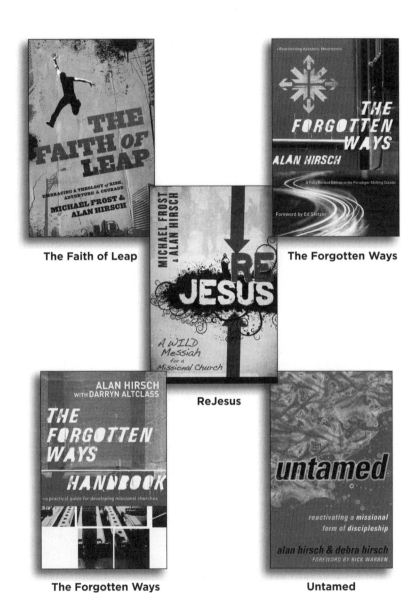

The Faith of Leap

The Forgotten Ways

ReJesus

The Forgotten Ways
Handbook

Untamed

ALAN HIRSCH & MICHAEL FROST